T0345226

SECOND SIGHT

SELECTED FILM WRITING OF ADAM MARS-JONES

REAKTION BOOKS

FOR SAM AND JOANNE

Thanks to the publications that have commissioned these pieces over the years

Published by Reaktion Books Ltd
Unit 32, Waterside
44–48 Wharf Road
London N1 7UX, UK
www.reaktionbooks.co.uk

First published 2019
Copyright © Adam Mars-Jones 2019

Printed and bound in Great Britain
by TJ International, Padstow, Cornwall

A catalogue record for this book is available from the British Library

ISBN 978 1 78914 154 2

CONTENTS

By calling this collection of pieces about film *Second Sight*, I'm not claiming any sort of psychic power as a reviewer. If I saluted emerging talents it was probably by accident. Writing for *The Independent* for over a decade, and then *The Times* for a year and a half, I had plenty of space on the page. It wasn't enough to say I liked a film, or didn't, I had to go into the why of it with some thoroughness.

There has never been an obvious career path to the job of film critic on a national daily (I'd better add 'newspaper', since print journalism has lost so much of its cultural centrality) – Derek Malcolm, *The Guardian*'s reviewer when I started on *The Independent*, started off as the racing correspondent and his successor, Richard Williams, also moved sideways from the sports pages. I wrote a memoir piece about my own sidelong, knight's-move advance on the job at the time of the twenty-fifth anniversary of *The Independent*'s founding (it was published in the magazine *Areté*).

My Independence

The Independent newspaper, launched on 7 October 1986 and bearing little resemblance to the paper which changed hands for a pound in 2010, was a strange institution, both radical and conservative, hi- and low-tech, but wholly benign, virtually avuncular, in its dealings with me. The paper indulged my quirks for over a decade and allowed me to get, and then service, a mortgage, something that would hardly have been possible for an unproductive writer of fiction who has only made money for his publishers on special occasions (and then in small amounts).

I was on a retainer until 1997 but still technically freelance, after a test case in which it was established that you could still be self-employed as long as you didn't have a desk and/or a telephone in the office of an employer. So I was both on board the ss *Independent* and able to splash about on my own to a modest extent, thanks to a lifebelt marked Schedule D. Early contracts sharply restricted what work I could do for other journalistic outlets, but as time passed and there seemed to be little (or no) extra money available, it seemed sensible to negotiate for extra latitude instead.

I had published fiction before I wrote my first review for the *Times Literary Supplement*, and had no journalistic training or ambitions. During three months spent in Perugia between school and university I had acquired the habit of regular film going. One cinema in the town showed a different film every day, mainly subtitled Hollywood films from a time of golden ferment in the industry. You just had to identify which film it was. Sometimes (*Easy Rider*) this was hardly a problem. Mainly it was just a matter of elementary Italian vocabulary: *Il gruppo selvaggio, Non si uccidono così i cavalli?* Occasionally a bit more work was required, to decrypt *Fragole e Sangue* (Strawberries and Blood) back into *The Strawberry Statement*; *Un Uomo sul Marciapiede* (A Man on the Pavement, or, more likely, Sidewalk) into *Midnight Cowboy*. In Perugia there were people who, surprisingly to me at first, went to the movies so as to argue into the night about, say, Peckinpah's grievous politics.

In Cambridge cinema-going could also be a thrifty treat, thanks to the Arts Cinema, which programmed seasons of classics as well as a fastidious selection of current releases. I remember going to see Polanski's *Repulsion* at the late-night showing, tickled by the paradox that I was technically breaking the law (this would be October 1972) by seeking admittance to an X-rated film while underage, but that my offence evaporated during the screening, when midnight brought my eighteenth birthday with it.

The cold hysteria of that film made quite an impact, and I went back to my room in Trinity Hall wanting to push it out of my mind. But then I reasoned that this was the mistake made by Catherine Deneuve. I must be careful not to disintegrate in my turn, though perhaps not in a west London flat surrounded by sprouting potatoes and a rotting rabbit carcass. You can't be too careful, and in a student's room entropy is never far away. I sat down on the bed and thought the film through, until I could be reasonably sure I wasn't repressing trauma.

I read writing about film only casually. My father subscribed to *New Society*, and I remember a piece expounding *Jaws* in terms of the fear of *vagina dentata*, not the sort of theory that is easily forgotten by anything short of the Catherine Deneuve method. I read *Sight and Sound* occasionally, and was very struck by an essay on the imagery of cleansing and atonement in *Marathon Man* (which starts on Yom Kippur, literally the Day of Atonement, has an important scene by a fountain and ends in a water-purification plant), a brilliant piece of interpretation which made the film seem richer, undoubtedly, but somehow no better.

The crucial difference between cinema and theatre has always been repeatability – that a film can be screened again indefinitely, while a play disappears from immediate experience at the end of the run. In practice the difference, in those days, was not so great. When a friend and I saw Claude Miller's *La Meilleure Façon de Marcher* (The Best Way to Walk) at the Arts in Cambridge, we disagreed about the ending and what it meant. Our dispute centred on a single shot; of a drawer containing a red dress being pulled open, and who it was that was doing the opening. The only way to resolve it was to go back to the Arts and stump up 40p to see the film again. I don't remember who was right, which presumably means (given the working practices of the editing suite we call the memory) that I wasn't.

In 1978 I went to America, in theory to study the Faulkner holdings in the Alderman Library at the University of Virginia in pursuance of a PhD. I never crossed the threshold of the Rare Books Room, but life in Charlottesville seemed to suit me and I stayed on for a couple of years. I could Xerox *The Times* crossword from the copies arriving at that splendid library, and the Vinegar Hill movie theatre was solidly programmed. Callard & Bowser's butterscotch was available in the foyer, an imported luxury so precious that it was sold by the individual tablet, like cigarettes in impoverished areas. In the same way that filmgoers used to categorise weepies by the number of hankies needed to staunch the flow of tears, my friends would measure out a film in units of butterscotch. *Les Enfants du Paradis* was a three-tablet film.

I worked a couple of days a week in a second-hand bookshop which stocked some current magazines, and so was able to read Pauline Kael's *New Yorker* pieces. I would rather have seen the film first and read her article later, but the wait was often long for a showing within reach and I didn't usually have the patience. I remember that her review of *The Deer Hunter* was almost as extravagantly proportioned as the film it anatomised. The colossal wordage she was allowed meant that she could explore her reactions without the cramping effect of enforced concision on a subtle verdict. She greatly admired the film (its ambition, construction and particularly its editing) but she made no bones about the weakness of Meryl Streep's role, the shortfall in the female hemisphere of a film trying hard to encompass everything. This was the boys' movie *in excelsis*, but a boys' movie still.

My other favourite film critic took an almost opposite approach to banty, contentious Miss Kael. The existence of *Christopher Street* magazine was a shock in itself to a British gay readership: a non-pornographic glossy magazine, complete with urbane cartoons and upmarket advertising that was guaranteed to make our humble, high-minded *Gay News* look shoddy. And now *Christopher Street* was employing Quentin Crisp as its film reviewer! A man who clearly disliked his own minority, memorably saying that those homosexuals who wanted him to be less flamboyant were like consumptives urging one of their number to refrain from coughing, because it was spoiling the fun of TB for everybody else. It seemed a baffling appointment. Please bear in mind that this was a time when the belief that Americans didn't understand irony was as close to a religion as some of us got.

Once the surprise had worn off, though, the fit between contributor and magazine was perversely perfect. Crisp always called film stars, and everyone else, by title (Mr, Mrs or Miss) and first name – 'Miss Madonna', even – with something that wasn't quite old-fashioned good manners nor quite camp but something in-between. He must have been the only critic since about 1900 to put into practice the old principle that if you don't have anything nice to say, you should say nothing at all.

Sometimes in the sacred cause of politeness he was reduced to complimenting the decor or the cleanliness of the cinema lavatories. His secret weapon was the longevity of his movie-worship. He remembered the time when cinema was a female cult, almost a matriarchy, while men were catered to only by a few specialised genres.

While I was in America I sometimes had the opportunity to see a film under ideal conditions, namely without having read anything about it. I was in San Francisco the week that *Alien* opened. I knew nothing about it, but was curious on the basis of Ridley Scott's first film *The Duellists*, which I had seen at the Arts in Cambridge. At the showing I attended, there was a couple sitting behind me, clearly on a date. She was saying to him, 'I *love* scary movies.' But after John Hurt's little on-screen tummy upset, I could hear her hissing, 'I know what I said. I don't care what I said, we leave *now*.'

Cinema was from its beginnings a communal experience, though that potential excitement has steadily leaked away. People used to 'go to the pictures', ritually, regularly, without necessarily knowing or greatly caring what was on. The closest I have come to film-going on this model was in Charlottesville in, I suppose, 1980. The cinema in the downtown mall cut its ticket prices from $2.99 to 99 cents. When the manager was asked by the local paper how he could possibly afford to do that, he replied that they should be asking how he had ever thought he could afford to charge the old price. Certainly the movie house used to be thinly attended, and now it was full, at least at weekends. For less than a dollar, audiences would take their chances. The films we were there to see would have to be pretty bad to make them feel cheated.

One such film was good, even extraordinary, but not right for the venue and the occasion. The bulk of the audience strongly resented the scrupulously slow pacing, the deployment of anti-climax, the bleak smooth mood. There were well-managed climaxes, but they obstinately refused to join up and acquire momentum. What we were watching seemed more like an austere meditation on the horror movie than an actual example of the genre. Of course it did – it was *The Shining*. But for most of the punters in the cheap seats on the downtown mall (and all the seats were cheap) the film seemed to be one long failure to scale the heights of *Friday the 13th*. These viewers might not have been able to place *The Shining* in Kubrick's filmography, but they were pretty authoritative about its appeal to Saturday-night gorehounds. There was scornful backchat, and a popcorn tub was thrown at the screen – an empty one, but still . . .

After the publication of my first book *Lantern Lecture* I was fractionally in demand as a reviewer of fiction, first of all for the *Times Literary Supplement*. I was still living with my parents, and when they asked if I was making a living I said that reviewing for the *TLS* was an honour rather than a job, and no fee was expected. The truth was that I didn't know. No money was flowing in my direction, even after several months, and the most likely explanation seemed to be the one I gave. I wasn't to know, and nobody was going to spoil my fun by telling me, that when Rupert Murdoch took over Times Newspapers and started examining his purchase, he found anomalies in the accounts department. While these were being investigated, and those accused were on suspension, that department was running at half strength. *TLS* monies were not high on the list of priorities. Eventually tiny cheques started to reach me. It was almost a disappointment. I wasn't operating in a world above money after all, just one where it dripped rather than gushed. I was too well brought-up to think of biffing the tap with a wrench, either then or later.

Then the *Financial Times* asked if I would review for them on a regular basis. This had to be a step up – they had 'financial' right up there in the title, so I was obviously onto a good thing. I didn't like to mention money. They'd look after me. And they did – I reviewed a pile of books (sometimes as many as seven) in a fiction round-up every three weeks and they paid me £55.

Radio work plays a part in a lot of writers' lives, since it is by and large conversational rather than gladiatorial and it demands the minimum of preparation in terms of wardrobe and make-up. It's not exactly a licence to print money, though, or else a licence to print it very slowly, as in some stultifying performance art piece. When Alison Lurie had the heroine of her novel *Foreign Affairs* keep afloat financially in London with freelance radio work, there was wild laughter in the British reviews written by people who knew better – and everybody did.

Paul Barker at *New Society* then asked me to review films, and from there I moved on to the *New Statesman*. The *TLS*, *NS*, the *Staggers*: a standard enough career ladder for a freelance reviewer, though not likely to impress a yuppie of the period, since my ladder gave access not to a penthouse but something more like a tree house, if not the upper accommodation of a split-level hamster cage. Then I was offered a foothold on a wholly different style of rung – belonging to the sort of ladder which descends from a helicopter, in high winds and lashing rain, as it rescues the survivors in the last reel of an action film. The first quality newspaper to be launched in this country for two centuries was looking for reviewers.

The entire newspaper was a novelty, but there was also going to be a novel approach to reviewing. We wouldn't be specifically a film critic, a theatre critic, a television critic. All of us would do everything – though it was acknowledged that assessing classical music and dance required the technical knowledge of a specialist. I wasn't the only one to be offered the chance of being winched to safety by *The Independent* helicopter, the paint hardly dry on its rotors. Others included Marina Warner, Stephen Games and Peter Kemp. We would be a Round Table of critical knights, who would ride out in search of the Holy Grail of excellence, as likely to be found in a hovel as a palace, at a Feydeau farce revival or a Prince concert.

It was this free-range aspect which attracted me. Why should critics be cooped up in a single speciality? I had been very vaguely considered for the job of film reviewer at the *Sunday Times* (in the last phase of Frank Giles's editorship), but hadn't been all that keen. Film reviewers see too many films – it's a fact. Book reviewers don't reel from one book to another, and theatre reviewers rarely see more than one play a day. Art critics can take things at their own pace so as to refresh their overstimulated eyes, but press screenings take place in the daytime, one after another.

The mediums work differently in themselves. There's no motor in a book to keep it moving on – or rather, your brain is the motor whose teeth engage with the sprocket-holes of narrative. No one has ever nodded off while reading *The Thirty-nine Steps* and woken up with the chase concluded, the mystery solved. It's true that theatre proceeds independently of the audience's will, but the presence of breathing people in a shared space delivers an invigorating reproach to drowsiness. There's always the risk that La Redgrave or Le Sher will meet your eyes as you open them after a yawn and strike you dead with a basilisk bolt of contempt. Even the actors on stage pretending to be asleep (or comatose, or lifeless) are decently awake – dare you insult them by falling below their standard of vigilance?

Film is agreed to be the art form closest to dreaming, which unfortunately means that it's also the closest to sleep. As this is the art form which most rapidly turns novelty into routine, watching films in succession is a numbing rather than intoxicating experience. What you notice very soon is not the difference between products but the much-of-a-muchness. Differentiation suffers, and the rave review shades into the perfunctory endorsement. Worse, the denunciation fizzing with outrage becomes a weary dismissal.

The Independent's parliament-of-saints idea would keep us all fresh. The only disadvantage of the system was that every assignment would have to be fought over, but even this could be turned to advantage by the institution of a weekly lunch at which the distribution of labour could be settled. I could look forward to haggling with Marina Warner over whether she could review the new Le Carré as long as I had first dibs on the Pet Shop Boys concert, as if we were 1950s schoolboys doing swapsies with our stamp collections.

The departures from the norm started with the appointment of an arts editor, Tom Sutcliffe, who had never worked on a newspaper. This procedure is fully as orthodox as appointing the village policeman to be the parish priest, and if things had gone a traditional way then I would certainly not have got a sniff of a job. A newspaper man would have brought in old colleagues to build the staff, while Tom recruited from his radio contacts. He himself writes journalism under the name Thomas Sutcliffe, to disambiguate himself from a Tom Sutcliffe already filing (Wikipedia's propagation of the splendid word 'disambiguate' is enough in itself to justify the existence of that site).

When Tom suggested a meeting, I proposed as the venue a place in High Holborn, near where I lived. I had never been through its doors, but knew it served claret, port and sandwiches. That choice is a mystery to me now. Its name was The Bung Hole. Did I really think it was a good idea to tease him with a place that sounded as if it would contain go-go boys in cages rather than a fusty financio-legal clientele?

To be recruited so early meant that I would be writing pieces for the paper before it was even a fledgling, in the last month or so before the launch; not dummy articles exactly but real articles for dummy issues.

The whole venture had a stubborn unreality up to and even after the launch date. I began to fantasise that the whole thing was a charade set up by a philanthropist who (overestimating my aversion to charity) wanted to subsidise me as a writer without taking away my dignity. This delusion seemed to be corroborated by the odd fact that there was no editorial feedback during the dummy-issue period. If there was much anxious fine-tuning being done on fonts, layouts and production processes, why not give your contributors guidance about how to achieve a house style suitable to the new paper? Of course I may have hit the right note of unbuttoned authoritativeness from the first word, and never deviated from it, but the voice that tells me so is the same one that urges me to inspect my mail for the Stockholm postmark.

I was keen to see the first issue – and after all, my benefactor could easily have faked a copy for my benefit. After that I felt oddly squeamish when I saw someone on the tube reading the paper. What if it turned out to be blank sheets inside a dummy cover? Then my benefactor would withdraw hurt, and the cheques would dry up. It was quite a while before I started buying it myself (avoiding only the days when my own stuff was appearing).

The Independent was an odd mixture of risk-taking and playing safe, high-mindedness and business-as-usual. To start a new quality broadsheet was bold, but as the first editor, Andreas Whittam Smith, said more than once at the time, newspapers are an inherently very profitable business – how else could so many titles have survived so long with the dead weight of restrictive practices hung round their necks?

Rupert Murdoch had been confrontational with the unions at Wapping. *The Independent* didn't need to be. As a new paper it wasn't bound by the old dispensations and didn't need to be anti-union, just discreetly, placidly non-union.

Traditionally the making of newspapers was a heavy industry, the yoking together of an office in which words were written and a factory where that opinionated ore was smelted into print. It was a familiar sight to anyone brought up near Fleet Street in the '50s to come across lorries in the evening laden with huge lashed-down rolls of newsprint, like a scaled-up version of the bus-conductor's ticket roll which small boys of the period so longed to be given. After the *Daily Mirror* headquarters was built on Holborn Circus, my brothers and I were treated to tours of the building, which culminated in the making of a sample slug of hot metal for us to take away, a line of type with hidden meaning. If you held it up in the bathroom, the boy in the mirror showed you your name.

Even before the launch of *The Independent*, the twin aspects of newspaper making had started to separate. They were only elastically conjoined, and the writing desk and the smithy carried different messages of class. At Cambridge I had met Charles Moore, who said at the time that his dream job would be to be a village policeman, but (perhaps after being rejected?) went on to work for *The Telegraph*. I paid him a visit one lunchtime, and we were turned away from El Vino's, whose dress code I had failed to anticipate: gratifying result. Before I left he asked if I would like to see the presses. Yes, I would. We moved towards a low throbbing noise, which then seemed to be behind us. It also seemed to be below us, so we went down some stairs, after which it seemed to be over our heads. We didn't manage to find them that day, though I'm sure given enough time we could have tracked them down.

No such embarrassments would afflict the new paper. Visitors wouldn't expect to see the presses unless they had the power to dive down an optical fibre in the same way that each day's issue did, to Bedford or wherever our current printers were located. *The Independent* signed contracts with presses which might be far from London (as long as remoteness didn't compromise the distribution of the product) and could shop around, at renewal time, to keep costs down. With the hiving-off of the heavy industrial aspect of newspaper-making, *The Independent* could be run from suites of offices on City Road.

There were a few of the touted lunches (Peter Hall attended one of them) in a dining room below ground level, with a canted view of Bunhill Fields, but the atmosphere of a salon didn't really develop, and the distribution of assignments became bureaucratic rather than conversational.

I would call by the offices to drop off copy. Once I watched as article headlines and pictures were being jigsawed together on a computer, and the whole screen started flashing with the caption FITS! To lock down a page seemed an achievement of the same order as docking vehicles in space.

I was issued with a personal computer (I wish I had it now, to make today's cyber-kiddies laugh) but I didn't use it. It wouldn't exactly have transformed my working practice anyway, since in those prehistoric days before connectivity text couldn't be sent direct to some vast and secretly conspiring HAL 2000 on City Road. What I delivered or faxed would still have to be typed in, keystroke by keystroke.

On one visit to the offices I coincided with our editor. The arts department had asked if they could have some space on the front page for an item about the arms of the Venus de Milo being found in a field outside Paris. Andreas Whittam Smith was quietly delighted, gave permission very willingly, and asked if the other papers had got hold of the story or if this was an exclusive.

Well, it was an exclusive in its own way. The assembled journalists had to break it to their top man that this was an April Fool. He wasn't at all embarrassed, saying he could always be fooled by such things – he had been taken in by the story about the Harrods cellars extending under Hyde Park, and the hereditary job of rat-catcher required to keep the vermin down. Perhaps he should have been just a little embarrassed, since childlike trust isn't the first quality we look for in a newspaper editor.

The parliament-of-saints format at *The Independent* didn't last more than a few months. We were all learning as we went along. Tom Sutcliffe himself made the beginner's mistake of coming in under budget in the first year. Of course he was hoping to demonstrate that he was fiscally rigorous, so as to have more to play with the next year. Fat chance! Any decrepit old hack could have put him right about that. He should have overspent, though only slightly. Then he would have been in with a chance. As it was, his budget for the next year was cut.

Now Tom broke it to me gently that the readers (damn them all! If it wasn't for the readers, journalism would be a lot of fun) turned out to prefer a single critic per art form, so that they could familiarise themselves with a consistent approach, factoring in foibles and prejudices so as to know what to see themselves. From now on I would be reviewing films.

It took me a while to realise that I had accidentally landed my dream job. As the job developed, I didn't have to review all the films, like my opposite numbers on other papers, just a major release or two. I could write, in effect, the sort of extrapolating essay I had enjoyed reading so much in *New Society* and *The Statesman*, but to a tight deadline, so these were essays written under the gun. I had a good allocation of space, not wordage as far as the eye could see like Pauline Kael, but a large paddock or small prairie. The 'round-up' of lesser releases would be done by doughty buckaroo Sheila Johnston (and later by Ryan Gilbey), which meant that I wouldn't have to see too many films. I could stay fresh as a daisy, keen as mustard, mean as a dead dog.

Film previews were usually screened in basements in Soho, some smart and some seedy. There was one (the Bijou?) which seemed to have been decorated to suit the tastes of Barbarella's dowdy older sister. The seats weren't fixed in rows but were free-standing, large oval chairs of orangey yellow that held you almost horizontal. The mood induced by such furniture was an odd balance of torpor and panic, particularly when foreign-language films were shown. Subtitles could only be seen reliably from the front row, and the jockeying for a workable angle could be quietly savage.

The atmosphere was more or less the opposite of what prevailed on Charlottesville's downtown mall. It was considered beneath us to laugh at a comedy or to flinch during a horror film. At the preview screening of the original *Nightmare on Elm Street* everyone was talking about Cannes and the new Woody Allen when the lights went down, and when the lights came up they started talking about Cannes and the new Woody Allen again. It's just that their shirts were wet in a wide area below the armpit.

I had already become familiar with the presences and personas of some of my seniors in this new trade. There was Alexander Walker of the *Evening Standard*, whose place was always in the front row, dapper and prickly, a willed precision of diction overlaying any hint of Northern Irish origins. As he sat down on a Monday morning he would dependably give an acidulated little sigh through his teeth. He was expressing weary distaste even in advance of the films which would justify it. That sigh said, 'And how will my intelligence be insulted *this* week?' I felt he had already seen too many films, whether he knew it or not, although he went on raising his face stoically to the screen every week.

Alex was a fanatical anti-smoker. Those who had phoned him at home (an act of insane daring, or so it seemed to me) reported that his answerphone message ended with the formula

'Thank you for not smoking.' It does seem extraordinary that smoking was permitted at preview screenings in those days, though tobacco addicts tended to sit meekly at the back. Punctuality was also very much part of Alex's code, and he didn't take kindly to films starting late or (worse) being preceded by a trailer for another release. Over the years one or two publicity persons got themselves singed in the course of duty, by a crisp and beautifully enunciated tirade. One day, though, Alex was almost late, and found to his quiet shock that a smoker was installed in his seat, a seat which seemed as integral to his working life as the Stone of Scone is to the coronation of a British monarch.

The intruder possessed, as well as a thin crimped tube of cigarette paper with a few strands of Golden Virginia loosely plaited inside it, a beard and a ponytail, yet Alex remained polite. He delivered no reproach as such, but a series of related statements which should by rights, properly assembled in the trespasser's mind, have resulted in his moving on, a sort of flat-pack eviction order.

That is normally my seat. I have a strong objection to tobacco smoke. Smokers normally sit at the back. If they wish to see the screen through a foul fog that is their business, but I don't see why the bad habits of others should nauseate me while I work.

The trespasser gave a surprisingly sweet smile and said, 'I should tell you now that nothing you can say will make me change my behaviour.' Perhaps he was thinking that this was all a fuss over nothing, since there was such a tiny quantity of tobacco in his roll-up, and when that was combusted he was hardly going to roll another while watching a film. But between Alex and the tobacco plant there could be no truce. He took a seat further from the screen with the exemplary dignity and stiffness of someone who has been cashiered in full view of his troops.

What we watched that morning wasn't *RoboCop 2*, though my memories of that film are part of the same strand. It's a very ordinary sequel, with none of the vibrant misanthropy of the original, but one moment made a particular impact on the screening room. A plot complication involving corrupt officials results in the cyborg lawman being reprogrammed to pursue minor offences rather than chase the real bad guys in City Hall. So we see Peter Weller firing hundreds of shots out of a hi-tech machine-gun towards a civilian standing innocently on the pavement. The wall behind him becomes pitted with impact craters, forming a sort of artillery silhouette.

The traumatised pedestrian, not at all sure if he's alive or dead, lets the cigarette drop from between gibbering lips. In his voice of metal RoboCop intones, 'Thank You for Not Smoking.' A moment of marginal drollery became a fiesta of suppressed hysteria in the screening room, thanks to the presence among us of someone who would really struggle to concede that armed response was disproportionate. In Alex's mind it was the Zippo lighter which had fired the first shot.

Another colleague was genuinely a veteran – Dilys Powell, then in her mid-eighties. Her memories of film-going went back as far as Quentin Crisp's, and she had the knack of conveying her opinion perfectly clearly without ever abandoning a neutral tone (something I keep on meaning to try). By this time she was reviewing for *Punch*, and perhaps she had almost reached the point of having seen enough films for one lifetime. She dozed off fairly often, her chin slowly rising, and if I was sitting near her I would be careful to resist the siren call of such calm and regular breathing.

Yet she didn't abdicate critical functioning just because she was asleep. She only dropped off during films that weren't worth watching. There was always a pilot light left burning in her brain, a pineal eye alert and lidless while the lower two closed. It didn't take much to make that little chin snap down and to rekindle the full beam of attention. I saw it happen during a film called *Black Moon Rising*, in which Tommy Lee Jones and a director called Harley Cokliss – though these days he prefers to go by Cokeliss – puddled their talents (if that's the opposite of pooling them) to tell the story of a car which could reach a speed of 350 miles per hour. All it took was a few seconds of inventive editing in a humdrum chase sequence and Dilys was suddenly fully present and wide-eyed, admitting every image down the educated rainbow tunnels of her optic nerves.

I was surprised one afternoon to see Dilys leaving the cinema in mid-showing. This was at the Institute of Contemporary Arts, and we were being shown a South African film called *Shot Down*. Dilys's walking wasn't always steady, and night vision doesn't improve with age. She made her way past me and approached the exit door which would release her into the Mall. Like all such doors it had a very decisive action, so as to prevent unauthorised entry. She fluttered in front of it, like a bee at a window, but could make no progress in pressing down the horizontal bar, equipped with a strong resisting spring, which would trigger the mechanism.

I made my way over to her and added my strength to hers. The effect was dramatic. The door was flung open and Dilys was expelled from the cinema into the Mall, in more or less the way that people in science-fiction films are sucked through airlocks into the infinite void.

I returned to my seat and tried to take in the implications of what I had just seen. If Dilys Powell felt she didn't need to see the rest of *Shot Down*, perhaps I should consider playing truant myself. If someone of her integrity could break the reviewer's oath to see every frame of every film, then why was I clinging so stubbornly to that samurai code? Who was I trying to impress? I had already made up my mind about the poverty of the film's achievement, after all.

Then I became aware of movement behind me. It was Dilys, making her way back to her seat after entering the premises all over again. She hadn't been trying to leave at all, when I had activated the sly catapult of the ICA's exit door. She was trying to find the Ladies'. After that I sat meekly till the end of *Shot Down*, ashamed of my moment of temptation. If she could serve her full sentence without complaint, so could I.

A colleague who would never have thought of going absent without leave was Philip French, whom I knew from his work as producer of *Critics' Forum*, a long-running radio discussion programme with its own suppressed element of sumo wrestling. Philip reviewed for *The Observer*. There was no likelihood that he would ever see too many films, or even enough of them. There was always room in his head for a thousand more. He was voracious without being undemanding, and his memory for what he had seen was extraordinary. Hesitance of speech overlaid a great sureness of knowledge, shared with a faint air of startlement. He was almost embarrassed on your behalf that you should be so lacking in basic information, playing without a full deck (fifty-two million cards).

In those days it was hard to do basic research in a hurry. The press kit handed out before the screening played a vital role in filling the gaps in a filmography. I had a few reference books, but often went out on a limb, reassured that there were very few people in my readership with better access to background material. Still, if there wasn't Google there was Philip's brain, a search engine ahead of its time, cooled by the breeze in summer, kept at ideal functioning temperature in winter by nothing more than a scarf or hat. It didn't seem too

unprofessional to ask Philip casually at screenings for confirm-
ation of my faulty rememberings, but I would rather have fallen
on my sword than have called him at home to put my fallibility
formally on record.

Philip had an unusually strict interpretation of the film
critic's oath of service, and would stay in his seat until the very
last of the credits had processed slowly by. I admit I was more
cavalier, and would often join the surge towards the exits the
moment I saw the words THE END, or heard valedictory music.
The few times I have stayed to watch the credits it has been
when I have been too pole-axed by a film, for good or bad
(usually for bad), to trust myself to stay upright if I tried to
walk before fully recovering. Which is how I know that the
Best Dolly Grip Boy Clapper Loader Wrangler (or something,
if only I could ask Philip) on *JFK* was called Ulysses Fred.

Most weeks I could write 1,200 words, though for an
important release such as *Schindler's List* it could go as high as
1,600. That particular film presented me with real difficulties.
If there was such a thing as a Distinguished Medal Service
for reviewing, I might have qualified for it that week. The
preview screening was on a Monday morning – the morning of Valentine's Day, as it happened, though it's hardly a
movie for a romantic date. I set off to Soho in good health
and spirits. There was snow on the ground in Upper Street,
and I remember helping someone up who had slipped on a
zebra crossing. Then suddenly I felt very sick. I was able to
take refuge in a friend's flat without public disgrace, but there
was no possibility of seeing the film that day. I phoned the
office, hoping that someone could deputise for me, but no
luck. The best anyone could suggest was that I should catch
a trade screening late on Tuesday morning. This was hardly
ideal, since my deadline was ten o'clock the next morning, but
there was no alternative.

I was still feeling very queasy when I sat down to watch the film next day, and by then I hadn't eaten anything for more than a day. Over the next couple of hours, I fought a battle to keep my response to the film separate from the way my body was feeling. If I was in a genre movie myself, I would be the geologist attending a music festival on a tectonic fault, unable to stand due to an attack of viral labyrinthitis, who must work out which reading on the seismograph application on his iPhone is earthquake and which is heavy-metal band (this concept copyright 2011 by YouThoughtIWasJoking Enterprises).

As the film went on, I was increasingly bathed in bodily well-being, and this – though I don't want to spoil the film for you – is not the standard audience reaction to *Schindler's List*. I was sitting down, to be sure, but there was a new spring in my step. By the time women were being herded into showers by armed guards my body was saying, 'Soup! Why not soup? We could have soup!'

When my copy was written (by hand, since I had long ago returned my little computer to the office) I would file the old-fashioned way, the *His Girl Friday* way, dictating over the phone to a copy-taker, verbalising punctuation ('initial cap', 'plural poz') like an old pro. I remember seeing Ingmar Bergman's production of *Hamlet* at the National Theatre for *The Independent* (in Swedish, without surtitles, and lasting over four hours) – in which Ophelia for some reason kept appearing on stage even after her death. Naturally I dictated all the tricky Swedish names. When I came to Polonius, the copy-taker asked crisply, 'Is that Polonius spelled the usual way?' When I said yes, he asked, rather plaintively, 'What is the usual way?'

I would sit in a café to write my copy. In the absence of any word-counting technology, I learned to keep my writing small so as to get roughly 1,200 words on a side of A4. Then I only needed to count up manually once, make length adjustments as necessary, and phone it in. I enjoyed the prestige of working for a new newspaper, one with a claim to be breaking a few moulds. Everyone noticed the excellence of the photographs and the quality of their reproduction. Our competitors soon took steps to close the gap.

The Independent's film-reviewing format (a lead piece and a round-up), established more or less by accident, perhaps had some influence of its own, though on other papers the same poor overworked critic sometimes had to write both pieces. These days the number of releases each week is so much greater (perhaps ten on average) that such a format becomes awkward, and a simpler solution is to give each film separate consideration, sometimes with two critics dividing the workload more or less evenly.

There was another innovation made by *The Independent* in those early days, not accidental at all but a matter of principle. The paper would not carry coverage of such trivial matters as royal love affairs (unless they had had constitutional implications) or celebrity gossip in general.

It didn't catch on.

Gradually it faded, my delusion that the paper was some sort of benign hoax cooked up for my benefit. Even so, there was an absence of feedback that sometimes made me wonder, though it was certainly restful. I doubt if I got more than a hundred letters in the eleven years I wrote for the paper. Such a small sample is hard to analyse meaningfully. Getting two responses to a single review should be significant – but not if they cancelled each other out, like the two I got after reviewing *Raising Arizona*. One correspondent said that I was wrong to think a scene of byplay with baby quintuplets went on too long, because five babies would be two-and-a-half times as funny as her own twins, the other that she was horrified (as a mother of twins) that I would write approvingly about a film in which, clearly, babies were abused.

The two letters I got on the subject of *Awakenings* were in agreement – the reason I had hated the film, apparently, was because I couldn't deal with the amount of emotion in it. My own idea was very similar – that they had been taken aback because they couldn't deal with the amount of emotion in my review.

Most of the films I saw as a critic were American, and I could safely speak my mind without worrying about running into the director or actors. The very day, though, of my rather unsparing review of *Sammy and Rosie Get Laid* (Hanif Kureishi and Stephen Frears's follow-up to *My Beautiful Laundrette*), I was sitting at the bar in a crowded café in St Martin's Lane when cast members started to drift in. The only spare seat was next to me, and a whole party seemed to be assembling round it. Frances Barber – kisses all round – then Roland Gift. Of course no one made eye contact with me, but I became convinced that they were only waiting for the writer and the director to turn up, and then the lynching would begin (though the scene is really more Greenaway than Frears). Very slowly I eased myself off the stool and moved politely through the little crowd, moving with an exaggerated slow smoothness, thinking of the trauma-tised group at the end of *The Birds* who make their way gingerly across a porch covered with not-quite-dormant birds, which they know only too well could turn and rend at any moment.

Twice I have had a written response from a director, and that did seem mildly remarkable, since in both cases my review had been warm but not gushing. Tony Palmer wrote to say that the difficulties of making *Testimony* (his film about Dmitri Shostakovich starring Ben Kingsley) had been so great that he was relieved there was enough of what he had intended up on the screen to be discussed at all intelligently. Patricia Rozema, whose film of *Mansfield Park* attempted to find a more central place for things which Jane Austen kept in the margins of her book (colonialism, slavery), sent a postcard from Canada, barely the size of a book of stamps, saying simply 'I don't know who you are, but I think I like you.'

Sometimes letters weren't sent to me direct, and were intended for publication. This could be painful, particularly if there seemed to be an element of contrivance about the statement, artificial dismay, so that it seemed my neck was just a peg to hang a placard round. I reviewed Pedro Almodóvar's *Kika*, making it clear that this was not one of that little master's great works. I referred to its comedy rape scene as a supremely bad idea, but thought the director just about got away with it. I was mortified when the paper published a letter reproaching me for my indifference to the sexual abuse of women. As a gay man I should have known better than to take sides against my sisters.

More people have seen a salted slug, writhing in ugly pain under the roses, than a critic reproached for a failure of solidarity, but the spectacles are similar. I was the more pained because I would have written as right-on a denunciation of Almodóvar's reprehensibility as anyone could have wanted, if I hadn't attended the screening with a woman friend. She didn't object to the rape scene, and told me she felt that what had been a euphemism in Victorian times, 'a fate worse than death', had become the encouraged perception of sexual assault. She felt that such rhetoric gave women no permission to recover. It installed rape as the defining event of women's lives. She wasn't speculating, by the way, but speaking from experience of rape.

This I could not put in a letter. So I just fumed and squirmed, turning on myself the reluctant catechism of the public figure (Arts section, Nonebrity division).

Did I like being talked about? No.

Did I like it when people ignored me? No.

Could I dish it out? I sure could.

Could I take it? Not really.

Would I stoop to any low jibe in hopes of a cheap laugh? I would.

Had I stopped to consider Gérard Depardieu's feelings before writing 'there have been plenty of film stars in the past with cleft chins, none with cleft noses'? I had not.

My next experience of the letters-page pillory almost made me nostalgic for the first. The Scottish director Bill Forsyth made some beguiling low-key British films (*Local Hero* perhaps the most fondly remembered) before making some more in America, where low-key is a virtue that is held in low regard – though his first film to be made in the U.S., *Housekeeping*, was wonderful. Back on home ground he made a belated sequel to *Gregory's Girl*, called *Gregory's Two Girls*, which was horribly disappointing and incoherent. Only respect for the makers of Pedigree Chum could veto the label 'dog's dinner'. John Gordon Sinclair played the schoolboy from the earlier film, now himself a teacher, idealistic in theory but entirely passive. He gets involved in a scheme to expose the sinister dealings of a local businessman, who supplies torture equipment to Third World tyrannies, but really only because he is attracted to one of the activists, a pupil of his.

It becomes a cause for official concern that he has been seen in her company in a park late at night. An interview is arranged with his headmaster, which the police will attend. The girl has already given an explanation, but Gregory doesn't know what it is. Luckily one of her friends slips him a piece of paper with a single word written on it, just enough for him to build his story round. The word names a mammal.

The detective asks: 'So what were you doing last night?'

Gregory's reply: 'Well, last night was pretty exciting, actually, because Frances had more or less promised us . . . You see, the thing is, I've never actually seen Frances's beaver.'

A silence quivering with horror.

What has gone wrong? There is another mammal that starts with the same letter as the one he meant to say. Under pressure he has substituted the name of a beast extinct in the wild with an unfortunate double meaning catastrophic in this disciplinary context. To be fair, it could happen to anyone, anyone in an unreal situation with a flailingly desperate script.

Gregory spots his mistake: "'Frances's beaver"! I mean Frances's badger . . .'

How to describe this? *Carry On Amnesty International* with a queasy subtext? The queasiness lying in the fact that Gregory is only technically innocent of taking an improper sexual interest in the girl, since he hasn't had a chance to act on it.

Every critic has a private Rogues' Gallery of things he or she would do anything not to see again (the option of never having seen it in the first place not being available), but it's unusual to have two of them in the same film. In this second scene, Gregory is again on nocturnal manoeuvres. By accident, a stranger's fingers get caught in a slammed door. His fingertips swell up. The stranger explains that this has happened to him before, when he was tortured in his home country, and that there is only one way to relieve the pressure on his fingertips. Someone must pierce the fingernails, one by one. This duly happens, though Gregory is too squeamish to face it and the honours are done by a teenaged girl. There is a spurt of blood each time a nail is pierced.

How is it supposed to work, this crazed cocktail of adventure story, shoehorned-in political commentary and horror film? It doesn't begin to coalesce. It would make more sense to feature a drive-by shooting on Tobermory as a way of sensitising children to the dangers of the inner city. Reviewing the film made me feel as if I was writing the obituary of a talented film-maker who had made too many wrong turns, in a business that punishes them heavily. Bit of a surprise, then, to read a published letter from the founder of a campaigning charity lamenting my failure to take the issue of torture seriously.

Most of the people who read the letter, not having read my review in the first place, would take my inhumanity as proven, but (the damage being done) it was pointless to think of writing my own angry letter of response. Shakespeare of course put it best, when he had Cassio exclaim, 'Reputation, reputation, reputation! O! I have lost my reputation. I have lost the immortal part of myself, and what remains is bestial. How will I face the lads down the Groucho now?' It certainly seemed odd for a humanitarian to insult a reviewer's integrity as a way of getting publicity for a charity. It so happens that the same organisation asked me to take part in gala events more than once afterwards, and I accepted, though always with some rage in my heart.

For the time being, the film review pages were established and possibly even respected. I remember receiving quite a few compliments for my review of Clint Eastwood's *Heartbreak Ridge*, although as it happened they all were compliments for Tom's headline, 'Macho Do About Nothing'.

At one point it turned out that *Variety* and the film page of *The Independent* went to press on the same day. Tom felt it would be polite and even politic for me to phone *Variety* to let them know my verdict on this week's films. *Variety*'s rating system wasn't tremendously sophisticated, so at least I didn't have to spend too much time paraphrasing my intricate judgements: thumbs up (Genius), thumbs down (Stinker) or thumbs level (Ho-hum). Anyone who has a thousand words to devote to a film will end up with level thumbs more often than not.

In weeks when I forgot to make the call, *Variety*'s experts won't have had any trouble guessing the verdict. Not hard to predict the behaviour of the Man with Horizontal Thumbs. Sometimes, though, I surprised myself. I remember ringing

Variety to say that the Coen brothers' *Barton Fink* had coaxed my thumb to quite a perky angle, then sitting down to write the review and finding that in fact I disliked it. I've enjoyed quite a number of those boys' pictures (*The Hudsucker Proxy* and *O Brother, Where Art Thou?* in particular), and *Barton Fink* wasn't obviously short on flair and brio. It was just the contempt with which the Coens regarded a different sort of artist, the one who wants to change the world, which rankled in my memory. Talk about easy targets! And a fraternal team writing/directing/producing can easily get lost in self-congratulation, missing that meshing of contradictory characters which made Powell and Pressburger so remarkable as a team.

Seeing the film again might settle the point, though in general my reactions are pretty consistent. In the first stages of re-seeing a film, I may wonder why I rated it so highly – or else, why I had dismissed it – but by the end I'm more or less where I was the first time round, even if my thumb-language has a lot more vitality and nuance than the exhausted hitchhiker gestures which make up *Variety*'s impoverished dialect. I'm more like the tic-tac men at the races.

I lasted at the paper for over a decade. There was a tenth birthday party, held at the Victoria and Albert Museum, with speeches – which I didn't hear because I had bunked off to the outdoor courtyard with some secretaries from the advertising department who valued their cigarette time. I didn't smoke myself, but was flattered to be asked along by the bad girls, the truants. They cross-examined me about a column in the paper which meant nothing to me. Everyone knew 'she' was written by a gay man, apparently, and that meant either me or someone I knew. I swore blind that I didn't know what they were talking about, and by rights I should have convinced them, unless they thought I was pulling off some brilliant double-bluff. From their point of view it was barely possible that there was anyone in the world, let alone anyone on the paper, who hadn't read *Bridget Jones's Diary*.

I lasted about another year before the new editor, Andrew Marr, decided he could manage without my services. He gets points for speaking to me directly, not delegating the task of giving a contributor the chop, though he has to lose some of them right away for using the formula 'change is good, at all levels of the paper' – which may have come back to haunt him a few months later when he too got the chop.

Later I learned that I had been hanging by a thread for some time, though a number of colleagues (stand up, Mark Lawson) had made the case that I was in some way an asset to the paper. They were certainly good years for me, though I can find it in my heart to be sympathetic to some directors. I imagine Ridley Scott, for instance, opening his *Independent* one day in 1988 in search of a review of his new film *Someone to Watch Over Me*, and finding instead my extended riff on the idea that he is the tame Eisenstein of Reaganomics, making wealth seem a natural state and subsistence living an aberration. So much for the trickle-down ideology of his entertainment.

Lower down on the page is the *Inside Eye* column, in which an expert in some field (in this case, a bodyguard) is invited to comment on a film dramatising his profession. From this he learns that no competent security operative would assign a man to protect a woman, since this would leave her vulnerable during bathroom visits. So much for his plot . . .

I don't have too bad a record in terms of recognising right away which films would be influential and even become classics, but I didn't see it as being my job. I wasn't paid to back a winner, just to make an argument. When the paper printed in 1994 a letter complaining that I had liked neither *Pulp Fiction* nor *Forrest Gump*, I can't say I was bothered. There isn't a quota system in place determining how many films a year a critic must like if he is to stay in post. Quentin Tarantino's film seemed to me smug in its perversity, while Robert Zemeckis's was rancidly wholesome. But don't mind me – feel free to watch them back to back for the rest of your life.

I learn from IMDb that Ulysses Fred was part of the 'swing gang' on *JFK*. I can't say I have any clearer an idea about what his job involved, but at least it's reassuring to know I didn't make him up. It's his only credit – perhaps he dropped something important and valuable, or was so much mocked for his lovely name that he changed it.

If there were acclaimed films that left me cold, there were others not generally liked that worked just fine with me. The second sequel to *Alien* was perceived as a disappointment, though I didn't see it that way.

Alien³ (1992)

Alien³ sets the seal on an extraordinary series of films, mainstream entertainment firmly in the tradition of can't-bear-to-look-can't-look-away which nevertheless touch on some incongruously ambitious themes. While, say, Tim Burton's *Superman* films sacrifice the dynamism of their genre to the look but not the reality of art cinema, David Fincher's *Alien³* delivers images of an often extraordinary beauty without letting the adrenaline level of its narrative drop much below the maximum.

A lot of credit for the success of the series must go to Walter Hill, a successful action director in his own right who has chosen to restrict his contribution to production and screenwriting but has been a far-thinking godparent of the project as it evolved.

It takes nerve in the context of modern Hollywood to wait for eight years before making a sequel to a highly successful film, and a further five before completing the triptych. On the other hand, there tends not to be a lot left standing at the end of an *Alien* film except the heroic Ellen Ripley (Sigourney Weaver), battered but finally triumphant, so there is no logical alternative to starting from scratch.

The story of the new film was written by Vincent Ward, himself a considerable director (*Vigil, The Navigator*). It would have been interesting to see what he would have made of *Alien³* if he had been put in actual charge. Certainly *The Navigator* contains a number of elements further developed in *Alien³*: a fierce focus on ordeal and redemption, and constant recourse to medieval images and spaces, Gothic vaults and galleries pregnant with darkness.

Ward's story deals with a prison world where the inmates have found religion, choosing to stay on after the end of their sentences and indeed after the closing of the 'containment facility'. Ripley crash-lands into a hostile, single-sex world, where she is treated as an enemy until it turns out that she has unwittingly brought a worse one with her. The Alien's habit of lunging from ducts and vents and biting people to bits has a certain foreshortening effect on character development, but something of Ward's vision survives: a grim world in which transcendence is still somehow possible.

What makes the *Alien* series modern, even (dread word) post-modern, is the way it has had critical reaction fed back into it, so as to become in reality what a few enlightened or simply over-excited viewers thought it was or might be. Was the dark feminist fantasia that some critics detected in Ridley Scott's original film planned or accidental? Cast your mind back to when Ol' Slime Chops was new. The late casting of a woman to play the eventual sole survivor suggests it was

accidental. But the film-makers have certainly learned to cap-
italise on a fluke of ideology. The first sequel, James Cameron's
Aliens (1986), duly incorporated a theme of motherhood, to
extend but also neutralise the images in the first film of Alien
infestation as a nightmare pregnancy. Ripley forged a maternal bond with a child living wild on a devastated planet, and
ended up fighting a duel for custody of her with the Queen
Alien – the Bad Mother.

Aliens now looks like the weakest film in the cycle, flawed
by a certain sentimentality and a relatively routine approach
to action. Ripley's heroism in the first film was a matter of
making the right decisions, striving to put the interests of the
group over individuals, while in *Aliens* the men who were the
natural fighters were progressively put out of action, leaving
her no alternative but to fill the role left vacant. It may be
that James Cameron genuinely admires strong women, but
then so do the men who pay to watch female mud-wrestling.
Women being strong is a sexy concept; women being right is
actually more threatening. In *Alien³* the emphasis is once again
on Ripley's willingness to accept loss and make sacrifices. It
would have been interesting to have female input on *Alien³*
behind the camera as well as in front of it (though admittedly
Weaver co-produced and presumably carries clout) but perhaps
Kathryn Bigelow, currently working her way through the action
genres, had other directorial engagements.

The new film contains, in effect, a critique of its immediate predecessor. The girl who was the sentimental focus of
Aliens is dead before the opening credits are over, and the first
thing Ripley must do is have her anatomised, for fear of a parasitic presence in the corpse. This scene amounts to a brusque
dissection of the previous film's heart. Only the intense grief
of Sigourney Weaver's reaction shots prevent it from being a
mocking in-joke. Weaver's performance throughout shows an

undiminished intensity in the role that made her reputation and has dominated her career.

Other episodes revisit earlier scenes with more respect. The moment in the first film when Ripley patched up the disabled robot who had been masquerading as the USCSS *Nostromo*'s science officer Ash (Ian Holm) to get answers to her questions is recapitulated in the new film when she rescues fragments of the android Bishop from a scrapheap, sliding electrodes into his head in order to play the flight recorder of a crashed ship. The conversation between Bishop (Lance Hendricksen) and Ripley is full of pain, tenderness and the dark humour that becomes more pronounced as the film goes on, without jeopardising its seriousness. Bishop comments on Ripley's hair, cut skull-short to forestall lice, with an oddly marital matter-of-factness. In *Aliens* Bishop won the status of honorary human by his readiness to sacrifice himself, but in *Alien³* that status is shown to be no more than a sentimental limbo. Bishop chooses death in preference. To be virtually human is to be nothing.

In the new film, though, Ripley has something remarkably like a soul. We have seen nothing in the world of the film that is worthy of her sacrifices, and as *Alien³* moves towards its apocalyptic conclusion she risks turning into a saint of the future. To the Roman virtues she adds Christian excellences, even Christly ones. This isn't just the most heroic female role in the movies; nothing the other gender can boast comes anywhere near it. At the end of *Alien³* Ripley puts herself in a maternal relationship with all humanity, not giving birth to the world but taking death out of it. All this is wildly over the top, but startling in genre terms, and visually persuasive from moment to moment in David Fincher's steady hands. *Alien³* is a technological film not ruled by technology, as well as a gory film not ruled by gore.

Not everything in it is quite so exalted. One punch, laid by Ripley on a man who has assaulted her, is there purely to raise a cheer from a Saturday night crowd, while one of the Alien's entrances, from a bath of boiling lead in which it was presumed dead, suggests only that *Fatal Attraction* forms a cherished part of its video library. But David Fincher conjures images of a strange, disinterested beauty out of a convincingly grim reality, and from its perhaps accidental beginnings the *Alien* series has turned into a fascinating, contradictory exploration of the themes of death and motherhood.

Alien³ was a 'troubled production', apparently, after which David Fincher felt no particular enthusiasm for directing another film. In an interview with *The Guardian* in 2009 he said, 'No one hated it more than me; to this day, no one hates it more than me,' which puts me in an awkward position. So I was wrong to like it as much as I did? – except that the director himself isn't always right, and many of them (Hitchcock only the most extreme example) have a habit of revising their verdicts once a film is released, either to fit in with the general opinion or to contradict it.

Kathryn Bigelow's *Strange Days* managed to be a controversial film, without having the commercial success that is often the consequence, intended or unintended, of that status.

Strange Days (1995)

With *Strange Days*, Kathryn Bigelow continues her rampage through the film genres. *The Loveless* was a biker movie, *Near Dark* was a (highly effective) horror film. *Blue Steel* was a woman-with-a-gun melodrama, and *Point Break* was Bigelow's contribution to the tiny genre of the surfing/skydiving/detective thriller/buddy movie. *Strange Days* is another hybrid, a futuristic thriller with an unusually complex agenda, based on one piece of imaginary hardware rather than a whole fictional world. The story, by James Cameron, is a great deal better than the one he last chose to direct – *True Lies* – or, by the sound of it, his next project – *Spiderman*.

The advance publicity for *Strange Days* has been negative, with Ralph Fiennes (excellent in the film) being interviewed as if a nice English boy who should have waited for the phone call from Merchant Ivory had gone and spoilt it all by making a snuff movie. For the record: *Strange Days* is less violent than, say, *Casino*, and certainly less offhand about violence than *RoboCop* or *Total Recall*.

Not only that: the film is largely preoccupied by the morality or otherwise of vicarious experience (which is one definition of art, or of pornography). The gizmo at the heart of the plot is the Squid – a little headset that records and plays back a person's sensations, originally developed as a refinement of the 'wire' that undercover police wear to obtain evidence. In 1999 the Squid is illegal for civilian use, but there is an underground and a vocabulary: users 'jack in', a sly mixture of the druggie (jack up) and the sexual (jack off). And the hero sells tapes, of sex, of crime. You want a nun to tie you up? It's all doable.

The first conversation we see that involves Lenny Nero (Fiennes) is precisely about the limits of entertainment. He agrees to buy a tape (a 'clip'), which, disorientatingly, we have seen without knowing what it was – but haggles over price because he's going to have to edit out the end, where the Squid wearer falls to his death. He doesn't do snuff. Everyone knows that. He's got ethics here. His supplier just says, 'Yeah, when did that start?' He seems to be standing in for the director when he says, 'You ask for excitement, for what's raw, and then you can't take it. And you blame me.'

In 1999 Los Angeles is a few steps further along the road to collapse. Lenny drives through streets where the police rely on tanks and where teenage girls beat up Santa Clauses. Some of this background is cartoonish (like the violence in Godard's *Weekend*, for instance), but Bigelow is also making a formal point. Lenny keeps changing stations on his car radio, and the streets look different with each style of music. Lenny filters reality as he goes along, as if the windscreen was just that: a screen. It's also a good joke that people should feel so bizarrely safe in their cars, according to the long-standing principle of LA life that nothing good can come of being a pedestrian.

Strange Days is a thriller not a lecture. Yet behind Bigelow's exemplary kinetic control of a complex plot, the hero keeps being offered moral choices, for all the world as if this were an episode of *Star Trek*. He can choose the past, and the used emotions associated with Faith (Juliette Lewis), his ex-girlfriend now making it as a rock star (sensibly Bigelow buys in some fierce PJ Harvey songs for her to sing). Or he can wake up to the present and the future, to the disapproving love of his old friend 'Mace', played by the magnificent Angela Bassett, who has one of the most stylish martial-arts routines since the heyday of Emma Peel.

Lenny always makes the right choice, but the argument for substitute experience gets a fair shake. Early in the film we see a new client of Lenny's being given a taste, only we don't see the clip, just the reaction to it. What we see is a fully dressed lawyer, eyes closed, slowly running his hands over himself in a trance of wonder. He's an eighteen-year-old girl in the shower. Lenny is smirking, but that's partly because he made a good guess when it came to giving this new customer a test-drive, and the lasting impression of the scene is pathos: the sadness of our hunger to be other than we are.

Later on, Lenny drops off a clip for a friend, who's in a wheelchair. When he plays it, we simply see footage of legs, legs reliably pumping down there at the water's edge. An early morning jog by the ocean – is that a pornographic experience for someone who can't walk? Or is it consolation, a workout for phantom limbs?

In the past, Cameron's screenplays have moved towards thunderous but linear climaxes: in the Terminator films it was merely a question of waiting for a dismantled cyborg to get its act together one more time. *Strange Days* has a more complex resolution, as a seeming sub-plot turns into the real thing after all. Cameron credits Bigelow with wanting to emphasise the race relations aspect of the story, but it's a bold move all the same. As the countdown to a new millennium starts – 2K, as people call it in the film – the world's biggest party could just as easily be the world's biggest riot.

Who would have expected a sympathetic black character in a mainstream Hollywood picture to say the line, 'Maybe it's time for a war'? When was the last time a rap artist was positively presented in such a film? As *Strange Days* moves towards its ending, it is filled with memories of the Rodney King beating, and the knowledge that in a racially polarised society riot is always in the wings.

Strange Days is loud and dazzling. It will take audiences a little while to get up to speed with it, but it is a stirring and surprising piece of film-making. Any apocalyptic vision of Los Angeles tends to look like *Blade Runner*, but Kathryn Bigelow styles the city confidently. A more important influence on the screenplay is certainly Michael Powell's *Peeping Tom*: the sequence in *Strange Days* that has been seized on as outrageous – of the rape and murder of a woman made to see her own death by being wired up to her attacker's Squid – is clearly modelled on the more low-tech sadism of Powell's murderer, who had only a film camera (with added stiletto) and a parabolic mirror to achieve the same goal.

Peeping Tom is an extraordinary film, but sometimes it seems the director has forgotten that it is a horror movie rather than an allegory of the artist's doomed attempt to fix beauty. *Strange Days*, for all its noisiness, doesn't gloss over the suffering of its victims. In its consideration of voyeurism, too, it is a lot less hypocritical than, say, *Henry: Portrait of a Serial Killer*.

The hostile reception to *Peeping Tom*, famously, killed Powell's career. An Englishman should know better than to dabble in such Americanised filth. Kathryn Bigelow's position looks secure, but it certainly seems that being a woman film director makes you a sort of honorary Brit, expected to take the genteel route at all times, and regarded as a traitor for making an action picture that offers no special exemption to your gender.

And here's the *Schindler's List* piece I mentioned, heroic reviewing against the odds:

Schindler's List (1993)

The surprise about *Schindler's List* is not that it comes from the maker of *Jurassic Park* or the *Indiana Jones* films, with their buffoon Nazis. Anyone is entitled, like Graham Greene, to undertake entertainments as well as more challenging projects. The surprise is that it comes from the maker of *Empire of the Sun*, another narrative of suffering and survival, and one that seemed in prospect perfectly chosen to help Steven Spielberg make the passage from entertainer to serious artist. Even those few years ago (when it was already his ambition to film

Schindler's List), he was unable to kick his addiction to spectacle. He cared too much that his extras be visible in their full numbers; he wanted the focal depth of his sets to be appreciated. He sought to convey extremes of human experience, but still he lusted after crane shots.

Most of *Schindler's List* is very different. Shot in black-and-white, and making extensive use of hand-held cameras, the film has in parts a pseudo-documentary intensity quite opposed to Spielberg's usual style, which is hyper-realistic (with all the paradoxes attendant on being exaggeratedly real) rather than merely realistic. The film is also three-and-a-quarter hours long, and as distressing as a conscientious film about genocide must be.

Some sequences have the force of ghastly newsreels, while others convey extremity by understatement. *Schindler's List* makes the setting-up of a little row of collapsible chairs and tables in the open air – a repeated image – the arrangement of typewriters, sheaves of paper slips, endorsing stamps, seem to contain the horror they represented. How chillingly casual it looks, how lightweight, the bureaucracy that administered a people into ash.

The screenplay, by Steven Zaillian from Thomas Keneally's fact-based novel, is like a mirror-image of István Szabó's great film from the 1980s, *Mephisto*. There, a moderately well-meaning actor who started off as a communist gradually became suborned by the Nazis until his soul was wholly owned. Though it was hard to identify the precise moment at which his rot became definitive, there could be no doubt that it had occurred. *Schindler's List* is about an inverted corruption. A moderately ill-meaning Nazi, content to profiteer, is thanked for good deeds he hasn't intended, saves lives half-selfishly and gradually becomes encrusted with virtue. Over time the base metal of his nature corrodes to gold.

Where *Mephisto* was cautionary, *Schindler's List* is inspirational, but that doesn't condemn it. It is as close to a feel-good story about the Holocaust as you can responsibly get, but that isn't very close. There's nothing wrong in emphasising that one person can make a difference, although it isn't true that absolutely anyone can always make a difference. Oskar Schindler wouldn't have had the power to save if he hadn't already acquired the power to exploit, when he took over a confiscated enamelware factory in occupied Kraków, and found that Jews cost less to employ than Poles. (Their wages also went directly to the authorities, which created good feeling all round.)

Early on, Schindler's argument against the destruction of the Jews was at least in part economic – it was bad business to kill a docile, in fact enslaved, workforce – and there is no clear indication of a moment at which it became moral. The screenplay is content to leave virtue a mystery.

Spielberg grants his audience intermissions of grief in the narrative of horror. John Williams's music is let loose, and emotion openly vented. Sometimes the effect is of deepening feeling, sometimes of reflex manipulation, when we are already in the state of mind that manipulation pimps for. In particular, Spielberg throws away the implacability of the sequences that show the liquidation of the Kraków ghetto, which Schindler (Liam Neeson) witnesses by chance from an overlooking hill while horse riding. Schindler's attention is caught by a child in a red coat, which the director tints for our benefit.

This gimmick is in every way counter-productive. It singles out a child from a panorama of violence, it insists all over again on the artificiality of images whose authority has been painstakingly earned, and above all it alienates us from Schindler's perceptions in the very act of dramatising them, since, whatever it is that draws his eye to the little girl, it can't be that she is the only splash of colour in a black-and-white world. It is as if the withdrawal symptoms of giving up his addiction to spectacle had become too much for Spielberg, driving him back to his habit for a quick fix of cartoonishness. Certain sorts of truth go stubbornly against his grain.

If the screenplay is content for Schindler to remain enigmatic, it is perversely curious about the psychology of Amon Goeth (Ralph Fiennes), commandant of the Plaszów forced-labour camp. *Schindler's List* shows no understanding of low-level evil, fellow-travelling evil. We see monsters laughing in the middle of the suffering they have created, monsters playing Bach on the piano mid-massacre. There is no acknowledgement that brutalisation is a fact, that if you force a group to live in inhuman conditions you can make them disgusting even to people who did not start off loathing them. Even perhaps to themselves.

And yet a large portion of screen time is given to an arch-monster, who added arbitrarily to the atrocities that were demanded of him professionally. The screenplay wants Goeth to have a psychology, but doesn't go to the trouble of supplying him with one. Schindler suggests that, in other circumstances, he might be a nice guy. Spielberg, with baffling crudity, cross-cuts between the two men's equally fastidious shaving on the day Goeth happily announces the end of Jewish Kraków, as if uncovering a profound correspondence. Zaillian writes a monologue in which Goeth expresses sexual attraction to his Jewish housemaid and then blames her for trying to seduce him, but Fiennes can do nothing with it. Spielberg adds more crass cross-cutting, between Goeth beating the maid, a ramshackle wedding in the camp and Schindler enjoying the high life. No film of 195 minutes is actively too short, and considerable economies could have been made in this unrewarding area.

In any case, the odd echoes are not between Goeth and Schindler, but between Schindler and Hitler (the syllables have a teasing parity). The poetry of the story comes from the fact that Schindler's neutralisations of Nazism looked like continuations of it. His counter-bureaucracy rhymed with what it opposed. Hitler set up death factories, and death camps served by death trains. Schindler's factory produced life for those who worked there, his sub-camp at Plaszów preserved people, the trains he filled took people to safety. The gas chambers were disguised as showers: Schindler's people-conservatory at Brinnlitz in Czechoslovakia, where he took his workers from Kraków, was disguised as a munitions factory, though the machinery was miscalibrated so that nothing it produced could destroy. Hitler caused Jews to be killed, and their teeth to be pulled from them for the gold lodged there. But Schindler caused a Jew to offer his own living tooth for the wrenching, so that a ring of thanksgiving might be forged in his honour. Hitler's legacy is a vast absence. Schindler's is a descendance of other people's children, people whose cancellation he cancelled. When in the film Schindler is given the ring, he is so moved that he drops it.

Liam Neeson has plenty of presence, which he must rely on in an all but impossible role. Schindler doesn't reveal his emotions much, even to his wife; he has a gambler's instinctive unreadability. Even the Jewish accountant Stern (Ben Kingsley), who makes the enamel business possible, has to deduce his goodness rather than observe it directly. Kingsley gives the film's finest and most necessary performance: he is particularly good in early scenes at conveying a man in deep shock, who only understands that for some reason those who are destroying his people demand that he not show he has noticed. He becomes the audience's stand-in, as his face slowly dramatises the dilution of fear by hope.

In the big scene at the end, when Schindler on the last day of the war takes leave of those he has saved, Neeson must send his performance into full reverse. In one sense this is a highly theatrical moment, of rhetorical address to a large audience, but it is also the opposite. A lifelong actor drops his mask at last, when it no longer matters, and speaks from the heart, but discovers a new sort of pain as he does so, blaming himself for keeping a car that was worth ten people, even a gold Party badge that would have bought two lives.

There are several separate big scenes compressed into this one big scene, and perhaps only in the theatre, on a good night with the right audience and everybody flying, could such a mixture of intimacy, community, relief, desolation and joy come off, once or twice in a long run. Spielberg seems to acknowledge this by supplying a coda, an alternative discharger of audience emotion, with present-day survivors from among the survivors paying tribute at Schindler's grave escorted by the actors who played their younger selves.

Schindler's List is three partial films in one: a harrowing pseudo-documentary, an effective melodrama, and an embarrassing piece of kitsch movie-making. Authentic intensity, emotionalism and botch: the first two marry unexpectedly well, and the third element is by far the smallest, but it is there, and it means that the film is less than the touted breakthrough for the cinema. But it is a considerable achievement for Spielberg, hyperbole addict on the long road to recovery, though still sometimes in denial about the scale of his problem.

I remember going to the newsagents the morning this review was published feeling quietly proud of myself, reasonably sure that I had made up the ground lost to flu. Weekly reviewing on the basis I was doing it, rarely seeing a film before the week of release, is necessarily a race against time, but one lacking the athletic elegance of sprinting. It's more like the egg-and-spoon race, and I'd managed to scramble to the finishing line without dropping my cargo of fragile impressions, despite a late start.

I was dismayed to find that the copytaker had misheard 'perceptions' ('it alienates us from Schindler's perceptions in the very act of dramatising them') as 'deceptions', making nonsense of an important part of the argument. I'd been tripped at the finishing line and not even known it. There was nothing to be done about it, but at least the mistake would be forgotten, newspapers being so ephemeral . . . except that the review is available online a quarter of a century later, still with the misprint. In fact, I now notice that 'rhetorical address' had become 'rhetorical redress', also mangling the sense. Perhaps the copytaker had a hangover?

Anyone who dictates copy over the phone is wise to avoid seeing what actually appears in print. I'm amazed that anyone could make head or tail of what ended up in the paper. 'Theme' and 'scene' replace each other on a regular basis, 'essentially' degrades to 'eventually', 'revoke' routinely trumps the 'evoke' I intended, 'beauty' is sternly moralised as 'duty'. The copytakers must have thought, *he seems to know what he's talking about, I'd better not ask* – particularly the one who greatly enriched the plot of *Notorious* when he typed 'Iranian' rather than 'uranium'.

It obviously bothered me at the time that the film didn't dig deep into Schindler's motivation, but over time I came to think I was importing irrelevant criteria. *Schindler's List* was, and is, unusual among films about the Holocaust for having a distinctly Jewish viewpoint.

In my review I had contrasted Spielberg's film with *Mephisto*. Another film, released a few years later, *Amen.* (2002), indirectly illuminates the point. The frame of reference shifts; Christianity places such enormous stress on motive, on clarity of conscience, making the interior experience the touchstone of good action. When you gave money to that beggar, was it to impress the person you were with? In which case your behaviour is compromised. Puritan self-scrutiny doesn't take effectiveness into account, is even actively suspicious of it, as if the sin of

pride lurked in any sense of achievement, while Jewish morality welcomes it. Schindler saved lives, and that's all you need to
know. The inscription on the ring given to Schindler in the film
('Whoever saves one life saves the world entire') is both mystical
and down-to-earth.

British culture in particular has a soft spot for the heroic
failure, but this characteristic is shared by other parts of the world,
other traditions. *Amen.*, for instance, is directed by an expatriate
Greek (Costa-Gavras), co-written by him for the screen with
a Frenchman (Jean-Claude Grumberg) from a play, known in
English as *The Deputy* or *The Representative* by a German (Rolf
Hochhuth). Both play and film present an indictment of Pope Pius
XII as being indifferent to the annihilation policy of Nazi Germany,
through the story (more central in the film than the play) of Kurt
Gerstein, an SS officer in charge of distributing Zyklon B – he
was head of the Technical Disinfection Services – who tried to
get news of the Holocaust out to the world, briefing a Swedish
diplomat and using Catholic contacts to send messages to the
Vatican. None of this activity was successful, and he was treated
as a war criminal after the defeat of the Reich, dying in French
custody in 1945, most likely by suicide.

Gerstein's intentions were at least as good as Schindler's,
but he didn't save a single life. If anything he added to the total
sum of suffering, since at one point (this at least is an incident
from the film) he supplied a weaker version of the gas used in the
chambers, which only meant that the victims' death was slower
and more agonising. It's hard to think of him as a coward, given
that he stood up in his seat to protest against the anti-Christian
prejudice of a play in 1935 (he was beaten up by Nazis in the
audience), and was expelled from the Party in 1936 after distributing anti-Nazi material. But it's also hard to think of a moral
system that would find an honourable place for both the heroic
failure Gerstein and the compromised but effective Schindler

– it seems almost perverse that Thomas Keneally, who wrote the book on which Spielberg's film is based, should also have written a theatre piece, *Either Or* (first performed in 2007), examining Gerstein's life in wartime.

My responses to Spielberg's films aren't always so positive – dismay comes into them on a regular basis. When *Prospect* magazine commissioned a piece on him to coincide with a retrospective at the National Film Theatre, I found myself going on the offensive.

'Thirteen Spielbergs' (2016)

'Steven Spielberg' has been some sort of global brand for over forty years now, but it's a strange old brand whose products run from the likes of *E.T.* to *Schindler's List*, from *Tintin* to *Jaws*. Perhaps it would be simpler to divide him into separate sub-Spielbergs, not all of them sharing a great deal with the others, and not all of them necessarily world leaders.

THRILL MERCHANT The first Spielberg to emerge (I realise this sounds like one of those multiple-personality movies) was the implacable thrill-merchant of *Duel*, a film originally made for television then extended for cinema release. He got the most out of limited resources in a lean road-movie thriller with tension but no psychology. One vehicle pursued another and we simply watched, siding with Dennis Warren more because he had a face (the driver of the truck that persecuted him being kept out of sight) than for any deeper human reason.

RELUCTANT MINIMALIST *Jaws* capitalised on the strengths of *Duel*, seeming to announce an heir to Hitchcock, someone who could manipulate audiences with an implacable technical control that still left room for subtlety. The most effective scenes were ones that kept the shark out of sight, like the masterly sequence of two drunks lobbing a joint of meat from the freezer off the end of a jetty on the end of a rope after hearing about the reward, and hoping to attract the killer Great White. They get their wish – but what we see isn't too explicit. The rope goes slack in the water, meaning that the shark is no longer pulling away from the shore. Meaning it's coming towards them.

Those first audiences weren't to know that the shoot had been behind schedule and over budget, and that the mechanical shark hadn't worked, forcing Spielberg to rely on inventiveness, like the 'dolly zoom' shot borrowed from *Vertigo* that conveys Chief Brody's shock of terror when he sees a shark fin enter the bay. In Spielberg's work since *Jaws* there has been an increasing investment in special effects that do actually work. Though indirect strategies haven't completely disappeared (think of the ripples in the surface of a drink that announce the approach of a T. Rex in *Jurassic Park*) there have also been frequent wieldings of the . . .

SLEDGEHAMMER OF SUBTLETY This was first on show in *The Sugarland Express*, the film released between *Duel* and *Jaws*, highly unusual for Spielberg in being a relationship drama, and having a female character in the lead, a desperate mother (played by Goldie Hawn) who springs her husband from jail so as to prevent their small son being fostered away from them. This is as close to the spirit of freewheeling 1970s independent cinema (the spawn of *Easy Rider*) as Spielberg gets, and it's not close. He keeps being distracted from the central relationship by the need to stage elaborate scenes with cars (a news van full of reporters, for instance, ploughing into a pond) and though there are moments of tenderness and insight there's also an image of a teddy bear being run over by the wheels of a police car. That's the Spielberg contradiction, the presence side by side of a great bold imagination and utterly safe, conventional sentiment. By this stage he was giving notice that he was . . .

NOT A MAN'S MAN BUT NOT A WOMAN'S MAN EITHER Spielberg's persona is of a nice Jewish boy, and it seems highly likely that he opens doors for female companions and is well brought up in every way, but there are virtually no interesting parts for women in his films. Martin Scorsese is a much more conflicted figure, what with being both a spoiled priest and a spoiled hoodlum, but he can point to *Alice Doesn't Live Here Anymore* as an unapologetic 'women's picture', while Lorraine Bracco in *Goodfellas* and Juliette Lewis in *Cape Fear* both have extraordinary moments. Set beside Spielberg, Brian De Palma seems pretty much a card-carrying misogynist, but *Carrie* is still electrifying, with outraged female sexuality having the power to raze buildings and flip cars over.

INNER-CHILD WRANGLER In Spielberg's early career there was no special status given to children, but that began to change with the wholesome initiative of *Close Encounters* and, above all, *E.T.* I recoil from forced wonderment and don't particularly respond to images of flying bicycles silhouetted against the moon, let alone *E.T.* coming back from the dead, but even I can see that *E.T.* is beautifully managed, certainly when compared with films that attempt to recreate the magic, such as *Super 8* (produced by Spielberg) or the recent *Midnight Special*. The use of François Truffaut as an actor in *Close Encounters* perhaps signals a shift in allegiance, from Hitchcock himself to a Hitchcock fan and advocate – whose own direct homage, *The Bride Wore Black*, was not a great success. Yes, there was a sentimental side to Truffaut, but there are wild children and delinquent ones in his work (*L'Enfant Sauvage*; *The 400 Blows*) as well as the lovable scoundrels of *Small Change*, and the director of *The Man Who Loved Women* (never mind that it's a horrible film) really did find women interesting.

In later Spielberg there's a great emphasis on children, and considerable indulgence of the theme of inability to grow up, as in *Hook* and *Catch Me If You Can*. A project originated by Kubrick, *A.I.* starts with some sense of the creepiness of humanoid robots (a synthetic child programmed to 'sleep' at night, though still watchful), until Spielberg realises it's a version of the story of Pinocchio and everything starts turning into marshmallow. Kubrick may have been a misanthropic control freak, but at least he kept his films Pinocchio-free.

MASTER OF GENRE WHO KEEPS FORGETTING WHAT HE'S DOING Sometimes it seems that Steven Spielberg has difficulty in distinguishing between childhood as a subject and children as a market. *Jurassic Park*, for instance, should by rights be a horror film as implacable as *Jaws*, but Spielberg was hell-bent on targeting the widest possible audience, so we have kids in traumatising action sequences (trapped in a car while a T. Rex chews it up) making do-you-think-he-saurus jokes minutes afterwards. It's a thrill ride that keeps wanting to hold our hand and tell us not to worry, until the velociraptors get into the kitchen and Spielberg remembers what he does best. Spielberg is also quite capable of making the same mistake in the other direction, spoiling what is meant to be a romp with grim material – see *Indiana Jones and the Temple of Doom*, with its overdose of death, child slavery and monkey brains.

HYPERREALIST WITH NO SENSE OF THE REAL For the splendid *Raiders of the Lost Ark*, Spielberg devised an apotheosis of the boys' action movie, highly detailed and dynamic though fundamentally cartoonish, every element punched up for maximum impact. Then, like somebody who has pulled a face when the wind changes, he was stuck with it. He went on applying what was essentially the same style of film-making to serious projects, or to projects he thought were serious. On paper, *The Color Purple* was an enterprise brave to the point of insanity, a film about black women and their sufferings without household names in it (though Oprah Winfrey and Whoopi Goldberg haven't exactly gone away since then). On the screen, it was hardly recognisable as a film about human beings, with the world being divided into brutal oppressors and cringing doormats, and the misery laid on so thick that it became almost funny.

Every sequence was exaggerated in one way or another. Sample: young Celie, newly married (though herself still a child – this is rural Georgia, 1909) to a brute who wants a mother for his children, enters the kitchen for the first time, carrying a mop and a bucket of hot soapy water, and stares in horror at the filthy rat-infested dereliction that faces her. So where did she get the hot water from, if not the kitchen? Later the same day – she hasn't changed the bloodstained bandage on her head, needed after one of her new stepchildren greeted her by chucking a rock – everything shines and you could eat off the floor with total confidence . . . and here comes Celie's husband to hit her for the first time.

A milder case of the same exaggeration disease damaged *Empire of the Sun.* The source book has few illusions about childhood, and it seemed odd that Spielberg should be attracted to it, but he found a way past the thorns and prickles. Near the end, young Jim (Christian Bale) plays dead so as to avoid the real thing. He flops down on the ground, just like any kid, completely unconvincing. Adorable! Except that Jim has seen plenty of real death, and identifies more with his Japanese captors and their cruel code than his fellow detainees.

LEARNER FROM HIS OWN MISTAKES For *Schindler's List*, Spielberg drastically stripped back his over-dynamic style. The violence was abrupt and disorienting, and finally he seemed to abandon his belief that the young are resilient and indestructible, with the sequence where children trying to hide in a concentration camp find the latrine already fully occupied. By the time he made *Minority Report*, too, he seemed to have realised that there was no place for a child's perspective in an exhilarating adult thriller, and the gains were obvious, particularly in the sequence of the black-market eye transplants, which introduced a new note of wild black comedy to his work.

FORGETTER OF THE LESSONS HE LEARNED FROM HIS OWN MISTAKES Spielberg's version of *War of the Worlds* went back to the bad old *Jurassic Park* idea of the horror film with kids at the heart of it, and the portrayal of children as somehow both vulnerable and indestructible. Admittedly Dakota Fanning's character was infinitely more spoiled and annoying than any previous Spielberg child, but that wasn't exactly good news. Many millions of human beings were vaporised, drowned or ground to powder, but at least feckless Dad and bratty Daughter learned to understand each other better.

After the abject failure of *1941*, Spielberg had seemed to learn the lesson that slapstick humour wasn't his strong suit, even though he had clearly been tempted by a style of comedy that seemed mechanical in the same way that a suspense sequence is mechanical, though in theory producing laughter rather than tension. But slapstick sequences keep on cropping up, with results that are just as grating – look at the sequence in *The Color Purple* when the abusive husband (Danny Glover) cooks breakfast in an attempt to impress the love of his life.

MUSIC LOVER WITH TIN EARS Forget for a moment that John Williams's approaching-shark cue from *Jaws* is roughly the second most famous bit of music in the movies (after Bernard Herrmann's stabbing violins from *Psycho*), with the alien-greeting melody from *Close Encounters*, also by Williams, most likely in third place. Steven Spielberg has a very limited idea about what a film score can do, and John Williams's work for him is mainly pretty poor. I don't blame Williams. A film composer doesn't call the shots. Spielberg's mother may have been a concert pianist, but that hasn't made him discriminating – perhaps it just gave him the idea that there should always be music going on in the background, for no particular reason.

Compare Williams's unfocused first score for Spielberg, on *The Sugarland Express*, with the one he wrote the year before for Robert Altman's *The Long Goodbye*, playful and inventive, with one song providing the material for the entire film in different transformations, as a tango, on sitar for a hippie party, in a mariachi arrangement when the action moves to Mexico. When Elliot Gould's Philip Marlowe goes into a supermarket, we even hear the same song being piped through as muzak. Presumably the approaching-shark cue was something Spielberg realised he absolutely needed in the absence of a functioning gnashy automaton – but after that it was back to business as usual. Williams isn't the only composer he has hamstrung, either. Quincy Jones provided the music for *The Color Purple*, excelling when asked to provide an actual number (blues singer in a juke joint, gospel choir in church), obediently churning out cotton-wool blandness the rest of the time.

NON-EXPLORER OF ACTORS There are directors who like to discover actors or to stretch them, and those, like Spielberg, who by and large expect them to get on with it. Hitchcock made out that he didn't value the contribution made by actors, but his films tell a different story. The actors he used repeatedly, such as Cary Grant and James Stewart, become partial self-portraits: Grant a figure of fantasy suavity, Stewart worn and decent but out of his depth, both personas being put under sly pressure. Spielberg too has his recurring actors – I don't mean Harrison Ford, who plays a single character in four films, but Tom Cruise (*Minority Report*, *War of the Worlds*) and Tom Hanks (in *Saving Private Ryan*, *The Terminal* and *Bridge of Spies*). Spielberg doesn't put them under any pressure, just turns to one Tom when he wants a strenuous blank and the other when he wants a regular guy. The only time that an actor has seemed under pressure in a Spielberg film was in the middle stretches of *Close Encounters*, when a miscast and underpowered Richard Dreyfuss struggled with a confused script.

PRODUCT PLACER In *E.T.* the children tempt out the strange shy visitor with a trail of Reese's Pieces, a modestly selling peanut-butter treat that benefited from a large boost in sales as a result. Hershey's, the parent company, didn't make a payment but agreed to promote the film. Later in the film, E.T. himself hides in a pile of soft toys, a sly nod to the fact that action figures of the character would soon be on every child's Christmas list. In *Minority Report* twenty years later, one of the futuristic highlights was a shopping mall where interactive hoardings, triggered by iris recognition, address the hero by name, having access to his purchase history. After the eye transplants, of course, the Gap hologram was asking Mr Yakamoto, not John Anderton, about how those tank tops worked out for him. So is this savage satire on consumer culture or just more product placement? Postmodernism can hide a multitude of sins.

By the time of *The Terminal*, in which Tom Hanks plays an Eastern European visitor stranded at JFK airport, what we seem to be watching isn't a Capraesque fable about the indomitability of the ordinary man, but the monetised swoop and glide of Spielberg's camera across an environment largely composed of commercial premises. It's tempting to imagine an actual tariff, with prices listed according to whether you want your business glimpsed, dwelt on, or mentioned in dialogue (Planters peanuts, sbarro fast food, Hugo Boss) ... though perhaps Borders (remember them?) got a special rate for happening to chime so nicely with the anecdote. It certainly takes some of the shine off the underdog-triumph theme that it should be sponsored by so many corporations. In this way Spielberg's films seem to trace the whole short history of product placement, from tentative beginnings through self-conscious sophistication to invisibility despite omnipresence.

WORLD CONSCIENCE Spielberg's status as a commentator on history soared after *Schindler's List*, though there were special reasons for his interest in that subject, and special reasons for the film's success. It had a stubborn integrity despite decisions of self-sabotaging kitsch, like a girl wearing a red coat in a black-and-white film, and its use of soupy music, as if viewers would sit there unmoved unless an orchestra wheedled for their tears. On first viewing I thought the film oddly incurious about Schindler's motives – about whether he was hedging his bets in some way, or acting according to conscience. He could hardly do both. I blamed this on the director's lack of flair for character, but since then I've wondered if it was actually a weakness. Most films about the Holocaust interpret events through Christian values, which prize integrity and self-sacrifice over effectiveness, as if what was in your heart was all that mattered. Christianity loves a heroic failure, and Schindler disappoints on two counts, by saving lives without immolating himself. Wot, no martyrdom?

The film marks Spielberg's engagement with Jewish ethical values, and a *mitzvah* is a virtuous act but not one of charity. It is judged only by the change it makes, while it also makes a change in you. If you saved Jewish lives then you are a righteous gentile – it's not a character reference but an ethical fact. The same logic doesn't illuminate other historical moments and other films – *Amistad* and *Bridge of Spies* seemed pretty hollow to me, starting off pseudo-critical of America (in the time of slavery and McCarthyism respectively) before suggesting that there will always be a man to speak up for what is right, whether it's a past president of the United States (*Amistad*) or a humble insurance lawyer (*Bridge of Spies*), making America a great country after all. Surprise! *Munich* was slightly different, in that this time it was Israel being pseudo-critiqued, for the unofficial campaign of revenge against those who had planned and carried out the massacre of athletes in 1972.

Again there was much manipulation, with the hero Avner (Eric Bana), burdened with guilt for the killings, asking his mother if she wants to hear what he's done. She says no – 'Whatever it took, whatever it takes. A place on Earth. We have a place on Earth. At last.' Which is changing the subject, really, but the scene ends there, so presumably this is a winning argument. Just in case there was doubt we see Avner toiling sexually on top of his wife, haunted not by the murders he has committed but apparently by images of the Munich massacre, though he wasn't there. (The role of Mrs Avner isn't a glorious one, even by Spielberg's standards.) Is this a superior piece of visual rhetoric to a teddy bear under the wheels of a police car? Hard to say.

I make that thirteen Steven Spielbergs – a baker's dozen. By your count, how many are worth celebrating?

If only to show that I haven't lost my cussedness, my habit of taking against the films everyone else likes, the *Forrest Gumps* and *Pulp Fictions* of a later day, I should reprint something recent. Here goes.

Three Billboards Outside Ebbing, Missouri (2017)

Martin McDonagh has made a name for himself as a playwright since the first production of *The Beauty Queen of Leenane* in 1996, and as a film director since the release of *In Bruges* in 2008. His status as the child of Irish parents brought up in London allowed him to use Irish material on stage but also to travesty it (a double game perhaps first played by J. M. Synge), in plays set in Galway and the Aran Islands. A taste for American subjects was announced in the 2010 play *A Behanding in Spokane*, produced on Broadway with Christopher Walken in the lead. The highly entertaining *In Bruges* took Irish characters away from their home turf, while its follow-up *Seven Psychopaths* (2012) had a mainly American cast and a California setting (screenwriters, gangsters, dog-kidnappers). This was much less fun to watch, a sub-Tarantino piece of work in need of much more flair to redeem the heartlessness. Under-motivated violence being announced in the title wasn't enough to make watching it exhilarating. Now with *Three Billboards Outside Ebbing, Missouri*, McDonagh has shifted away from his home genre of black farce to confront real, bleak emotion – grief, rage, pain – as experienced by a bereaved mother.

Mildred (Frances McDormand), dissatisfied by the lack of results in the investigation of her daughter's rape and murder, takes the unusual step of paying for posters to be put up near her home taking the local chief of police to task. McDormand is the film's great asset, with an unusual ability to layer complex emotion, conveying flinty blank alertness one moment, harsh tenderness the next. She is mainly known for her work in films by the Coen brothers but has also played a major role for Ken Loach (*Hidden Agenda*, back in 1990) and minor ones for Alan Parker, Robert Altman and Wes Anderson.

In a small town like Ebbing the reactions, both of support and condemnation, are inevitably intense. Mildred's billboard ploy is vindicated, in the sense that the case becomes news again, but the repercussions go beyond anything she could have anticipated. She is braced for a certain amount of backlash, even so, but her son Robbie (Lucas Hedges), suffering in his own way, isn't grateful for the increased stress. Hedges is an outstanding young actor, who will be carrying films on his own before too long, even if here he is playing what amounts to a variation of his role in *Manchester by the Sea*.

It happens that Chief Willoughby, far from being negligent, is conscientious and popular, so this is a conflict between two rights rather than a right and a wrong, with the makings, as you might think, of true tragedy. He is also terminally ill, with his own sort of mortal questions to answer – people aren't supposed to know, but you can't keep a secret in a small town. (People know, for instance, that Mildred can't afford to keep paying for the billboards indefinitely.) Chief Willoughby is a peach of a part for Woody Harrelson, but a rotten peach, one that bursts with sickly juices under his teeth. Well-controlled folksiness has always been part of this actor's professional equipment (as it is of McDormand's), but it isn't enough to sell so preposterous a character to an audience. One day Willoughby devises a complicated game for his young daughters to play on a picnic, unsupervised, so that he and his lovely wife can sneak off for a valedictory bout of love-making *en plein air*. Back home he engages in cute suggestive literary banter with her – it's noticeable that McDonagh's characters get a sudden boost of IQ when he wants extra sparkle for the dialogue. Willoughby composes so many wise letters of farewell ('Love is all you need to be a detective' a fair sample) that he seems to be adding a new symptom to the pains of pancreatic cancer, cramp of the writing hand.

When he comes to remonstrate with Mildred about the billboards she receives him on the porch, refusing him the hospitality of the house. It's true that she reassures him the billboards won't be there forever, but the reason she gives is unmerciful: 'They won't be so effective when you croak.' At this point Carter Burwell's music spells out Willoughby's desolation, but then Mildred's face loses its fixity and turns sad too.

Burwell got his start on the Coen brothers' first film, *Blood Simple*, where they specifically asked for a score that contested the mood of each scene rather than corroborating it. He has scored subsequent films of theirs in an unusually responsive way, sometimes intervening strongly, as he did with *O, Brother Where Art Thou?*, where the music was almost the hero of the piece, sometimes holding back with extraordinary discipline, as he did on *No Country for Old Men*. He has also done strong work for other directors, such as Todd Haynes, and if he produces an utterly undistinguished score for a film, as he does for *Three Billboards Outside Ebbing, Missouri*, then the simplest explanation is that the director who is employing him doesn't know what to ask for. A great film composer like Burwell is as powerful and as helpless as a genie, being unable to grant wishes that haven't been made.

Willoughby is by all accounts a good guy, yet one of his underlings at the police station, Jason Dixon, played by Sam Rockwell, is an unrepentant violent racist. Rockwell has played brainless for McDonagh before, in *Seven Psychopaths*, where he was the beneficiary of a mighty IQ boost, almost a brain transfusion, at the very end of the film. In *Three Billboards* there seems no limit to the crassness of his comedy mugging. He throws a peanut up in the air and tries to catch it in his mouth. He misses. He gets tangled up in furniture. In one ludicrous shot Dixon dances idiotically to an Abba song on his headphones (it's 'Chiquitita') ignorant of the fact that everyone in the police station behind him and out on the street is acting out extremes of grief after hearing some bad news. Is this the same film that was supposed to have real emotion in it? And is this still the police station that takes its cue from the virtuous Willoughby?

You can't choose a serious central situation and then have everything around it be crassly cartoonish – or rather you can, and *Three Billboards Outside Ebbing, Missouri* shows what happens when you do. The sheer falsity of the situations starts to corrode parts of the film that might have been emotionally powerful. Mildred's murdered daughter appears in a single sequence of memory. An accomplished production designer (Inbal Weinberg in this case) can rig up a plausible facsimile of a rebellious but essentially wholesome young woman's bedroom for Mildred to perch in, overwhelmed by painful memories, ready for her flashback, but then the writer-director doesn't deliver anything but atrocious kitsch irony, in the form of an argument over the use of a car that ends with the girl saying she'll walk instead, 'and I hope I get raped on the way'. How's that for cruel fate, or screenwriter's shamelessness?

Dixon's violence is served up for an audience's horrified condemnation, but Mildred's, admittedly on a smaller scale, is apparently just fine. Someone throws a drink can at her car when she's driving Robbie to school, and she charges in among the kids demanding to know who did it, kicking one in the groin to show she means business. In another scene she goes to the dentist, not a stranger to her but someone who nevertheless chooses to express his disapproval of her actions not in words but by using his drill on her without anaesthetic and then, when she insists on being numbed, tries to start work before the drug has taken effect. Her response is to grab the implement from him and to drill into one of his fingernails. She concludes with a grotesque version of the dental patient's end-of-session routine, rinsing out with mouthwash and then spitting it over him while he cowers on the floor. This is not made less ugly a scene by being played for laughs. Something like the 'riro' principle in computing applies – rubbish in, rubbish out. If distorted psychology (abruptly psychotic dentist) is where you start, you can't end up with anything else.

In one scene Mildred, brooding at home after her campaign has met a setback, looks down at her pink bunny slippers, wiggles her toes and does funny voices for them – voices saying things like 'I'm gonna crucify those motherfuckers!' She quite cheers herself up – it's one more preposterous moment to add to the collection. The tonal extremes and touches of Surrealism that can be so powerfully effective in, say, a Sam Shepard play are likely to fall flat in the work of an interloper on that cultural territory. It's on the cards that Martin McDonagh knows nothing much about small towns in Missouri and is busking it, hoping to get by if he musters enough tropes of Americana.

Three Billboards could be passed over as a failed exercise in hybridising farce and tragedy, if there wasn't such an unattractive contrast between the liberal views of society expressed by the approved characters in the script and the actual interactions depicted. The bigot Dixon asserts that homosexuals are put to death in Cuba, allowing someone more enlightened to remark that he must be thinking of Wyoming – a clear reference to the 1998 murder of Matthew Shepard, discovered still just about alive after being brutally beaten and left tied to a fence overnight in temperatures close to freezing (the cyclist who discovered him at first mistook him for a scarecrow). But of course there are no gay characters in the film, though Shane Black's *Kiss Kiss Bang Bang* a few years back showed that such a thing could be managed in a mainstream entertainment – Val Kilmer having a whale of a time – without causing public unrest.

In the role of James, Peter Dinklage (best known as Tyrion Lannister in *Game of Thrones*) has the inverse problem, of visibility without dignity. This actor can't play tall or long-limbed, but he has done his best to resist reductive casting, and his roles in *Game of Thrones* and *The Station Agent* are hardly one-dimensional. In other words, he has tried to avoid sad-sack loser roles like James in *Three Billboards*. James has no characteristics except dwarfism – though dwarfism isn't a character trait, that's the point – and a sexual desperation presented as self-explanatory.

As for the few non-white characters (if characters is the word), they have virtually nothing to say for themselves. Some are essentially walking talking pieces of litmus paper, whose function is to indicate the attitudes of the white ones. Mildred works in a gift shop alongside Denise (played by Amanda Warren) and since we know Mildred doesn't own the business she's a plausible candidate – there are no others in sight. How did she get her start? What's it like not being white in a racist town? The film takes no interest. Denise is a manifestation of Mildred's liberal credentials, a sort of ideological hologram.

Abercrombie (Clarke Peters), Willoughby's replacement as police chief, is black, though again he has no back story – and the lack of reaction on his part to the bigotry he is inheriting is confounding. Perhaps he's in shock, which would be understandable, or perhaps the part was written white and cast black without rewriting – or else the newcomer is the counterpart of Steve Martin's character in *The Jerk* (brought up by a loving black family) and likewise misidentifies his ethnicity. Whichever is the case, this part of the film makes *Blazing Saddles* seem like a work of sober realism.

Towards the end of the film it even seems that non-white characters need help to find each other. Denise's eyes light up in wonder when she sees Jerome (Darrell Britt-Gibson) in Mildred's company – he's been putting up the posters on her billboards. What, the lady from the gift shop has never seen the guy who does jobs for the advertising agency directly across from the police station? I thought this was a small town where everyone knows everyone. It's quite something for a film's racial attitudes to seem as wrong-headed in the week of release as the ones in *Guess Who's Coming to Dinner?*.

The bad-faith bleakness of McDonagh's film isn't a new thing in cinema. In 1999, though I was no longer the resident film critic for *The Independent*, I wrote an article for the paper, somewhere between a linked pair of reviews and the dreaded *think-piece*, about a little rash of similar films.

'Slavish "Independents"' (1999)

The relationship between mainstream and independent cinema in America is a complex and shifting one. Sometimes they're like classmates from very different backgrounds, with the rich dumb kid sneering during school hours and then turning up late at night on the wrong side of the tracks, throwing pebbles at the window of the poor smart kid and begging for help with homework. And sometimes they're like siblings from the same dysfunctional family, one desperate to be liked and unable to make friends, the other perpetually scowling and setting fire to waste-paper baskets.

We're all familiar with the conventions of the Hollywood movie, the sheer level of contrivance, the targeting of adolescent values, the way issues are raised and then shelved. But there can be conventions to the independent film also, so that supposedly personal visions are constructed according to a set of rules. The result, typically, is a film that reverses the despised formulas of Hollywood, without having any superior contact with reality.

Evidence for this is supplied by the second films of two writer-directors whose debut work was acclaimed: Todd Solondz and Neil LaBute. Solondz's *Welcome to the Dollhouse*, which won the 1996 Grand Jury Prize at the Sundance Film Festival, told the story of Dawn Wiener, a homely, unpopular girl at a junior high school. Essentially this was a suburban version of 'The Ugly Duckling' without the transformation (a false Dawn) and though Solondz's determination to avoid a happy ending was admirable in its way, he offered nothing that could take its place.

Neil LaBute's no-less-feted first feature, *In the Company of Men*, took a simple situation and followed it through: two businessmen conspire to worm their way into the affections of a deaf co-worker, raising her hopes to dump her with maximum destructive effect as a way of revenging themselves in the abstract for the damage supposedly done to men by women on a routine basis.

There was a plot twist of sorts – the nastier of the men is also trying to destroy his male colleague – but no let-up in the misanthropy. If there is really such a thing as the writer's writer or the designer's designer, then Chad, played by Aaron Eckhart, was the bastard's bastard, both entirely psychotic and perfectly functional. Chad was offered up to an audience's hatred like no character in the movies since Glenn Close in *Fatal Attraction*. The psychology in LaBute's film was no less sensationalist than in Adrian Lyne's, but the critics took *In the Company of Men* at the director's valuation and found in it an unflinching exploration of the dark side of the male psyche.

LaBute's second film, *Your Friends and Neighbors*, aspires to a larger range, with a cast of three men and three women, and the subject is sexual rather than emotional manipulation, but the tone is familiar. At the beginning of the film we're presented with two couples in bed, either wrangling or failing to communicate. What is shocking, given that neither pairing has enough in common to justify a shared cappuccino, let alone a one-night stand, is that these jarringly incompatible people are supposed to be established couples. LaBute posits a ludicrous situation, and then develops it with what we are intended to see as rigour. But to draw grotesque conclusions from a grotesque premise is not an achievement so much as a law of logic. From a grotesque premise no other sort of conclusion can be drawn.

In twenty years' time, people will watch *Your Friends and Neighbors* and ask, *My God, was sex really like that then?*, not realising that the question is unrhetorical, and that its answer is No.

The level of observation in the film is low to non-existent. For instance, the men in the film want to talk during sex, carrying on their seductive arias right up to the moment of orgasm, while the women want silence, one because she's interested only in the basic mechanics of pleasure, two because despite being a journalist she flinches from four-letter words. Sound familiar? I doubt it.

In the film's most emptily provocative sequence, Jason Patric's character (obvious heir to Chad in the earlier film), when asked to describe his supreme sexual experience, reveals that it was when he and some friends raped a boy from their high school for revenge. He romanticises the assault, as if there were deep communication within violation. It has never been like that with a woman, or so he says – and yet he has never doubted his heterosexuality. The camera meanwhile slowly zooms in on his handsome face, as if this were the sequence in a Hollywood movie where a character thinks back to the summer when he was eight, the family dog got ran over, and nothing was ever the same again. It's a retread of a *Company of Men* theme, the hollowly scary notion that psychotics can be well adjusted at the same time. Yes, and cannibals are often vegetarians.

Any claims that *Your Friends and Neighbors* can make to providing a portrait of modern mores are supplied by that flatly generalising title, and by the annoying way that none of the characters call each other by name – as if no other effort were required to make them representative.

Todd Solondz's follow-up to *Welcome to the Dollhouse* is less mechanical than *Your Friends and Neighbors*, although it shares a certain hatefulness. The screenplay is something of a mess, but then mainstream and independent films differ sharply in the way scripts are developed. Before a screenplay can be accepted for production by a major studio, it is likely to have had so many nips and tucks that any original features are all but obliterated. A writer-director, on the other hand, one who has received a prize for his first film, is unlikely to take a script to a doctor even if it has broken bones and internal injuries.

The structure of *Happiness* seems to be a numb variant on *Hannah and Her Sisters* – except that Woody Allen knew better than to make a film 140 minutes long. The *Happiness* sisters are a shy and unsuccessful singer-songwriter, a glamorous but secretly self-hating poet, and a housewife and mother who thinks of herself as the lucky one, the one who has it all.

The plot of the film is a succession of humiliating or degrading encounters and revelations. The singer-songwriter has a disastrous date with a man who then, after her rejection, kills himself. The poet, dissatisfied by the bimbo sexual athletes her celebrity brings her, seeks an encounter with a maker of abusive phone calls, but finds him too tame. The housewife discovers that her husband has been drugging and raping their eleven-year-old son's classmates. The trademark act of sex in this film seems to take place between a conscious and an unconscious party (an obese woman brokenly caressing a dead-drunk man, for instance, before he comes to and throws her out) – necrophilia without the sincerity.

The big scene in *Happiness*, counterpart of the romantic rape-reminiscence in *Your Friends and Neighbors*, shows young Billy asking his father what exactly his father did to those boys, whether he'd do it again, whether he'd do it to Billy. All very heart-rending – except that America is hardly a country where accused paedophile rapists are left alone to have heart-rending conversations with their sons.

The last scene of *Happiness* demonstrates that a work of art can remain inert even while doggedly breaking taboos. Little Billy achieves his first ejaculation on the balcony, while watching a sunbathing neighbour rub herself with cream. The family dog licks up this offering from the railing where it has landed, and Billy's mother promptly nuzzles the affectionate animal, unaware of the freight on its tongue.

The mission statement of the independent film is to explore areas from which the mainstream excludes itself. These days, it's true, that's not so easy. The look of independent film is no longer as immediately identifiable as it used to be in the days when the starkness and intimacy of every frame marked the films of John Cassavetes as an antidote and a reproach to Hollywood gloss. These days a mainstream film may affect rough edges of technique, and technical breakthroughs in affordable equipment mean that even low-budget films don't need to look raw unless they want to. Nor is it necessarily subject matter that sets independents apart. Even the secretion that's supposed to shock in *Happiness* featured in *The Silence of the Lambs* (flung at Jodie Foster by a prison inmate), and 1998's *There's Something About Mary* proved, if nothing else, that visual jokes about semen need not put people off their popcorn.

The thing that American independents still do well is to portray intimate relationships without romanticism or reflexive cynicism. The men and women in a film by Whit Stillman or Hal Hartley are engaged in mating dances and rituals that are shot through with awkwardness and uncertainty. Behaviour that in Hollywood would be the province only of minor characters is moved from the edges to the centre.

It's this that makes films such as *Your Friends and Neighbors* and *Happiness*, with their callow determination to be unflinching in matters of sex, seem like betrayals of their tradition rather than merely failures. A reaction against cosmetic prettiness produces merely cosmetic ugliness, and the hollow 'heartwarmingness' of Hollywood is answered by a faux nihilism for which there is no excuse.

I shouldn't reprint pieces hostile to what seem to me pseudo-independent films – essentially reactionary pieces of work – without honouring at least one great success in the area, criminally underrated: a film that shows it's possible to withhold genre cues, avoid 'character arcs' and three-act structures and deliver a haunting work of art. The budget of Todd Haynes's 1995 film *Safe* was about a million dollars (*Happiness* cost about three million, *Your Friends and Neighbors* five – all figures from IMDb) and made about half of that at the U.S. box office. Of course the reason it's underrated is that it doesn't fit an obvious category, a sort of horror film without special effects, where if there is a monster (hard to be sure) it's an abstract one, the whole modern environment. Films that offer you an experience unlike what you're used to are at a disadvantage in the marketplace, compared to films that give you more of the same – the words that studio executives want to hear in the title of a projected film aren't words at all but numbers, 2, 3, 4 . . . even if a few sequels, just a few, have matched or excelled the original film without repeating it (*Godfather 2*, *Aliens*, *Terminator 2*, *Gremlins 2*).

Safe (1995)

Todd Haynes's mysterious and beautiful film *Safe* tells the story of a woman who becomes sensitised by her environment to the point where exposure to the routine chemical insult of a perm can trigger symptoms, or even a seizure. As Haynes, whose first feature was the talented but irritating *Poison*, has been associated with queer film-making, there is an assumption that with *Safe* he is using his protagonist's condition as a stand-in for AIDS.

This mildly demeaning suggestion can't survive even a few minutes of the film itself. AIDS has a fixed set of cultural meanings, which must either be allowed or contested, while what happens to Carol White (Julianne Moore) is something that she must make sense of as best she can – and so must we – as we watch. On one level *Safe* works as the most deadpan possible satire on Californian suburbia. Carol lives in a luxurious house in a hillside development that looks like an advertisement for itself. When she is referred to a shrink she describes herself as a 'housewife', before substituting the term 'homemaker', but neither word seems to apply. She claims to be working on some designs for the house in her spare time, but we see no trace of this activity.

The total of her domestic workload seems to be making coffee for her husband, after a dinner that the maid has cooked and cleared away. When she talks to the shrink about being stressed, she particularly mentions an 'important client dinner' that is looming. Is she going to make the meal herself? But no, the big event takes place in a restaurant, and her contribution is restricted to laughing at the clients' jokes.

Carol goes to aerobic classes but no amount of exercise seems able to make her break out into a sweat. Not that her daily life requires much more exertion than a sideways flip of the head to allow the telephone access to her ear without disturbing the fall of her hair. In bed with her husband, she is passive and rather non-committal, waiting for his excitement to be over and then dispensing a maternal kiss. Her social circle is no more dynamic than she is. At a baby shower attended by a dozen tastefully frilly women, the question 'Did you wrap that yourself?' receives the answer, 'Are you kidding? I wish I was that creative.'

On a satirical reading of the film, Carol's surroundings become dangerous to her precisely because they are too safe. Her life contains no roughage, and so her ability to digest it breaks down, as blandness acquires a paradoxical toxicity. She traces her sensitisation to the arrival of a poisonous new couch, but significantly the first problem is the colour of the item. She ordered teal and they delivered black. She almost goes into shock. It is as if she can't tolerate any surprise, any unannounced stimulus.

There's comedy in the moment when the delivery team installs the right couch at last, the trio in overalls stepping back to allow an appreciation moment, as if they had just hung an Old Master. Yet a satirical reading of *Safe* only goes so far. Carol with her little-girl voice and her pale suits is not so much trivial as unformed. With her addiction to milk, which chimes so nicely with her bland surname, she might best be described as unweaned. She is at a distance from everything, starting with her husband and stepson. But the camera does not claim an intimacy with her either. It glides towards her without crossing any threshold. The director's slow tracking shots are studiously neutral rather than stealthy, and Julianne Moore offers herself to the camera's gaze with no effort at animation.

Carol makes a pilgrimage from the suburbs to the desert, pulling behind her an oxygen cylinder on a trolley like a little golf cart, to a centre called Wrenwood where environmental illness is treated – or rather, allowed to flower. One of the staff members at Wrenwood offers a little aria of self-healing: 'This was a gift. This whole thing was a gift, everything was taken away from me, everything in the material sense. And what was left was me.' Yet she offers only disconnected maternal gestures and a rhetoric of reclaimed strength that is subtly entrapping. First of all Carol is told, 'All these feelings you're having are just fine. They're just natural.'

But then Peter (Peter Friedman), who runs Wrenwood and who works on an audience like a mixture of stand-up comedian and fundamentalist preacher, has a slightly different message. He asks people why they think they got sick and prompts them to their therapeutic breakthroughs. 'The person who hurt you most was . . .?' he hints, and a patient will obediently reply '. . . was me.'

Under this regime Carol's symptoms are both relieved and intensified. They go into remission, yet can be set off by ever-smaller triggers. When her husband visits, he gets to pull her oxygen cart but his cologne makes her recoil even though he is not wearing any. A clean shirt's history of fragrance is enough to set her off. She starts using the jargon of the institute, and casts longing glances at a porcelain-lined igloo up the hill, the safest place in this whole safe place.

In some ways her condition improves. She is able almost to flirt with another resident and to collaborate with him on the making of lasagne for a group meal. This relatively straight-forward Italian dish is her most ambitious project in the whole film, yet it hardly seems a triumph over adversity. The overall impression that *Safe* leaves is that the heroine has disappeared inside an illness that she may have invented.

Safe seems like a European art movie in its avoidance of forced climaxes. The film has a continuous fascination that is not to do with getting answers. Ed Tomney's synthesiser score mutates from ominous throbbing to New Age reassurances without ever quite helping us to know what to feel. But if the film seems to come from nowhere in recent American cinema, perhaps it does have identifiable ancestors. Where else have we seen a love of surfaces coupled with an indictment of superficiality, meticulous camera work that does not expect the clichés of revelation from faces or gestures, alienated women disappearing from their lives or embarking on quests that are valued as much for what they leave behind as where they lead? Perhaps only in the classic period of Antonioni. *Safe* may not quite belong in that company, but it's a breakthrough for Todd Haynes, and a satisfyingly strange experience for audiences willing to risk it.

I hope the ability to respond to strangeness on the screen isn't dying out. I remember watching David Cronenberg's version of *Naked Lunch* in a cinema in Washington, DC (this must have been 1991) and gradually realising that I was the only person laughing, like the ghoul in the Charles Addams cartoon in stitches while the rest of the audience is weeping at a tragedy. It wasn't that others were crying, but the film showed you some horrifying things and some funny things without clearly labelling which was which. Some of them were both in any case, and I enjoyed being pulled this way and that. I didn't actively enjoy being the odd man out. You don't go to the cinema to feel superior.

Of all the films I reviewed for *The Independent*, *Awakenings* (1990) was the most consequential in terms of my own character arc. I already had a passing interest, perhaps more, in issues of disability – I remember interviewing Daniel Day-Lewis at the time of release of *My Left Foot* (1989), after he'd finished filming *Eversmile, New Jersey*. He was mortified that despite all the time he spent riding a motorbike in character for the film, he had still failed his test for a British licence. I was impressed that he had at first refused to play the part of Christy Brown, on the basis that an actor with the same condition, cerebral palsy, should do it, until it was pointed out that such a film, even supposing an actor of sufficient skill with cerebral palsy could be found, was never going to get funded without an established name like his own attached to it. His sense of scruple would simply block the project.

I suggested that there was another way of approaching the problem. If the part of Christy Brown needed to be played as an adult by an able-bodied actor, then at least Christy as a boy, a much less demanding role, could be played by a performer with cerebral palsy rather than the able-bodied one who was chosen (Hugh O'Conor). Then at least there's one disabled actor with film experience, thanks to the film, with an increased likelihood of more work, perhaps even something approximating to a career. Of course there would be difficulties, since an actor with cerebral palsy can't dial the disability up and down as an able-bodied one can, but they could in principle be overcome. The idea, though, hadn't occurred to anyone involved in the production, not even Day-Lewis. It's true that he would have had to model his performance on the junior actor's, but that would seem to be just the sort of challenge he relishes.

After I'd done my review of *Awakenings* I felt I had more to say on the subject, and approached Faber to suggest a book about the representation of disability in film. I hadn't got going on the project before two somewhat overlapping books were published, addressing the topic from different angles, so that I felt my proposed study was holed below the waterline long before it could be launched. Instead I wrote a mighty essay drawing on material and ideas from both books, about half of which was published by the *London Review of Books* under the title (suggested by Howard Schuman) of . . .

Cinematically Challenged (1996)

The film is a well-known one from the early nineties, a touted return to form by a famous director. The hero's lawyer, representing him in connection with a murder, is in a wheelchair. There is no particular symbolism to his condition – he isn't for instance an Ironside, paradoxically powerless champion of the truth, a person possessing moral force exclusively. Nor is he presented, like so many wheelchair-users in films, as having a special affinity with technology, whether by supposed virtue of being a disembodied brain or as a person who is already in part mechanical.

The character is in a wheelchair, essentially, because some people are. The chair says no more about its owner than, say, a bicycle or a skateboard – except that its user doesn't ride a bicycle or a skateboard. The actor playing the character may or may not use a wheelchair when the camera isn't turning. The hero's lawyer occupies only a brief time on screen, measured in a high number of seconds or a low number of minutes. If there is a more than casual point about his disabled status, it must be that by this stage of the hero's experiences, his life is so out of control, so free of an unfolding logic, that nothing can surprise him.

This is that rare thing, a neutral portrayal of a disabled character in a Hollywood film – a film about Hollywood, at that – and perhaps that's why, perversely, it's so easy to forget. It makes the point that it's not making a point, and then it vanishes from the memory. This is the double-bind governing representation of minorities in cinema: distortion resonates, while matter-of-factness leaves no trace.

It isn't a new observation that being cast in a physically disabled role does no harm to an actor's Oscar chances. A feigned impairment can be a real boost. But does anyone imagine there is anything particularly difficult about sitting in a wheelchair for short periods, about pretending to be blind or deaf? Part of the hysterical applause is of course self-congratulatory, saluting the presence of an 'issue' that has been properly distanced from raw experience – though perhaps there's more to this great need to emphasise the gap between the actor and the part.

Why single out these performances for praise? Actors act. The performer is not continuous with the role. Isn't that the point? Not always, apparently.

One other set of portrayals is given a somewhat frantic endorsement: impersonations of homosexuals by actors certified straight. Sometimes the most inert caricature receives frothing acclaim (case in point William Hurt's turn in *Kiss of the Spider Woman*). Here the thinking behind the brouhaha is most transparent: having defined homosexuality as a set of stylised gestures, Hollywood thereby creates the fear that anyone reproducing the gestures, for the best of reasons, will become homosexual. What follows is hyperbolic insistence on how hard it was technically (but really how risky, morally) to loll the wrist and simper. Somehow contamination was avoided.

So what is it about the able-bodied stars in their wheelchairs, beyond the fluffy feeling that Hollywood Cares? Perhaps it's something to do with the particular characteristics of the minority (the substantial minority, if we accept the figure of 10 per cent) made up by the disabled.

The majority values crispness of contour in a minority, clarity of definition. Disability does not oblige. There is considerable fuzziness of boundary involved, even when there aren't institutions with different agendas doing the assessing. This moreover is a minority that grows by osmosis across a membrane, as the hard-of-hearing become definitively deaf (the partially sighted blind, the residually mobile wheelchair bound), but also appears to recruit by catastrophe. The minority also loses members across its membrane, as people are successfully treated or rehabilitated, but miracle cures aside, the journey between motorcycle and wheelchair is made in one direction only. This is a minority for which all non-members are on a waiting list, with a real prospect of jumping the queue.

Anyone can speak for the rights of the disabled, but disability is not a unitary experience, and nor is fear of disability. It condenses many fears – of age, of dependence, of mutilation. What the Academy voices from time to time on Oscars night is perhaps a willed exoticising of disability, making it something that exists at a vast distance from real life, a remote territory that can only be reached by the most intrepid of cinematic explorers.

Hence the particular *frisson* behind the press coverage of Christopher Reeves' riding accident and consequent paralysis. An actor professionally identified with invulnerability lets the able-bodied side down, and allows repressed fears to return. Everyone out of a wheelchair needs to believe in Superman, in vigour that is self-sustaining and endless.

A book called *The Cinema of Isolation* (1994) by Martin F. Norden sets out to trace the history of disability in film. By its own admission the book goes for breadth over depth in its survey. Like many a cultural archaeologist coming upon a rich site, Norden does what Heinrich Schliemann did at Troy and sinks his shafts in haste, turning up many treasures but profoundly disturbing the strata in the process.

Norden lists a vast number of early silent films featuring people with disabilities – slapstick offerings such as *The Invalid's Adventure* (1907) or *Near-sighted Mary* (1909) – which would have to come into the category of mocking the afflicted. He is sometimes moved to sarcasm in his descriptions: 'Gaumont also found it necessary to share with the world its enlightened views on the subject of disabled people and marriage'. He even calls such films 'assaults' on physically disabled people in the name of humour.

Norden's Introduction to *The Cinema of Isolation* has the feeling of a historico-theoretical framework run up after the event, but at least it touches on an explanation. He quotes from Freud's 1919 essay, 'The Uncanny': 'anxiety about one's eyes, the fear of going blind, is often enough a substitute for the dread of being castrated' – fear of castration being 'what gives the idea of losing other organs its intense colouring'. If disability raises in the able-bodied viewer the spectre of castration, the so-called humour of those early films becomes not more attractive, but at least more intelligible, as a form of compulsive disidentifi- cation. This refusal of empathy is perhaps symmetrical with the attitude prevailing later, of sympathy offered as if from an invulnerable height, sympathy that denies any claim of kinship. Those who murmur 'There but for the Grace of God go I,' after all, disclaim their entitlement to an able body on a humble plane, while reasserting it on a more elevated one. God wants them as they are – and God wants the others other.

If Norden has an overall message, it is that the representa- tion of the disabled in films confirms their status as inherently different: 'most movies have tended to isolate disabled char- acters from their able-bodied peers as well as from each other.' The social ideal would be for the two not so very different groups to mix on a regular basis. Norden cites studies such as Nancy Weinberg's 'Modifying Social Stereotypes of the Physically Disabled' (1978), which have shown that 'as contact between able-bodied and disabled is intensified, the stereotype of the disabled as different diminishes . . . There is a positive relationship between contact and perceived similarity: as contact increases, perceived similarity increases.' It isn't clear how this attempt on the social level to reverse the mutual impoverishment of minority and majority could be realised or abetted by films.

As a consequence of his unrealistic expectations, some of Norden's judgements seem faintly absurd. No doubt *The Invalid's Adventure* and *Near-sighted Mary* are lamentable pieces of entertainment, but how many other films of the period 1907–9 are congenial to modern taste? It seems a little quixotic to expect higher standards of artistic achievement from films that happen to have disabled characters in them.

There is the occasional whiff of good intention even in early films, but the results seldom tickle Norden's nostril. *Deaf Mute Girl Reciting 'Star Spangled Banner'*, a single-shot film of about 75 seconds made in 1902 (perhaps at Gallaudet, the famous institute for the deaf), can make some faint claim to progressiveness, with its Old Glory backdrop and patriotic performer of American Sign Language. What is it saying, if not that the deaf are also citizens? Yet Norden sees only the 'desire for freakish entertainment', and a pandering to that desire. The deaf girl had novelty value, to be sure, but is that really the same as 'freakishness'? He is at risk here of presupposing the attitudes he seeks to rebuke.

A leitmotif that Norden discovers in early cinema is of the disabled person as fraudulent. Silent films swarm with beggars feigning. Again, he becomes incensed that the able-bodied world should libel a disadvantaged minority in this way (though it is the fate of minorities to be libelled). It might be rewarding to characterise this motif in another way: the desire to represent the disabled in movies is constantly shadowed by the desire not to represent them, somehow to separate the person and the disability. To expose a disabled person as a sham is the antagonistic version of this desire, while an insistence on curability (never entirely absent from films, but having, as Norden shows, definite seasons of prevalence) expresses the same drive in an apparently more sympathetic version.

Norden looks for a social-realist depiction of disability in films, with particular reference to economic conditions, which again seems a little naive. Hollywood cinema has only ever had spasms of realism in these matters – why would it make an exception in favour of the disabled? The workings of money are fairly thoroughly suppressed in mainstream cinema.

He also seeks to assess 'audience positioning' – whether viewers are encouraged to identify with disabled characters or with the able-bodied ones who look at them. With particular reference to blindness, he doesn't explain how a visual medium could appropriately accommodate the priorities of the sightless. In general, his judgements have an insensitivity to tone that can sometimes verge on the deranged: 'Though commendable for its explicit recognition of the able-bodied exploitation and relatively balanced in its representation of character gazes, *Heidi* otherwise deals with issues of physical disability in a simplistic and facile way.' But *Heidi* deals with *the Alps* in a simplistic and facile way. It's a simplistic and facile film. Who ever thought any different? We're not talking about *Persona* here!

With other films, by contrast, Norden's rudimentary analyses, particularly of camerawork, don't do justice to sophisticated strategies. A case in point would be *The Elephant Man* (1980), a still from which appears on the cover of the book. David Lynch's film may indeed demonstrate 'time-worn points of view' in some ways, and its central figure may indeed combine the stereotypes of the Sweet Innocent and the Saintly Sage (Norden is inordinately fond of categories like these and the Elderly Dupe, Noble Warrior, Civilian Superstar and so on). But his camera plays an ambiguous game, in two stages.

First of all it withholds the full sight of John Merrick (John Hurt), tantalising the audience with reaction shots, glimpses, a silhouette against a screen. The viewer's appetite for freak-ishness is played with, worked up and then strangely shamed. After Lynch has shown Merrick at last, the camera dwells on his appearance until it acquires its own integrity, if not actual beauty. Lynch questions in turn both of the rights that make up our position of privilege – first the right to look, and then the right to look away.

In his watchfulness about 'ableism', or able-bodied bias, Norden sometimes overstates his case, precisely where one might expect him to acknowledge distinctive efforts. This, for instance, would be a fair comment about a great many films: 'the fulfilment of actions ordinarily associated with mainstream members is an acceptable substitute' for miraculous recover-ies temporarily out of fashion. 'In other words, the characters should start acting like majority members if they cannot be cured outright.' It's just that this verdict is passed on *The Miracle Worker* (1962), of all films. When Helen Keller made her first communication with another human being, it wasn't a lot like selling out a considered political position. What it was like was a painful birth, and Arthur Penn's film doesn't play down the pain of her entering into language. The distinctive element in *The Miracle Worker*, which makes it still so eminently watchable, is the acknowledgement that in her isolation Helen Keller's resis-tance to communication was all that she had. Before she could express No explicitly, she was entirely clenched round a No that she had to give up. The film does what it can to honour that.

Martin Norden isn't the first cultural commentator to dis-cover that Freudianism works wonders in small doses, but small doses aren't available. The Freudian scaffolding rigged up to buttress the Introduction ends by threatening to pull down the whole building. Norden spoils a valuable point about the way disabled characters are arbitrarily inserted into screen adaptations of literary originals – he singles out the deformed lab assistant in Rex Ingram's *The Magician* (1926), drawn from a Maugham novel, mysteriously incorporated into the James Whale *Frankenstein* and subsequently acquiring the generic name of Igor – by his grudging response to one of the few occasions when a disability materialises as an aspect of the hero. Howard Breslin's short story 'Bad Time at Honda' has an explicitly able-bodied protagonist, while Spencer Tracy in *Bad Day at Black Rock* (1955) is famously one-armed. All Norden can think of to say is that Tracy's character is '"remasculated" through his heroic deeds'. Since when was he demasculated? He looks pretty tough from the word go (even Norden describes him as 'a self-assured, goal-orientated fellow'). The dismal equation of disability with an internal defectiveness is so thorough that it seems to have bewitched him into overlooking a rare exception, where the character who is physically impaired is the one to embody integrity.

Norden seems not to notice the film's theme: that difference need not be the same as otherness – you can be one of them and still be one of us. Its self-consciously liberal message is that xenophobia cannot plausibly be the philosophy of the melting-pot. It cannot, in other words, be an American value. The town's secret is that during the war some of its inhabitants murdered a farmer of Japanese descent. The guilty parties assume that Tracy's John Macreedy has come to investigate the crime, when his mission is much simpler: to deliver a bravery medal to the father of the man who saved his life in combat. The two quests, though, the feared and the real, necessarily converge since the father in question is the murder victim.

Bad Day at Black Rock also includes an early appearance of Oriental self-defence techniques: Macreedy fights off his attackers with some basic judo and karate. This is a more plausible resource for a one-armed man than Hollywood fisticuffs, and has the advantage of showing the hero's willingness to absorb non-Western skills without compromising his Americanness. Perhaps it even signals to the viewer the possibility that minorities in general might be able to use the majority's strength against itself. But all Norden sees is the disability platitude he projects onto it, and a highly unlikely Freudian reading of geography to bring about that redundant recovery of virility: if film-makers 'did not provide female figures to accomplish this remasculation, they at the very least offered female-like environments that allow the males to engage in heroic acts (e.g. the hostile landscape that John Macreedy penetrates in *Bad Day at Black Rock*)'. Since when is a hostile landscape a female environment? Are women deserts? Since when, come to that, is Spencer Tracy a phallus? Someone who has taken on the task of exploring our complicated investments in the bodies we see on screen should be able to provide a less preposterous gloss.

It's never explicitly stated in *The Cinema of Isolation* that commercial films can be made exclusively – or even primarily – for a disabled audience, but the assumption lurks in many passages. In his discussion of *The Heart Is a Lonely Hunter* (1968) the author remarks:

> anyone who knows [sign] language can readily tell when the hearing actors who play deaf characters are basically fumbling their way through it . . . A scene in which Singer interacts with a black deaf person played by Horace Oats [*sic*], who truly was deaf and knew the language well, only accentuated Arkin's lack of facility with the language and underscored the impropriety of casting a hearing actor in such a role.

Yet Norden has just finished telling us about the five-year struggle to get Carson McCullers's novel filmed (the industry reaction was: 'It's absolutely beautiful and I wouldn't touch it with a bargepole'), and the decisive contribution made by Alan Arkin, who had long coveted the role of John Singer, and told the screenwriter: 'You gotta give me the part now ... I've gone to all the trouble of becoming a star just so I could play it.' Arkin is clearly more fluent in Hollywood hyperbole than in American Sign Language, but he deserves more than a ticking-off for his 'impropriety'. No doubt his signing was substandard. But there's little point in comparing the film that exists with one that could never have been made – the same project with a deaf actor.

Perhaps the makers of *The Heart Is a Lonely Hunter* deserve praise for the fact that Arkin's faulty articulation of ASL is the only barrier to a deaf audience's understanding. Consider these strictures on *Children of a Lesser God* (1986): 'many signings were cut off by the edges of the frame, executed in bad lighting, or obscured when the performer, [William] Hurt, usually turned away from the camera, and hearing characters would some-times talk without signing.' Norden doesn't spell out what is implied here: that for signing to be properly intelligible it must take precedence over lighting, composition and editing. It isn't insulting to suggest that many deaf viewers (whose exclusion from movies, after all, began only with *The Jazz Singer*) might consider this a bad bargain.

Deaf critics of *Children of a Lesser God* seem to have been less hard-line than Norden, and to have taken it for granted that this was a mildly progressive film aimed squarely at hearing audiences. Clearly there's nothing more tedious for a minority than to be offered overwhelmingly grotesque or sentimentalised images of its existence, but it might also be said that minorities are under no obligation to bond with the positive images they are offered.

It may be, for instance, that a deaf viewer watching a properly captioned print of, say, *Edward Scissorhands*, will identify with difference as expressed in a strongly poetic register. Something similar might even apply to the sequences in *Planet of the Apes* where Charlton Heston is abused by monkeys who refuse to understand what he's saying, regarding him as, by definition, stupid. It is also possible to prefer negative images over positive ones, provided they offer some bonus of power. The fatal woman in film noir magnetises female viewers as well as male. Rod Steiger, playing the murderer in *No Way to Treat a Lady* (1968), impersonated a campy hairdresser in one scene, responding to the insult 'Homo!' with a serenely queenly 'Doesn't mean you're a bad person.' A grating caricature, but still a tempting catchphrase for the film's gay audiences.

So, too, with the stereotype that Norden calls the Obsessive Avenger. Clearly it is not the case that disabled people seek revenge on the able-bodied, but there might be times for finding that fantasy delicious. Norden can't bring himself to appreciate Tod Browning's *Freaks* (1932) because of the notorious finale, in which an entire community of circus performers undertake to punish a pair of sinners (they kill the man and mutilate the woman). They're not by any stretch of the political imagination 'role models', that desirable thing, but it certainly makes a difference that the disabled on screen at this point are in the majority, that wrongdoing was associated with able-bodiedness first, and that there is no comeuppance for these particular Obsessive Avengers. The subversions of *Freaks* are more thoroughgoing than Norden is prepared to admit.

Norden points out in his survey of recent films with a disability theme that it is particularly dramas with disabled people at their centres that are 'problematic': 'they have registered mostly regressive qualities with many of the old stereotypes still in force.' Less direct approaches are likely to be more rewarding.

An old episode of *Hill Street Blues*, for instance, dealt with disability issues in a glancing way. A police car on urgent duty was parked so that it happened to block one of the cutaway sections which have been required on American pavements since the '70s, and an activist in a wheelchair sprayed angry graffiti on its bodywork. He was arrested. Later in the episode he was found guilty of vandalism, but his punishment – with soap-opera glibness of closure – was to give the police classes in disability awareness. Nevertheless, between the arrest and the cutely didactic resolution was an extraordinarily painful sequence, in which the man in the wheelchair needed to use the lavatory. The facilities in the police station were not accessible to wheelchairs, so a policeman had to grudgingly escort him. Trying to hold the disabled man upright at the urinal, the policeman lost his grip. The two men's encounter with shame, loss of control and urine was powerful precisely because it wasn't part of some standard parable, some patronisingly smooth learning curve. The issue wasn't neatly aligned with the dramatic structure: there was a welcome element of syncopation.

Oddly, it is in cameos and bit-parts that ragged shards of reality are more likely to show through the Hollywood gloss. In Viggo Mortensen's brief appearance in *Carlito's Way* (1993) – he plays a wheelchair-bound criminal – two points are made with surprising force. Referring to his wheelchair, the character says that when they really want to punish you, they don't put you in a grave, they put you in one of these. The idea that life in a wheelchair is worse than death, actually a form of torture, is unusually stark for a thriller that is routine in most respects. And when the character is found to be wired for sound, and to have been hired to entrap Carlito, his defence of his actions is also striking: what else can I do to earn a little money, except sell out my friends? The economic powerlessness of the disabled, with the corollary that certain moral choices can become unaffordable luxuries, is rarely addressed by a cinema predicated on the power of individuals to transcend fate.

One film which receives no mention in *The Cinema of Isolation* nevertheless uses disability themes in a uniquely disorienting way: Michael Mann's *Manhunter* (1986), best known as a sort of prequel to *The Silence of the Lambs*, with Brian Cox doing a turn as Hannibal Lecter. The serial killer in the film is an Obsessive Avenger with a vengeance, murdering entire families of strangers carefully selected on the basis of the perfection of their normality. His psychology is obliquely explored in the film – the murders are transformational rituals – but the source of his (to put it mildly) alienation isn't explicitly stated.

In the middle of the film, after following the police investigation exclusively, *Manhunter* switches abruptly to the murderer's world – his professional world, not his handiwork. He is tall and odd-looking. He works in a large-scale film-processing plant. We see him talking to a female colleague, offering her a lift home after work. The part of us that is already unsettled by the film shrieks silently: 'Noooooo! Don't accept a lift home from the monster!' She says thanks, but she doesn't need a lift. He explains that his offer was selfish, since it would give him pleasure to drive her home. She accepts.

The viewer has been deprived of a piece of information known by both parties: the woman is blind. And yes, in her way she is a grown-up (and sexually competent) version of the Sweet Innocent. But in her discussion of her blindness and her job she shows a wry political awareness, of the sort that Norden searches for in vain in so many films: corporations in America must hire a quota of the disabled to be considered for government contracts, and employing a blind woman in a darkroom doesn't require much in the way of modifications to the premises. No expensive wheelchair ramps, for instance.

It's too much to expect the film to allow this character to wield the power of the gaze, but she does something remarkably similar. She wields the power of knowledge at a distance, which the sighted equate with sight. She congratulates her colleague on the clarity of his articulation, and on the excellence of the corrective surgery to his harelip. She remarks that he has trouble only with a few consonants – no one who hadn't worked as a speech therapist, as she has, would even notice. This is one of the most forceful pieces of self-presentation by a disabled person in all cinema. She goes on to make a request: may she touch his face? He refuses, and she doesn't insist.

He mentions that if she has time, he has a surprise that he would like to show her, on her way home. Again we bite our tattered tongues so as not to shout, in a crowded cinema: 'Noooooo! Don't let the monster show you a surprise!' She says yes. She likes surprises.

When the killer shows his colleague the surprise, *Manhunter* enters a territory of perverse and extraordinary richness. The surprise is a tiger, anaesthetised for the removal of a wisdom tooth, flanks stirring faintly as it comes round after the operation, its threat for now suspended. The blind woman touches the beast with wonder and then something like greed, an *amour fou* of the fingers and the sensing skin.

This is an astounding sequence quite apart from its almost Surrealist strangeness. We are being shown that evil can be imaginative, can identify with other people's lacks and desires. We are being reminded that blind people are particularly cut off from nature, our access to wild things being so largely ocular. And the murderer is conveying to her without using a word that he, too, is dangerous, but not to her.

It should come as no surprise that the romance on which these two people embark does not turn out well – if this is Beauty and the Beast, then the Beast can't rise above his bestiality. But what is salutary about the film's approach is that the murderer chooses to draw the dividing line differently, not as we do between her and him, representatives of good and evil, but between both of them and us – they with their difference, we with our defective normality.

Martin Norden has praise for a handful of films in Hollywood history, but there are two pieces of work that elicit outright acclaim: *The Best Years of Our Lives* (1946), directed by William Wyler, and *Coming Home* (1978), directed by Hal Ashby. Both films represent responses to a recent war and are perhaps part of a surge of awareness in different decades about a class of newly disabled men: wounded soldiers – people with an interrupted sense of entitlement, recently dispossessed of privilege, and a feeling of having kept their side of a bargain with their country. In a sense, then, these are films about the honouring of – or reneging on – a social contract that may or may not extend to all disabled people, including those who cannot present their condition as manifestations of sacrifice, negative trophies of patriotism.

Both films seek to address the intimate aspects of disablement, with a comparable mix of forthrightness and equivocation. Wyler's film, highly unusually, uses a disabled person, Harold Russell, in a major role. For once, disablement in the movies is a matter of visible absence rather than disguised presence, unlike Lon Chaney's strapped-up legs visible in profile in *The Penalty* (1920), or Spencer Tracy's theoretically missing arm bizarrely present in publicity stills for *Bad Day at Black Rock*. *The Best Years of Our Lives* goes as far as a bedroom scene, in which Russell's character is helped by his girlfriend to prepare for the night.

This sequence is, in its way, highly daring in what it invites an audience to contemplate. Yet it is striking that there is one area where the film-makers made the character of Homer Parrish less functional than the actor who played him. Russell could put on his prostheses by himself, and wasn't helpless without them.

Could anything signal more clearly the reassuring fact – in this context – of impotence?

The character's girlfriend reacts with true love rather than pity, but this need not mean more than that in a '40s film caring for men was still felt to be the female destiny – 'nurse' being only a special case of 'woman', and a nurse who married her disabled patient making a satisfactory contract between two people exempted from desire.

In *Coming Home*, by contrast, the wheelchair-bound veteran played by Jon Voight can give Jane Fonda's character sexual pleasure in a way her macho husband cannot. Here the equivocation is in the casting rather than the screenplay. The other inhabitants of the Veterans Administration Hospital in the film were disabled in real life, while Voight is a familiar face (best-known for *Midnight Cowboy*) attached to an able body. *Coming Home* contains sequences that are almost documentary, but it is the familiar actor in the standard triangle with whom audiences are expected to identify.

In films like *Coming Home*, or Brando's early film *The Men* (1950), the paraplegic supporting cast guarantee the seriousness of the lead actor in the wheelchair, which is only to say: the disabled people in the background certify the excellence of the star's performance. We never forget that performance is what it is. When Jon Voight pleasures Jane Fonda on the screen in front of us, we know we're not really being invited to imagine the sexual experiences of the wheelchair-bound.

The logical next step from the actor-surrounded-by-real-sufferers strategy of *Coming Home* is represented by the Gary Sinise character in *Forrest Gump* (1994). Here the actor and the 'real' disability have been fused by special effects. Sinise's legs aren't there because some expensive digitised manipulation of the image has seen to it that they're not. There is no strapping-up to be seen in a profile shot. This is one of the most visible absences on screen since *The Best Years of Our Lives*, but its significance is the opposite of the earlier one's. It becomes less and less likely that actual disabled people will appear in films, now that anyone can be a temporary amputee. The authoritative visual shock of seeing the body Harold Russell inhabits is lost when kids seeing the film that earned him his two Oscars (one of which he was forced in time to sell off) may only be impressed that special effects could be so good back then. After virtual disability realised to such high specifications, who will have (screen) time for the real thing?

It only takes common sense to understand that the sex lives of the disabled are a taboo subject because this private area is one where the majority sensitively prefer not to trespass. So much for common sense. In reality the able-bodied imagination intervenes with great intensity in this area. The disabled are insistently sexualised – it's just that they are sexualised in a highly particular way. What is sexualised is not the life but the loss. For the majority, the disabled are by symbolic definition unable to function sexually. If on the level of individual fantasy we equate disability with impotence, as if the wheelchair or the white stick were only outward and visible signs of an inner castration, we can hardly expect more realism from our films.

It should tip us off to the way our thoughts are being shaped that the limbs of the disabled in movies – Lon Chaney's legs, Spencer Tracy's arm, Gary Sinise's reverse prosthesis – are body parts that both cannot and must be there; a formulation classically applied in psychoanalytic theory to that necessary phantom, the mother's penis.

Yet Freudian theory is problematic in its own way. The Oedipus complex may contribute to an explanation of our compulsive disidentification with the disabled, but its root-myth itself both begins and ends with disabilities viewed symbolically. Oedipus is 'orthopaedically impaired', to borrow a recurring phrase of Norden's, as a result of being exposed on the mountainside as a baby, an impairment that is commemorated in his name. As an adult he blinds himself in a highly expressive piece of self-mutilation: he has seen too much, and at the same time, up to the day of his blinding, he has seen nothing at all.

The Oedipus complex is not an optional experience. Freud proposes it as universal and unchanging. But if disability is symbolically viewed by the able-bodied as castration, how is it viewed by the disabled themselves – by the estimated 15 per cent who were born disabled, but also by the remaining 85 per cent, those who became disabled later in life? Do they negotiate the complex in its female version, irrespective of gender, viewing themselves as already castrated? (And does this also mean that Freudian theory in effect constructs femininity as a disability?)

The theory of the Oedipus complex depends fairly heavily on seeing, on the glimpse of the mother naked that reveals her genital anomaly. Freud presented his theories as contributions to science, but if he had really wanted to test them scientifically, he might have taken an interest in the sexual development of those born blind.

Freud features only intermittently in *The Cinema of Isolation*, in the Introduction and then in the concluding pages, but he's present quite enough to destabilise the whole enterprise. Freud is invoked in the first place to explain hostility towards the disabled, as if this was a minor thing that could easily be disposed of, but then Freudian analysis itself seems to endorse able-bodied fantasies about what disabled bodies represent, and even to be composed of them.

The final paragraph of the book tries to put the genie from Vienna back in his bottle. It starts with a tone of modest confidence: 'Though the Oedipal crisis cannot entirely account for the construction of movie images of physical disability, there is little question that the Cinema of Isolation – good films, bad, and everything in between – is heavily indebted to it.' The confidence reaches a peak a few lines later: 'Though the Cinema of Isolation has hinged so strongly on this retrograde male fantasy, it need not continue to do so. The Oedipal framework remains a formidable challenge to movie-makers wishing to represent the physically disabled experience with some measure of equity, but it is not insurmountable.' At this point, on page 323, we are four lines from the end of a long book, and it begins to look as if the author has left it rather late to show us how the future can be made to differ from the past.

Here is his attempt at it:

> If movie-makers, disabled and able-bodied alike, can break away from this narrative structure that has served as the foundation for the whole of mainstream narrative media (and indeed the whole of patriarchal society) and pursue alternative strategies for telling their stories, we may at long last see some real progress.

In the course of a single paragraph the Oedipus complex has gone from being one factor among others in the shaping of cinematic images of disability, to being the strong hinge of the genre and, finally, to being the foundation of the entire society that makes and consumes the films. The Freudian tail has wagged the critical dog throughout *The Cinema of Isolation*, but with this particular convulsion even a sympathetic reader may wonder whether the doggedness which is the book's chief virtue is merit enough.

There's one question not asked in the book, apparently stupid but actually necessary, and that is: What are films about disability about? On the first page of Norden's Preface, even before his Acknowledgements, he refers to the mainstream movie industry's 'fascination' with 'the physically disabled experience'. This last formulation bears tell-tale traces of euphemistic embarrassment but if it is sincere it is already crucially wrong.

As all the evidence adduced in the book goes to show, if Hollywood has attempted to represent the disabled experience it has made an astoundingly bad job of it. Why not take another approach, and suggest that what is being represented is not disability? – Or certainly not disability as an experience. The movie camera shows us the outside of things, and the outside of people. In this sense film is a literal medium, and a literal medium has a crying need for metaphors. So when cinema wants to show a state of mind, it tends to show a state of body instead.

Films with a blindness theme tend to be about trust, films with a deafness theme tend to be about isolation. Both genres express the simultaneous fear of and need for other people. Films with a theme of wheelchair-boundness tend to be about a metaphorical powerlessness. Disabilities on screen stand in for negative mental states, and clearly it's a good thing to turn a negative mental state into a positive one. But where does that leave real-life people for whom the conditions are not allegorical? When disability is metaphorical, there is no such thing as incurability. Cure becomes a moral obligation.

Gender intervenes in the metaphors, not as it does as a factor in real-life disability (as part of a triad with race and class) but in accordance with well-established fantasies. There can be something especially appealing about a blind woman on screen, someone who can't meet the gaze that appropriates her, while a deaf woman is practically advertising her need for a male intermediary between her and the world. Powerlessness is felt to be more threatening for a man than a woman, since power is inherently his domain, and so wheelchair-users in the movies are with rare exceptions male.

If this is exploitation by metaphor, then it doesn't have to be signally pernicious. To object to the various blind-woman-in-jeopardy thrillers would be to object to the thriller itself. If we have devised a genre that arouses and then dispels fears, we have to accept a vulnerable central figure (the body-builder-in-peril genre has never got off the ground). In the case of *Wait Until Dark* (1967) or *Blind Terror* (1971) the supposed blindness of Audrey Hepburn or Mia Farrow is more of a gimmick than a metaphor.

We know where we stand: the appeal for a director is that the heroine's unawareness of her danger, which must normally be conveyed by cutting from her danger to her unawareness of it, can be compressed into a single shot, with great consequent intensification of *frisson*. (It takes a different class of director to attempt a similar trick with deafness, but Hitchcock manages it in *Marnie* [1964], when he shows the heroine robbing a safe while an office cleaner gets on with her work in the same shot on the other side of a partition. The scene builds a mighty suspense as it moves towards Marnie's 'inevitable' detection, which is inevitable only if the office cleaner can hear.)

In recent years a new trend has more or less driven out the established cinematic ideology of disability. Far from saying that disabled people are creatures of a different order, this trend sees no barrier to the consumption of any lives whatsoever. The catch, of course, is that *we* can be like *them*, but the proposition is not reversible. They're not allowed to be like us. Call it not the Cinema of Isolation but the Cinema of Specious Sharing.

There are traces of specious sharing even in fine and much-loved films. At some point in *My Left Foot* (1989), for instance, Christy Brown's psychological survival became a triumph of the human spirit. Obscurely it accrues to us, just as (in this context perhaps an appropriate comparison) an Irishman who wins an international prize immediately becomes British.

Many people have walked out of screenings of the film inspired and energised, to the point of not noticing that the cinema where it was shown was about as wheelchair-accessible as a lighthouse.

The classic example of the Cinema of Specious Sharing, though, would have to be Penny Marshall's *Awakenings* from 1990. There are very many bad films, but *Awakenings* is significant in its badness. Its badness is its only significance. It isn't merely bad but positively teeming with bad things, repugnant in its strategies and the manipulative meanings it imposes on real-life disabilities.

Between 1916 and 1927 there was a worldwide epidemic of encephalitis. A third of those affected died. The majority of those who survived developed forms of Parkinsonism which made them progressively contorted and paralysed. It was a peculiar paralysis, resulting from a deficit of dopamine in the brain, which could sometimes be outwitted in certain circumstances by those who suffered it. Over time, nevertheless, most of the sufferers were placed in institutions.

Then in 1969 a young doctor, aware of the paradoxical nature of the paralysis, had the idea of prescribing L-DOPA, a new drug which promised to restore dopamine levels and therefore physical function. The results were spectacular in the short term but not sustainable in the long.

Penny Marshall's film tells the story of the Parkinsonism patients, particularly of one played by Robert De Niro, but also of the doctor, played by Robin Williams. The doctor is shown to be almost as self-enclosed as the paralysed people he tends, pathologically shy sexually and easily flustered by the most routine social approach from the charge nurse played by Julie Kavner. Over that eventful summer doctor and patients come out of their different trance states. They share a learning curve, except that at the end of the film the patients sink back into their previous condition, while the doctor has attained a minimal but secure ability to function socially. He can go out to coffee with a woman.

To link the two 'awakenings' is of course a wholly grotesque narrative device: to suffer from a dopamine deficit in your brain is not a form of shyness. But the film has more crassness to offer. Much, much more. When the charge nurse is convinced that the post-encephalitic patients, though seeming little more than the living dead, might be worth some treatment, she rallies her forces. But the nurses are absorbed in watching soap operas on TV: she has to clap her hands to break into their absorption. Here in effect the director adds the helpful gloss that we're all in a trance. We could all be more fully alive. Which makes this viewer want to growl: Sure, Penny, we're all of us in wheelchairs. But some of us can walk.

What makes *Awakenings* more than simply a schlocky piece of Hollywood tear-jerking is that it was based on a very powerful book of the same name, written by the doctor, Oliver Sacks. *Awakenings* the book was even a sort of landmark. Without being the product of a hippy sensibility, it offered an interpretation of illness that was in some way holistic. At first Sacks could give his patients back their animation with L-DOPA, but over time their reaction to the drug became unstable. It was impossible to find a maintenance dose.

Sacks's conclusion was as much philosophical and psychological as narrowly medical: that an illness endured over decades, especially one that straitens sufferers' lives to the point of vegetation, becomes effectively part of the person. His patients couldn't resume their lives where they had been left off, often as much as half a century before. They could discharge energy and emotion, they could make a brief return to a changed world, but they had made an accommodation to their illness, and were dispossessed when it was taken away.

To coincide with the film, a new edition of *Awakenings* was published, with a cover chiming with the film poster and a new and rather star-struck appendix in which Sacks wrote about being on the set with the lead actors (whom he called 'Robin' and 'Bob'). But if the film people had made an impact on the book, there was no sign of a reciprocal invasion in the movie. What went missing from the film version were the people the book had been about.

In the book there were twenty or so patient case histories – after all, Sacks wanted 'something of their lives, their presence, to be preserved and live for others, as exemplars of human predicament and survival.' In Steve Zaillian's screenplay twenty-odd had effectively become one: the character played by Robert De Niro, Leonard. This wouldn't be so bad if this character was left unprocessed by the screenwriter. The real Leonard L. was a highly articulate man – when finally he could speak – a Harvard graduate who had been closing in on a PhD, aged 27, before post-encephalitic disease closed in on him. He also had a backlog of libido. In May 1969 he was masturbating for hours every day, not concealing what he was doing. In June he wrote his memoirs – 50,000 words' worth.

Of this complex human being virtually nothing survives into the film, certainly not those twin enemies of sentimentalism, the intellect and the libido. The twenty-odd have been boiled down into one, and then the one has been diluted with many times the original volume of syrup. If you ask someone to bring you two dozen free-range eggs, and he comes back with a can of Coke, you're likely to point out that this wasn't what you asked for. In Hollywood, you say instead, 'Thank you for the sensitive screenplay, Steve. It taught me a lot about myself.'

There was a time when awkward inmates of institutions would be lobotomised or castrated by their keepers. Dr Sacks would never dream of such a thing – so why does he give his blessing to a film which makes the same subtractions on the symbolic level? Leonard L. in his book had an unruly body, which subjected the nurses at Mount Carmel hospital to insistent sexual harassment, and a sophisticated mind which had done little for decades but reflect on its own experiences. 'Leonard' in the film is all heart. The original has been mutilated in the interest of greater wholeness.

'Leonard' is an ordinary-Joe-regular-guy, whose sudden quoting of a Rilke poem, of all things, comes across as a bizarre aberration. And of course he doesn't, you know, touch himself *that way*. He has a chaste romance, mainly in the cafeteria of the hospital, with the daughter of a patient who has had a stroke. She thinks that he works there, that he's maybe a doctor. Doesn't that just make your heart *break*?

When he starts to be able to move and communicate, the nursing staff line up to be introduced to him. They use his name now, now that he's a person and not a dreary zombie. Now it's a privilege to meet him, where before he was just a sack of unresponsiveness. But the 'Leonard' to whom they are introduced has been turned into a child.

Before he published *Awakenings* in 1973, Oliver Sacks had written a single book, a technical book of less than universal appeal, on the subject of migraine. *Awakenings* put him on the map culturally. He did a lot for his patients, but in that sense they did a lot for him too. Their lives were the material that gave him his reputation. They were hardly known, unexplored territory, and he was the explorer of that territory. When he sold his book to Hollywood, all that changed. If Sacks didn't mind being represented on screen as a virtually autistic virgin, every bit as removed from life as the people he was trying to help, that was an eccentric choice but it was certainly his privilege. He did not however have the right to feed his patients' lives into Hollywood's blender of kitsch.

What Sacks did when he let the rights to the book be bought was a betrayal and also a fraud of a rarefied kind. He sold on that which he did not own: the lives of his patients, who trusted him not just to medicate their bodies but to tell their stories. He continues to refer to them in the current edition of *Awakenings* as 'not only patients but teachers and friends', which is charming unless you feel that you shouldn't take any of these categories of person to market.

The post-encephalitics tended to be elderly at the time the book was published, and only one was around at the time the film was made. Sacks and the stars visited her, and so did the director. 'Bob, Robin, Penny and I,' he remarks in his 1990 appendix, 'all marvelled at her toughness, her humour, her lack of self-pity, her realness.' Ah yes. Her realness.

It isn't even the case that Oliver Sacks sold the rights to the book and then kept his distance from the trivialisation of his work. He was employed by the production (hence his access to 'Bobby' and 'Robin') to teach De Niro and other actors how to behave physically as his patients had. How to 'do' post-encephalitic Parkinsonism.

The great strength of the book had been that it insisted in patients being more than the sum of their symptoms. Now Sacks was defining them as symptoms all over again, and showing actors how to impersonate their restricted movements, with no interest in their individual lives. He gave classes.

> I showed the actors how Parkinsonian patients stood, or tried to stand; how they walked, often bent over, sometimes accelerating and festinating; how they might come to a halt, freeze, and be unable to go on. I showed them different sorts of Parkinsonian voices, and noises: Parkinsonian handwriting; Parkinsonian *everything*.

Well, not *everything*. Just a crash course in the gimmicks. The more photogenic gimmicks, at that. Sacks's patients tended to drool, but he gave the actors no drooling lessons. The film-makers wanted authenticity, sure, but not drool. Drool would be icky. They wanted, like, the broader picture. The nicer picture.

Perhaps Sacks wasn't aware of the use to which the director would put the tricks he showed the cast; perhaps he doesn't even notice when the movie is screened. But for instance there's a moment when De Niro is using a flight of steps in one direction, carefully, tentatively, and we are shown a toddler going in the other direction with a similarly touching gait. The disabled are really children, you see. Children at best.

Sacks even went on the publicity tour for the film. When asked, he did not seem to understand that he might be thought to be endorsing the film in any way, though he would be delivered to televisions studios for interview in cars sent by the film company, and ushered on set by the company's publicity people. Cuddly adorable bear-like man as by all accounts he is, Oliver Sacks seemed to be insensitive to the rights of the people he had, so long ago, been employed to look after. Yet that same season he was promoting his excellent book on deafness, *Seeing Voices*, which includes an account of the Gallaudet disturbances of 1988, when the deaf students had decided that enough was enough.

The film of *Awakenings* is an extreme case, because the same person who wrote a classic account of illness, and tried to imagine some very inaccessible interiorities, also benignly watched over the turning of his work into an obscenely sentimental confection, and did what he could to help.

The appendix about the various adaptations of the book survives in the current paperback edition. The Acknowledgements thank the actors, the producers, the director and the screen-writer, though the movie tie-in cover has been replaced by

something more classical. It no longer shows the doctor indul-
gently watching from the prudence of the jetty while 'Leonard',
the patient who is also his friend and teacher, stands triumphantly on a rock in the ocean, trouser legs rolled up, reaching
out to the sky with the sheer joy of being alive. The big kid!

An important subject, which perhaps accounts for the occasionally grating self-righteous tone – though it may be that the
academic tone of the book I was reviewing infected my manner.
I dare say it was intentional that I omitted the name of the film
described in the opening passage, the 'well-known one from the
early nineties, a touted return to form by a famous director' –
Robert Altman's *The Player*.

The slightly oblique references to Oliver Sacks being on the
publicity circuit for the film of *Awakenings* is explained by the fact
that I interviewed him for *The Late Show* on television at the time
of release, and a thoroughly disconcerting experience it was too.
I took it for granted that he was aware of the disillusionment
and even hostility of my *Independent* review, and for once I don't
think this is the standard egotist's expectation that what you
write will be of urgent interest to everyone in the whole world.
He was promoting the film, even if he chose to be unaware of
the fact, and his minders will certainly have known that they
were leading him perhaps not into an ambush, but certainly into
something rather more searching than the standard exchange of
politenesses, given the cultural prestige of the programme and
the amount of time at our disposal.

I half-expected that he would make some sort of plea for
clemency in advance. I tried to imagine what adequately com-
pelling excuse might be made – 'Have a heart! Go easy on me!
I needed the money to endow a medical research foundation . . .

in honour of my late father.' Something along those lines. I would go easy on him. Relatively easy anyway, leaving some edge on the questions but not seeking to draw actual blood.

In the event he didn't seem nervous. Normally I try not speculate about people's sexual orientation, on the basis that I'd rather accept their self-descriptions than contest or override them (also my gaydar is very bad). But I'd assumed Sacks was gay from the shape of his life – he left London for America on the basis that there were already two Dr Sackses working in London (his parents, father a physician and mother a surgeon), moving to California in the first instance as if to maximise his distance from where he started. There he became a committed weight-lifter, a regimen he explained by saying he wanted to prove that Jews could be strong.

I even imagined there might be a micro-vibe of affinity to be tuned into between interviewer and interviewee, something to complicate or make piquant the likely clash of views. In person, though, Sacks hardly seemed to inhabit his body. Big burly furball though he was, he had zero physical presence, as if this frame was no more than a virtual-reality avatar controlled from elsewhere. His manner didn't change as I made the case against the film and his involvement in it, though he said that he wasn't anything to do with its promotion – this was when I pointed out that he had been escorted to the studio by representatives of the film company. Then without anything much in the way of transition he seemed to accept the critique in full, saying undramatically 'I think I had this coming' and suggesting that later in the day (he was due to appear at the ICA that evening to discuss *Seeing Voices*) he would most likely talk about the criticisms I had made rather than his new book, after which, he said, the film company would send him home 'on a banana boat'.

The odd thing was that there was no detectable shift of mood to accompany the apparent intellectual capitulation.

He was as emotionally disengaged at the end of the interview as he had been at the start, and took his leave without either effusiveness or rancour. I wasn't at the ICA that evening and have no idea whether he denounced himself there, as he had predicted. It doesn't seem likely. But in any case the programme received a phone call saying that the interview couldn't be used.

Hah! Personal and commercial interests trying to muzzle the independence of the media – we'd fight tooth and nail to tell the truth. I'd seen too many films in the vein of *All the President's Men*. Actually we wouldn't be fighting tooth and nail, we'd be rolling over and wanting our tummies tickled. I don't know whether it was Sacks himself who applied the pressure, when his emotions finally kicked in after a strange lag, or the film company that was making use of him to endorse the film, but either way the interview was re-edited before being broadcast. It wasn't exactly toothless in this revised form, but it bore no relation to the startling document it had been. As transmitted, the most remarkable thing about it was not the discontinuity but the opposite. Although the order of the questions had been altered, so that segments recorded late in the interview now came early on, it was impossible to tell any difference in Oliver Sacks's manner. His manner was just the same before and after the moment when he had said he had it coming, and agreed with the accusation that he had exploited his patients.

From that point on, I had a bee in my bonnet and an axe to grind (proper health and safety nightmare) on the subject of disability in film. When I was asked to deliver a lecture at the Royal College of Art, I chose this as my subject, though back before the arrival of the DVD it was hard to co-ordinate clips with an unscripted talk. Videotape was a clumsy medium. More recently I've started giving a revised version of this presentation, using sequences from a number of the films mentioned in the essay (*The Best Years of Our Lives, Forrest Gump, Awakenings, The*

Miracle Worker, *Manhunter*, *The Player*). There are more people attuned to the relevance of the subject than there used to be. The low attendance mentioned by Martin Norden as inevitable when addressing the subject of disability is no longer quite such a problem.

I use as an illustration of my argument one film that didn't feature in the original essay, John Carpenter's 1982 remake of *The Thing*. It was a film I had seen on first release, and very effective and oppressive it was too, though it had seemed a mistake to cast doubt at one point on the human credentials of the main character (played by Kurt Russell). Audiences had enough to handle when an alien shape-shifter infiltrated a scientific survey in the Antarctic without being estranged from the hero, led to anticipate a twist that never came.

After watching the DVD of the film, I did some idle online research (I can't guarantee there wasn't a glass of wine involved) into how some of its famously gruesome special effects were achieved, in the days before computer-generated imagery took so much of the magic and the mystery of such things away. It was a bit of an eye-opener. So I use a sequence from *The Thing* after showing extracts from *The Best Years of Our Lives* (disability looked at directly, without stand-ins) and *Forrest Gump* (simulated disability, both realistic and entirely unreal). In the clip I show, there's a tense standoff between Russell's character MacReady and other members of the crew, who think he may have been taken over. Suddenly one of them collapses, plausibly with a heart attack – he's not breathing. The expedition's doctor, played by Richard Dysart, has him laid out on a table so as to administer electric shocks with defibrillating paddles and thereby, with any luck, restore the rhythm of his heart. We've seen the scene hundreds of times on screens large and small. *Clear!* Down come the paddles. No response. Try again. *Clear!*

This time something happens that is a lot worse than no response. As the paddles descend again, a wide mouth of sorts, complete with tooth-shaped edges, opens up in the chest of the (supposedly) sick (supposed) man. It's too late for the doctor to pull back – his momentum means that his hands and part of his arms enter the alien cavity. The dentition closes, severing his arms near the elbow. He screams, understandably, and waves his spurting stumps in a frenzy of dismay.

It's all very exciting, and the next minute or so contain some astoundingly baroque images, designed by Rob Bottin, so ugly they approach some sort of beauty from the other side. But it's that moment of defibrillation gone so horribly wrong that I focus on. What are we looking at? What are we being shown? This isn't computer-generated imagery – it can't be, at that date. But nor are we watching Richard Dysart being mutilated for our entertainment. He's not an A-list actor, true, but he's not *that* expendable. This is what's going on, according to Michael Truly in the podcast 'The Art of the Scene' on the CineFix channel:

> To achieve the effect of Dr Copper's arms being chest-chomped, Carpenter cut from Dysart . . . plunging his arms into the fibre-glass chest to a pair of fake arms affixed to a stuntman who was a double amputee . . . the hydraulic chest snaps shut, mangling the prosthetic arms, which were made of gelatin with wax bones and rubber veins inside. With fake blood and gore flying, Carpenter and Bottin knew the audience would not notice that Dysart had been replaced by a stuntman with a prosthetic Dr Copper mask on . . . in fact the mask was so realistic that Joel Polis, who played Fuchs, thought the production had simply found a double amputee who looked exactly like Dysart. The subsequent shot of Norris's chest spouting viscera, just before the Thing

emerges from the gaping hole, was designed to be a single take – the prep time for that shot alone was ten hours . . .

Can we wind back a bit, please, to before that mention of 'spouting viscera', and before we get on to the celebrated *head-spiderisation* and indeed the legendary *tongue-lasso*? It makes it hard to concentrate. Filter out the tech triumphalism, and what we're being told is that someone who had lost his arms (circumstances unknown) was hired to re-enact that injury on camera, with as much spurting of blood as the director felt was required to distract audiences from the substitution of one performer for another. Is it fair to describe such a person as a 'stuntman'? A stuntman or stuntwoman is essentially an athlete, after all, and there's not a lot of work on offer for someone whose only marketable asset is a physical deficit. He won't get the call for regular stunt work, in fact he won't get the call for anything but the re-enactment of the event that disqualified him for regular work of any description. Can we be brutal? (Given that the circumstances are all the more brutal for not being directly addressed.) Isn't he just a guy who has lost a large part of his arms? It would be strange to characterise that as a skill.

There are a dozen credited stuntmen on *The Thing*, as listed by IMDb. They all did work on other films, which rules them out as the stand-in for the chest-chomp sequence (if you want a search term for this part of the film, 'chest-chomp' is the way to go) – what made the performer perfect for this gig would debar him from most other stunt work. No credit and no name. There are the crack troops of stunt work, and there is cannon fodder. I hope at least the performer was paid for the re-enactment of his injury, but if he had lost his arms in an industrial accident or the military then he would likely to be receiving some sort of benefit, conditional on having no other source of income. In which case the anonymity may have been a necessary precaution on his part, as much as a decision by the film-makers.

It's rhetorically more effective to show the chest-chomp in *The Thing* out of historical sequence, after the excerpt from *Forrest Gump*, to trace first the disappearance of the disabled body that had been so directly addressed in *The Best Years*, replaced by a special effect thanks to computer-generated imagery, and then the return of disability without a person attached to it, again on the level of a special effect. There's nothing wrong with rhetorical effectiveness, rhetoric being no more than the performance of an argument.

Next time I give my *Cinematically Challenged* presentation, I'll point out the similarity between the injuries sustained by Harold Russell in *The Best Years of Our Lives* and Richard Dysart's stand-in on *The Thing*. I may even find myself saying – since rhetoric can so easily get out of hand – that it was the Second World War itself, an honourable war, that licensed the showing of Russell's wounds, even though he hadn't as a strict matter of fact suffered them in combat, while the Vietnam War, a conflict lived by America as dishonourable even while it was going on, could yield only dishonourable wounds, injuries to be shown off in a horror film as if it was a carnival freak show. Though I don't even know that the not-quite stuntman in *The Thing* was a Vietnam vet. And all I would really be saying, anyway, would be that in 1946 it wasn't technically possible to represent the disabled without showing them, in a medium that sets higher standards of realism than the sort of theatre matinée in my childhood where Long John Silver has his leg tied up behind him and an equally perfunctory parrot.

Awakenings was indeed some kind of wake-up call. A broader interest in what you might call exclusionary represen-tation, where an issue is staged in a way that is reassuringly free of the people actually affected by it, surfaces in some surprising places – for instance my 2000 *Times* review of *Nutty Professor II: The Klumps*, in which Eddie Murphy donned a fat suit. (Yes, I reviewed *Nutty Professor II: The Klumps*. No, they didn't quote me on the poster.) The last paragraph should be plenty:

> Obesity and ageing join the ranks of issues which Hollywood handles with reverent tongs. We have had films where the value of gay lives is asserted through the efforts of performers certified straight (William Hurt in *Kiss of the Spider Woman*, Tom Hanks in *Philadelphia*); films that use male stars to celebrate female experience (*Tootsie*); films that stand up for dowdy waitresses, starring Michelle Pfeiffer (*Frankie and Johnny*). Now the right to self-esteem of the fat and the no longer young is defended in the only way possible, given that in Hollywood putting on either pounds or years is unforgivable – by an expert special-effects team, and a taut-bodied actor in his whippet prime.

Shallow Hal, with Gwyneth Paltrow taking her turn in the fat suit, came out the year after *Nutty Professor II*, though this was a different case of obesity-borrowing. The story line required the heroine Rosemary to be shown both as very fat, as she really is, and as slim and lovely when seen by Jack Black's Hal after being hypnotised into being attuned to inner beauty exclusively – it's hard to see how that could be accomplished without a slim performer padding up. The cinematic ban on obesity is still in force, but the taboo on ageing has relaxed to an amazing extent, just as long as you're a man. Can I come back to that? I'd like to chase a few more rabbits just now.

The special effects man on *Nutty Professor II*, Rick Baker, disappears in IMDb's rigorously alphabetical listing of people in the 'Make-up Department' (itself a rather slighting description of a contribution crucial to the film) but had been well known for his effects work for a couple of decades before 2000. He was responsible for the famous vulpine transformation scenes in *An American Werewolf in London* (1981) and the less well-known ones in *The Howling* from the same year. My guess is that the work on *American Werewolf* came first, since even at the time I thought the effects were patchy – there's one particular shot in the transformation sequence in which the hero's big wolf legs look entirely inert, despite the actor's agonised gurning. Or perhaps it's just that Joe Dante was more of a perfectionist than John Landis.

There was black comedy in *American Werewolf*, particularly with the Griffin Dunne character, but the humour in *The Howling* was more distinctive, perhaps thanks to John Sayles's contribution to the script. The idea of a group of werewolves camouflaging themselves as a therapy community in California whose guru (Patrick Macnee of all people) preaches getting in touch with your inner wild beast is delightful. The mixture of comedy and horror is inherently unstable, and most films that attempt the hybrid come down on one side or the other fairly decisively, but *The Howling* managed to keep the balance right to the end. At the climax of the film the heroine, a television presenter played by Dee Wallace, went off-script during the news to warn America about the werewolf danger it faced, while also transforming into a wolf herself – but a rather elegant, feminine creature, in contrast to the massive killing machines we've got used to seeing, with a tear sparkling on her furry cheekbone.

Before the release of *The Howling* the *New Yorker* ran a piece (one of its 'casuals') on the making of the film. Sayles, who subsidised his directing career by taking on script-doctoring assignments, said that the first thing he did when he was brought in on *The Howling* was to compile a sort of handbook of how lycanthropy was supposed to work in the film. What happened if you were scratched by a werewolf? Bitten? Killed outright? What happened if a werewolf was injured while in human form? Internal consistency is what keeps fantasy rooted, not in realism as such but in its own reality.

Rick Baker worked, uncredited, as a special effects assistant on *The Exorcist* (under Dick Smith), where he was in charge of making Regan's revolving head, and claims he still found the result terrifying when he saw it in the cinema. He was employed on the first *Star Wars* film, earning a credit but not much glory (make-up second unit), working on one of the few sequences in the film that to my jaundiced eye has any vitality, the 'cantina' scene on Mos Eisley. Despite his own lowly status, he seems to have taken on Rob Bottin – later of *The Thing*, then still in his teens – to assist. Physical special effects, though the industry term is 'practical' effects, whose touchstone is tangibility, require an awful lot of labour. After *An American Werewolf in London* Baker got the call from Michael Jackson to work on a video (also directed by Landis) to feature dancing zombies – I forget what it was called.

Well-thought-through special effects can give fantasy a real boost of imaginative energy. My favourites are Jean Cocteau's, which are often very simple. You can work out how they were done – or see the trick immediately – but the shiver of delight survives knowing how the moment was created. Cocteau likes to film things backwards, by which of course I mean he films them in the ordinary way and then reverses the footage. In *Testament d'Orphée* (1960) he 'makes' a flower, by methodically tearing off petals and then showing the sequence backwards. At one beautiful moment, a spear, thrown at Cocteau's back by a statue, transfixes him, but when we see him from the front what protrudes from his chest is an old-fashioned dipping pen. Visual imagination is enriched by aural inventiveness, with the moment of impact accompanied by the sound of a jet plane taking off.

There's something eerie about Death's kingdom in the film *Orphée*, accessed through mirrors in a wonderful trick shot, the mirrors liquefying as the gloved hands of Death's motor- cycle outriders touch them. Brilliant! I can take any amount of preening poetic voiceover as long as there's visual poetry too. 'I shall tell you the secret of secrets. Mirrors are the doors by which death comes and goes. Just watch yourself all your life in a mirror and you will see death at work, like bees in a glass hive.' ... Actually that's pretty good. It takes a little while for the eeri- ness to make sense – the actors have been filmed performing all their actions in reverse, so that when the film itself is played backwards they look normal (well, normal-ish), while the laws of nature are suspended elsewhere in the frame, with scraps of paper falling upwards, for instance.

Some of Cocteau's effects remain mysterious, it's true, par- ticularly in *La Belle et La Bête* (1946), or at least I can't work out how they were done. When Beauty first arrives at Beast's castle, she is lighted along the passage by candelabra in the form of human arms – well, that bit I get! Arms reaching through from the other side of the wall of the set. But I don't understand how the candles can light spontaneously as Beauty approaches, and quench themselves when she has passed. But please don't write in. It must be that I don't want to know.

Later in the same part of the film Beauty moves smoothly, without seeming to move her feet, which are out of shot, across a space where draperies are blowing. She must be being pushed, or pulled, on a trolley. It's an influential invention, as much so as Hitchcock's famous 'vertigo shot', visible in any number of pop videos and in unexpected corners of cinema, like Lisa Marie's pneumatic gum-chewing alien in *Mars Attacks!*. It's there in Melville's 1950 film of Cocteau's *Les Enfants Terribles*, too, used extremely effectively, in a way that makes me wonder if Cocteau wasn't more involved in the production than is normally assumed (there's a tendency to praise the film at Cocteau's expense). It's almost his signature.

Cocteau's special effects have a lightness and simplicity about them, seeming to express his love, both adult and childlike, of film as a medium. In a stylised interior a statue may suddenly move, not for any sinister reason but just to remind you that the barrier between the living and the inanimate may not be fixed. There's a moment in the story when Beast's attention is caught by a deer in the grounds of his castle while Beauty is talking to him. His ears prick up – he can't help himself. This was not a slick shoot by Hollywood standards: I imagine that the actor playing Beast, Cocteau's lover Jean Marais, activated the ears of the costume with the help of a little hand-squeezed bulb, sending a puff of air down a tube – special effects created with the sort of trick you'd find in an old-fashioned joke shop. That's all that was needed. Perhaps someone else squeezed the bulb to produce this little displaced arousal, but it would be easier for Marais to do it him- self, so as to co-ordinate his performance with the moment of inflation. The result is sweet and funny. Josette Day as Beauty adds to it by saying, in a miffed, scolding tone, '*Oh, la Bête!*' Men are all the same. Can't take their eyes off a prey animal.

When the Beast turns back into the Prince, he and Beauty simply leap into the air, taking off into the realms of happiness. Once again, this is a trick shot reversing the filmed actions. Marais must actually have jumped down from a little height, with Day in his arms. As it was originally filmed, it took a second or two for the folds of Beauty's dress to settle into the new position, with the beautiful result, not planned but adding to the overall effect rather than detracting from it, that when the footage is reversed in the final film those folds start to stir first, and the costume itself seems to join in with the impulse of flight. In Cocteau's vision the distinction between living and non-living matter comes to seem arbitrary, a matter of convention rather than a law of nature.

The special effects of Kubrick's *2001: A Space Odyssey* (1968) are at the opposite extreme from Cocteau's, awe-inspiring and chilly. Again the division between animate and inanimate is called into question, but from another angle, with human beings, irradiated with intelligence (as it turns out) by a monolith, seeming to be a special case of mineral – ape-shaped stones that think and talk. The film foresees a future where moments of grandeur must be paid for by eons of rapt boredom, in a cosmos without personality that Kubrick explores by means of a narrative consciously avoiding the trappings of character and incident. Arthur C. Clarke, co-author of the screenplay, may have thought he was prophesying a thrilling future for humanity beyond the stars, but Stanley Kubrick made sure we register more keenly the amount of time spent waiting for things to happen, in intermediate places that are not like places at all.

To get to the site on the Moon where something astonishing has been dug up, Dr Heywood Floyd (William Sylvester) makes a trip in four stages – a shuttle from Earth (with seatback videos that anticipate the present-day splendours of Virgin business class), a layover on the space station, another shuttle to the Moon, where he gives a bureaucratic presentation which is mysteriously applauded by a room full of scientists, and finally a sort of flying jeep. At each change of vehicle there is small talk ('Hi, everybody – nice to be with you' is as memorable as it gets), and a slow, slow drip of plot information. In philosophy, Zeno's paradox states that a shot arrow can never reach its target, since first it must cover half the distance, then half that distance, and so on. Dr Floyd seems to be travelling on Zeno Airways.

On his previous film, the highly economical *Dr Strangelove*, Kubrick had already shown technology as having its own logic and momentum. On *2001* he enormously expanded the grandeur of his canvas, and scaled down the urgency of human concerns. The public-address system on the space station announces that a lady's cashmere sweater has been found, but there's no trace of anyone who might wear something so frivolous and sensual. It's knitwear from another world, the world of perfume, lipstick and dinner dates. It trembles on the edge of an in-joke – it might be an item Sue Lyon left behind at Shepperton during the filming of *Lolita*. *2001* doesn't attempt to cater to any aspect of sensory experience but the cold curiosity of the eye. In fact, the single most person-centred thing about the whole film is the provision of an interval after ninety minutes or so, a recognition that human beings in their unevolved state are still tied to the demands of a bladder. A similar amenity was offered by a film that could hardly be less like *2001*, *The Sound of Music*.

Though Kubrick had started his career directing lean little thrillers, on this project his ambitions were huge – *2001* starts with the oldest art form, mime (the apes in their fake fur), and ends with avant-garde visual effects. Storytelling is not a priority. If anything, Kubrick used his formidable manipulative skills to keep audiences from caring too much about the human action. Audiences feel distanced when they watch the film, up against the fact of distance.

Human interest shrivels under the gaze of the stars. Kubrick is parsimonious with the elements of film language that might nudge audiences towards identifying with the people shown. There's a little hand-held camerawork, as Floyd and his party approach the monolith on the Moon, and again when Bowman moves through the *Discovery* to disable HAL. At various stages there's footage from the viewpoint of the computer, but not of the people – although sometimes Kubrick emphasises their perspective (point of hearing rather than point of view), with an astronaut's amplified breathing dominating the soundtrack.

When Bowman and Poole climb out of service pods, they're filmed from above, so that the pairs of circles on the top of their helmets look like insect eyes. How many other directors would show the characters, at their moment of maximum vulnerability, with only spacesuits standing between them and the interplanetary void, resembling bugs as much as heroes?

It's only in the last, baffling scenes – set in a rococo bedroom whose translucent floor, divided into large squares and lit from underneath, has inspired a thousand discos – that Kubrick uses point-of-view shots for Bowman, and then they're part of the puzzle. Each time the camera takes up a position that matches where he was a moment ago, the next shot shows there's nobody there. Kubrick uses the machinery of cinematic identification largely against itself.

There had been films before that had staked everything on special effects (*King Kong* for one) but they began looking corny very soon. The effects on *2001* are as lustrous and alienating now as they were on release, apart from the apes – perhaps ape effects are a special case. In particular the model work is unprecedented in its precision, overcoming the great drawback of working in miniature, the way infinitesimal flaws become impossible to ignore on a big screen. (One designer for the stage was puzzled, when attending the premiere in Tokyo of a production on which he had worked – he had put his finished model onto a plane from London – by a curious translucent plastic hose stretching across one corner of the set. It was a thread of glue from his glue gun that he hadn't wiped off, dutifully scaled up by the fabrication crew.) On film the fault-finding eye can be hurried or distracted, either fooled by a fast pace or drawn in to the characters' predicament, perhaps with the help of some emotionally unambiguous music. None of these resources is tapped by *2001*.

Kubrick's use of music in *2001* is celebrated, disconcerting either by being unfamiliar and unwelcoming (the unearthly choir on Ligeti's *Lux Aeterna* sounding like some coldly boiling metal) or by matching familiar classical showpieces to overwhelming new images: the *Blue Danube* making a docking in space look like a mating dance, the infinity fanfare of *Also sprach Zarathustra* saluting the hidden order of the universe. There was also silence in the film – lots of silence.

It's not just that music goes missing, counter to every Hollywood rule, from the most dramatic part of the film, the computer HAL 9000's bid to eliminate the crew of the *Discovery*. *2001* puts to shame all those space operas where explosions go *BOOM!* without an atmosphere to transmit their vibrations, and every starship in the fleet has its own vacuous rumble. Actions outside the *Discovery* take place in the absence of sound. *2001* made such an impact over time that it's easy to forget the bafflement and boredom of its first audiences – Kubrick was taking a huge risk by starting a film with a futuristic title in the deep past of the planet. The first section overlaps with wildlife documentary, so that audiences must have felt they had been promised *Astounding Stories* and been given *National Geographic* instead. They laughed at the apes and left in large numbers during the final scenes. This was before word got round that it was worth the wait for the psychedelic light show of the last section, and that recreational drugs enhanced the effect of something that defied straight logic anyway.

Kubrick became alarmed at the apparent failure of his long-meditated and extremely expensive project. He cut nearly twenty minutes from the prints being shown, and even put film editors on international flights with a list of the relevant cuts so that the versions being shown around the world harmonised. Myself, I'd like to see those sacrificed minutes restored. How could there be more nothingness in *2001* than there is in the shortened version? Kubrick left in plenty of longueurs, perversely slow-paced shots like the ones of Bowman setting off from *Discovery* to retrieve his colleague, at what is in theory the climax of an adventure. But then the future as imagined in the film is awe-inspiring rather than interest-inspiring.

The cut footage turned up a few years ago, so restoration is a practicality, which isn't the case with other films that had major elements removed. Would I want to see the original five-hour version of von Stroheim's *Greed*, if it somehow surfaced? Not really, but I'll say I would just to keep up some sort of professional front. But I'd love to see the gas chamber scene from *Double Indemnity*, which Billy Wilder thought was the best thing he'd ever done, except that it skewed the whole picture into a debate about capital punishment. And the original twenty minutes' worth of Dalí dream sequence filmed for *Spellbound* would have to be worth anyone's time, no? I don't expect it's going to appear on a DVD anytime soon.

Dalí's work on another collaboration, with Disney on *Destino* (1946), surfaced a few years ago and is well worth watching online, showing that his mannerist imagery married beautifully with animation. Dalí and Disney, the masturbation merchant and the dispenser of syrup, could have worked remarkably well together. It's our collective loss that the project was cancelled, since the Disneyfication of popular culture has been a dismal process overall, despite the occasional recent reprieve from oversweetness with the sugar-reduced products of the corporation's Pixar wing.

The association between animation and childishness is both real and conventional (and childhood itself is hardly a fixed category). It's real because the world of animation is one in which there are no necessary consequences, so that irreversible experiences such as sex and death, the knowledge of which turns us into adults, have no place in it. The ruling impulse in animation is the id, but an id with no conception of inflicting lasting harm, the destructiveness of a tantrum not a vendetta. You can Taser an audience with pathos if that's really what you want (Bambi's mother, Mufasa in *The Lion King*), but only if you short-change the possibilities of the medium and present an animal society that closely mimics the human. Sexual feeling is even more against the grain of animation – chaste romance, mere togetherness, is the most that can be managed.

In America, historically, animation has always meant drawn animation, though everyone remembers the fighting skeletons created by Ray Harryhausen for *Jason and the Argonauts* (1963). The stop-motion technique has played a larger part in Europe, and its history goes back a long way. The pioneer animator Ladislas Starevich (1882–1965) spent most of his working life in France but started off in Russia, and his *The Cameraman's Revenge* from 1912 is still pretty startling. The characters in this drama of marital dissatisfaction are pretty obviously dead insects, but the movement compares well with live-action film of the period. Hmm. A beetle hero on the screen in the year Kafka wrote *Metamorphosis* – I feel a PhD thesis coming on.

When I started reviewing films the conventions were clear and the audiences distinct. A (drawn) American product like *FernGully: The Last Rainforest* (1992) was for children, though it dealt with grown-up issues like ecology. Not that you'd learn a lot about the struggle for existence from a film whose total body count (unless you include trees, as perhaps you're meant to) is a single snail. A European offering using stop-motion, like Jan Švankmajer's *Alice* (1988), could only be marketed as an art film, even if it was based on a classic children's book. It's true that Švankmajer's is a perverse imagination, who represents Carroll's Caterpillar as a sock with a pair of glass eyes and a set of false teeth, sitting on a darning mushroom from an old-fashioned sewing box. After it has finished speaking the Caterpillar falls asleep, spitting out its false teeth and darning its own eyes shut.

Years before *FernGully*, *Who Framed Roger Rabbit* had shrewdly appealed to audiences that wouldn't have paid to see a cartoon on a Saturday night in the ordinary run of things, but that was a unique project. It helped that there were human faces to be seen on screen, and names to go on the poster. (This was still a time when filmgoers would feel cheated if the names in large type on the poster didn't correspond to filmed face. The slow process whereby the phrase 'with the voice talents of' shrank in font and finally disappeared, so that posters for *Shrek* could list MIKE MYERS, CAMERON DIAZ and EDDIE MURPHY without apology, was a stealthy coup on the part of advertising executives, but also testified to a shift in expectation. An animated feature was no longer second best.)

Who Framed Roger Rabbit (1988)

Who Framed Roger Rabbit is the sort of film that gives block-busters a good name. At least five people deserve congratulations on a thoroughly satisfying entertainment: director Robert Zemeckis, animation director Richard Williams, producer Steven Spielberg and actors Bob Hoskins and Christopher Lloyd. All the film lacks, in fact, is a question mark in the title.

The film's mixing of animation and live action is not new, as anyone who can remember as far back as *Mary Poppins* will appreciate, nor does *Roger Rabbit* represent the state of the art in animation terms, exactly. These days computer graphics can generate images with a startling three-dimensionality, while *Roger Rabbit* harks back to the Golden Age of cartoons and a flatter, more childlike approximation to life. Computer-generated images can occupy human space very convincingly – but the pleasure of *Roger Rabbit* comes from the collision of the two worlds, not their blending.

The story is a sort of film noir pastiche, featuring corrupt business deals and a drink-sodden private eye (Bob Hoskins as Eddie Valiant) in a mutated Los Angeles of the 1940s, so that the human action has a stylisation of its own even in the absence of the animated element. The conceit of the film is that cartoons (known as Toons) are a sort of Hollywood underclass, restricted to working in the entertainment and service industries and living in their own sealed-off area, the DayGlo ghetto known as Toontown.

The world of cartoon is a vulnerable one, highly unstable when exposed to reality: when a cartoon rabbit breaks real plates, the audience can find even so harmless an action troubling. The plate fragments will not go on, as they might in a cartoon, to mount a song-and-dance number of their own, and already the rabbit has stopped being a disembodied spirit of anarchy and become a sharer in human destructiveness. A film like *Who Framed Roger Rabbit* risks reaping diminishing returns when cartoons lose too much of their innocence.

Anyone who is danger of missing the beginning of the movie would be well advised to wait for the next showing, since the opening sequences most perfectly demonstrate its virtues. *Roger Rabbit* starts as pure cartoon, with Roger left by the lady of the house to look after her baby. The next five minutes – featuring flame, kitchen knives, chilli sauce and rat poison – are like a compendium of every *Tom and Jerry* ever made, with added distortions and a wildly careering point of view. Then an unseen voice yells 'Cut!', the baby, revealed as a truculent brat, stalks off to his trailer, and Roger, who has failed to produce the right stars when knocked unconscious, pleads with the director for another chance, hitting himself repeatedly over the head but producing mainly birds and bells.

Action and animation cannot always fire off each other so dizzily. Filmed and animated special effects, for instance, tend to mix rather poorly, each showing up the weaknesses of the other. And there are some things that *Roger Rabbit*, for all its manic visualising energy, cannot realise. Valiant's brother, for instance, was killed by a Toon, who dropped a piano on him

– an incident which yokes human and cartoon, tragedy and comedy, too harshly, and so can only be narrated not shown.

There is something slightly ersatz about Roger Rabbit himself, a little too much like an assemblage of animated spare parts. But as an animal with human characteristics, and no obvious sexual identity, he can at least interact with humans in a number of ways – it is noticeable that at moments of high emotion he becomes unobtrusively human-sized.

His wife Jessica, on whom the private eye develops a crush, is more problematic, since she is given a purely human and voluptuous shape. The three of them constitute a triangle of taboos that make the Kong–Fay Wray romance seem smooth-running. Rabbit husband and human wife are of different species, but filmed man and drawn woman are of different media. These are formidable bars to happiness.

In practice Jessica Rabbit represents sexuality less successfully than coy little Betty Boop, who makes an envious guest appearance. The film's oddest junction of the knowing and the innocent, its most ragged piece of tailoring, comes when the private eye takes pictures of Jessica misbehaving. She turns out only to be playing pat-a-cake with another man – but Roger reacts as if pat-a-cake was the last word in carnality.

Jessica may refer to Roger's prowess as a lover, but her final promise of a carrot cake is more maternal than amorous. Her very curves seem projected rather droolingly from outside, for all the ostentation of their gravity (as she puts it, 'I'm not bad, I'm just drawn that way'). Since the human characters are allowed their worldliness (Valiant's girlfriend even asks, 'Is there a carrot in your pocket, or are pleased to see me?'), it becomes clear that the audience's innocence is being protected only selectively. There are certain kinds of knowledge that must be kept from cartoons, for their peace of mind or our own.

The film's cleverest idea – and the most economical – is the bucket of solvent (a cocktail of turpentine and acetone that eats paint) into which the villain Judge Doom drops Toons, thereby killing them. The scene where Doom casually dips an innocent Acme Squeaking Shoe cartoon, no more than a scrap of animation with trusting eyes, achieves the impossible of bringing a cartoon across the barrier into mortality. Something that was never alive has just died before our eyes. Its residual pigments swirl hauntingly on the surface of the dip bucket.

This is a hard breakthrough to follow up. *Roger Rabbit* goes on to complicate things by giving some of the cartoon characters souls, internal likenesses carrying harps that flutter out of their bodies. But cartoon characters are more convincingly amortal (if there is such a word) than immortal, just as they are amoral rather than moral or immoral. The plot's revelation of the evil that can lurk in the heart of cartoons seems hollow compared to the moment when Tweety Bird unmaliciously prises Valiant's fingers one by one from the flagpole from which he is hanging – innocence revealed not as purity but as indifference to consequences.

Who Framed Roger Rabbit is exhilarating in its excesses and fascinating in its limitations. It is poignant, for instance, that the climactic scenes should depend so heavily for their excitement on heavy machinery in motion, on a steamroller and a lumbering solvent-cannon, the momentum of solid bodies being the quality farthest removed from the unbounded levity of the cartoon.

Toy Story did more than anything to consecrate the status of the cross-generational cartoon, though the name of Tom Hanks didn't feature on the poster the way it would now.

Toy Story (1996)

Toy Story rolled off Disney's production line of wonder with two major advantages: it has a remarkably high quotient of jokes, both visual and verbal, and at 81 minutes it's one of the shortest films of the season. Brevity is the soul of animation. *Toy Story* is as much of a landmark in cartoon as *Who Framed Roger Rabbit*, without being quite so hectic with novelty. It's fast, but not loud or confusing.

In the years since *Roger Rabbit*, there have been many technical breakthroughs in representing the solidity and texture of the non-existent – the ghosts in last year's relatively workaday *Casper* had a more palpable aura than anything Bob Hoskins encountered in Zemeckis's movie. *Toy Story* makes life difficult for itself, though, by choosing to show us two worlds – the human world and the world of toys – through the same medium.

Flesh is still beyond the animators. Scud the dog has dead eyes. The kids in the film have toy hair, as if it was made of individual rooted strands of plastic fibre. If you shook their hands, it looks as if you would leave squish-marks and pressure dimples. The mother in the film is a trim statuette of walking dough – her gait shows none of the visual polyrhythms of human progress.

Better, perhaps, to have taken the *Tom and Jerry* route and shown only fleeting details of the people; though the story, given to director John Lasseter by the writers – enough writers for a law firm, Whedon Stanton Cohen & Sokolow – demands a final confrontation of the toys with Sid the bad kid. This scene, with deformed toys taking revenge on their torturer, suggests that at least one member of the firm is an admirer of Tod Browning's *Freaks*.

When it stays within the world of the toys, *Toy Story* is utterly assured in its flicking back and forth between the modes of adult and childish pleasure. When Mr Potato Head expresses his contempt for the Slinky Dog subservient by pulling his lips off and applying them derisively to his own undivided potato buttock, adults will smother their giggles in the presence of children, while children will feel free to laugh hysterically, knowing they can't be criticised for being amused by naughtiness not expressed in language. Anyone who shushes them has to explain the joke.

The adult references in the film are delicately managed, and don't exclude children. Woody the Cowboy (splendidly voiced by Tom Hanks) finds himself at one point in an arcade game inhabited by squashy three-eyed aliens, who have built a religion round the Claw that comes down now and then to pick one up. The chosen one makes speeches of devout hope as it is winched away from its fellows. When Woody is chosen, and resists, he shouts to the aliens who drag him back to the Claw, 'Let go, you zealots!' - a single sophisticated word giving an extra comic spin to the situation.

There are human verities that animation can't easily inhabit, and for which it struggles to find equivalence: sex and death. In *Toy Story*, Woody has a synthetic crush on Bo Peep, but that isn't it. Sex (at least in its aspect of longing for fulfilment in union) and death are both defined by the film in relation to the toys' owner, Andy. To be Andy's chosen toy is to experience fulfilment in union, to be superseded in his favour is toy death. Woody has Andy's name written on the sole of one boot, and his place looks assured, until Buzz Lightyear arrives one birthday.

Over the course of the story, Woody sins against toy solidarity by trying to eliminate the competition, and is redeemed by a deeper understanding of it. Along the way, though, Tom Hanks gets to express vocally what must be to him, the big screen's Mr Nice Guy, a gratifying quantity of pettiness and rancour. Meanwhile, Buzz must accept his own limitations. He isn't really an astronaut. He can't really fly, though plausible wings flick out of his shoulders at the touch of a button. Buzz discovers these things when he happens to see an advertisement for himself on television. Now he knows why, when Woody pummels his head, it lets out that tell-tale squeak of inauthenticity.

This is a nice cod-existential moment, not overplayed. Buzz briefly despairs, and when he is adopted by a little girl and recruited into her genteel tea party games, he accepts his new identity as Mrs Nesbitt. Only gradually does his self-esteem return, and the knowledge that toys, too, have a purpose.

Oddly, the film's score, by Randy Newman, is intermittently as mushy as the one he provided for *Awakenings*. For someone who writes rather dry songs, and delivers them in a cracked drawl, Newman's writing for orchestra is weirdly hushed. *Toy Story* includes some of his singing, to bizarre effect – nothing could seem more incongruous than the apparition, in this techno-shiny world, of the roughest vocal cords in the business.

In the eternal triangle of boy and toys, only the apex is exempt from the imperative of personal growth. Andy has nothing to learn. This should be a cause for celebration, in the overwhelming didactic world of children's cinema, but the inertness of Andy in his family situation is a troubling flaw of the film. Can *Toy Story* be a great kids' movie without including anything of children's experience?

The film starts with a birthday in one house and ends with Christmas in another, but we never learn the reason for the move or its meaning in social terms – is it a move up? Down? Inwards to the city? Outwards to the far suburbs? Above all, one word is never mentioned by Andy or his mum, even at those family festivals. The word is Dad.

Is Dad dead, divorced, away on business? Or were Andy and his drooling little sister raised from pods? Did Mom buy genius sperm on the Internet? It's impossible to tell, since Andy's family life has no feeling-tone. It's completely neutral, and this may be the strangest innovation of all in *Toy Story*. There was a time when Disney films showed us families that had no characteristics, apart from being luminously normal. Now Disney shows us a family that has no characteristics apart from the fact that it's not.

I may not have been the first to notice the absence of Andy's Dad from the film, but I'll take all the credit I can get. That absence holds good for the two sequels, and there are plenty of theories about why this should be.

The dramatising of family values in the *Toy Story* films is firmly a matter for the toys rather than the human beings. The development of themes in *Toy Story 2* even came in handy when I undertook to write for the *New Statesman* about gay men's changing attitude to family in 2000. Civil partnerships were still some years off, and Clause 28 prohibiting the presentation in schools of gay relationships as equal in status to straight ones was still in force, but I thought I detected a shift. Now that shift has gained enormously in momentum – it can only be a matter of time before gay men who don't want children will be asked why they're fighting their nature.

I outlined the situation in the film, with the toy cowboy Woody being the decision-maker in the group of Andy's toys. Then he's stolen by an unscrupulous collector,

> and comes face to face with a group that has a differ-
> ent claim on him. There's Jessie the cowgirl, Stinky Pete

the prospector and Bullseye the horse. Now that Al McWhiggin the collector has a complete set, he can sell it to a Japanese museum. But if Woody makes his escape, as he wants to do, the others will go back into storage. So what will he do?

It's a conflict between family as a chosen peer group and family as a fact of nature. Complementarity – we're a team – against completeness – we're a set. Set family can be brought over into team family, but there's no traffic possible in the other direction.

Team family in the film is linked with maturity and acceptance of loss (since sooner or later Andy will outgrow toys altogether), set family with the denial of change – that museum in Japan.

I suggested that for instance a father whose marriage breaks up will have to renegotiate his status as a team player, to earn his place in the family rather than taking it for granted.

Parenthood is now a matter not of entitlement but of performance . . . his playing of the role may become more scrupulous – the workaholic who would not have dreamed of taking a day off for his child's birthday now scheduling it months in advance. Family is as family does.

In other respects the piece seems hilariously dated, as when I refer to a decline in the appeal of identity politics, saying that 'defining ourselves by our differences may not be the most interesting way to live. I feel uncomfortable re-reading my reference to the original *Toy Story* as having 'enough writers for a law firm, Whedon Stanton Cohen & Sokolow', since this is an early shared credit for Joss Whedon. By the time of *Toy Story* Whedon, the son and grandson of successful television writers, had already served an apprenticeship on *Roseanne* and written the script for the film version of *Buffy the Vampire Slayer* (with Donald Sutherland as Buffy's watcher) but hadn't yet found his distinctive style. Early episodes of *Buffy* the television series observed the convention that being turned into a vampire simply eradicates any previous personality, creating an undifferentiated being, no more than a soldier in the undead army . . . and a dead end in terms of character drawing. Somehow Whedon was able to reshape the formula, and the liveliness and daring of the show became extraordinary. The key to its balance seemed to lie in what might be called Buffy's Law of the Separation of Realms, summed up in the formula I imagine written in huge letters on the wall of the writers' bunker: TAKE EVERY SITUATION SERIOUSLY, TREAT ALL DIALOGUE AS COMIC. The balance has become a sort of industry standard, but *Buffy the Vampire Slayer* set that standard.

The special effects on *Buffy* were well managed, but it's a rare thing these days for special effects to let a television programme, let alone a feature film, down. (It used to happen all the time.) Is there a 1950s film whose special effects pass muster, apart from *Fantastic Planet*? The broadcast climax of the first *Quatermass* serial wasn't recorded, but it's unlikely that the 'wiggly gloves' worn and wiggled by the show's writer, Nigel Kneale, over a model of Westminster Abbey would still have the power to terrify the nation. I have a soft spot for that sort of bodging – like the giant scarab beetles calmly chewed by a character in one episode of *Buffy*, which were hand-carved out of Tootsie Rolls. Who wouldn't rather be sculpting confectionery than Cutting and Pasting one more horde of orcs?

Perhaps there was a certain amount of boffin improvisation even in the preparation of the effects for *2001*, though the production gave every sign of meticulous planning. It wasn't just Kubrick's perfectionist temperament that called for such intense concentration. The effects on *2001* were qualitatively different. They would be looked at with full attention, and for more than seconds at a time. There were no competing elements to distract an audience: no dynamic plot, no character identification, little dialogue. In *2001* the special effects were what there was to see, and the slightest skimping would be fatal.

Tracing the genealogy of cinematic special effects in any detail would be to enter the territory of the fantastically complex and entertaining Rock Family Trees that Pete Frame used to draw, originally for *Zigzag* magazine. Shifts of context would be even more startling – Brian Johnson's trajectory isn't atypical, from working on *Thunderbirds* (filmed for television in 'Supermarionation'), then as part of the team for Kubrick on *2001* before ricocheting back to television for *Space 1999*. He signed up for the second series, which meant he had to turn down George Lucas's invitation to work on the first *Star Wars*. After that Johnson supervised the special effects on *Alien*, until Nick Allder took over.

Animal bones. Plasticine in vast quantities. A fork-lift truck covered in black velvet. 'Nottingham lace' – caul fat, with its delicate tracery of fat above the membrane. KY jelly, in vast quantities. A fork-lift truck covered in black velvet – I'm sorry, I just wanted to type that sentence again, mentally caressing what must be the supreme Surrealist object (making Meret Oppenheim's famous fur-covered cup and saucer seem rather mimsily transgressive, provocation at teatime). An eight-inch piece of wood, carved to resemble a body in a shroud. A bait-feeder or fisherman's catapult, used to propel the carved figure through a slot in a model. Fresh oysters and kidneys. The director's hands in washing-up gloves waggling in jelly behind a thin sheet of fibreglass to suggest ominous movement. This is a partial list of what went into the effects for *Alien* (1979), according to a documentary available online. 'Practical' effects – it doesn't get much more practical than Ridley Scott waggling his hands in rubber gloves to simulate alien activity inside an egg-pod. The criterion of tangibility is certainly met when the internal tissue of an alien's facehugger stage is represented by a display of items from Shepperton's butcher and fishmonger.

We're back to a bodging, everything-but-the-kitchen-sink approach, little changed from the days of *Quatermass*, even if the final impact is so much more intense. The carved piece of wood, for instance, stood in for the body of the unfortunate Kane (John Hurt) being consigned to space. It was only by running the footage at a slow speed and cutting judiciously, to hide the fact that the trajectory was wrong for an object travelling in outer space, that the scene could be made convincing to an audience already firmly held by the mood and story of the film.

Well-managed special effects in the pre-digital era involved a canny combination of models, DIY improvisation and the indispensable guy-in-a-monster-suit. In the case of *Alien*, a tall skinny guy – very tall, close to 7 foot, and thin enough not to rupture the rather fragile, low-grade latex that was available – who turned up in a Shepperton pub one night: Bolaji Badejo, a graphic designer (strong North London accent, but the alien has no lines). Give him lessons in mime and *tai chi*, bung him in the monster suit and you're laughing. The audiences who see the film, though, won't be laughing, as they might have been if the co-writers of the original story, Dan O'Bannon and Ronald Shusett, had gone with Roger Corman's production company, which at one stage seemed to be the best they could do. Corman would only have been able to fund basic effects, not much more technically demanding than the ones on O'Bannon's first film, *Dark Star*, a collaboration with John Carpenter. The alien in that film was a beach ball with clawed gloves under it, passing muster only because the film was a comedy, though there was a great moment when the alien expressed impatience by drumming its fingers (its toes, I suppose).

It's worth pointing out that the overall impact of the special effects in *Alien* has less to do with individual elements (even H. R. Giger's seductively vile designs) than with Ridley Scott's control of atmosphere and dynamics. At the moment before the alien bursts out of John Hurt's chest you can clearly see that blood – 'blood', anyway – is being thrown down onto Kane's T-shirt, not welling up from underneath. Tangible, yes, but moving in the wrong direction.

Tangibility isn't something that either Cocteau or Kubrick would have valued as a touchstone for their special effects – Cocteau because his were enchantments of the moment, Kubrick because his were conceived as existing beyond human reach. And it's in horror films that tangibility becomes crucial – the point being not that you could touch these manifestations but that they could touch you. Touch you and hurt you. Body horror films of the 1980s like *The Thing* or David Cronenberg's *The Fly* were rich in viscous glimpses. What made *The Fly* unusual was the thread of emotional continuity provided by the off-kilter pairing of Geena Davis and Jeff Goldblum. The moment in the film that made audiences gasp (as I remember from a screening in Elephant and Castle) was the one where the heroine moves towards the crumbling horror and hugs it – just as the most startling moment for audiences of *The Silence of the Lambs* was when Anthony Hopkins, under cover of passing a sheaf of documents to Jodie Foster through the bars of his cage, briefly stroked her finger. It's effective almost on the level of an electrical experiment – to build up a static charge of otherness, and a fear of touch, and then to discharge the accumulated tension.

Otherness is a huge theme in cinema, above all in science-fiction, the home genre of special effects. The Other isn't necessarily hostile or sinister in its designs on us (if any), though that's how it normally works out on the screen. Benevolent otherness, as shown in Spielberg's *Close Encounters* and Cameron's *The Abyss*, tends to be insipid because it is intangible. The blurred beings in both films, composed largely of light, have a family resemblance – I don't even remember which bunch were described at the time of release as resembling bald anorexic Barbra Streisands, though I do remember that the underwater spacecraft in *The Abyss*, which surfaces near the end of the film, looked like a coffee table the size of the Isle of Wight. Spielberg's sense of wonder isn't exactly forced, though I rarely find it contagious, but for most of Cameron's film wonder took a back seat behind thrills. There was one very exciting action sequence, with storms making a vast platform on the surface break loose, so that it plunges towards the research station far below in a sort of natural slow-motion, taking a significant amount of time to reach them.

Horror effects tend to be wet, the slow menacing drip of gore, violated entrails, mucus and KY jelly, while wonder effects tend to be dry, insubstantial, approximating, as in *Close Encounters*, to the condition of light itself. An exception is the wonderful moment in *The Abyss* when the alien beings send a probe of disembodied intelligence onto the submarine craft, a liquid optical fibre. It's a finger made of water. As it approaches the face of the heroine, played by Mary Elizabeth Mastrantonio, it swells and becomes face-like itself, reflecting her features as if to reassure her, clearly seeking to make contact. She is beguiled rather than frightened, but a paranoid and militarised member of the crew takes fright, closing the siding security doors and cutting the finger into pieces, which fall to the ground like the water they always were. This exquisite effect is tangible only in a subtle way, representing a liquid rather than anything solid, recalling the remark made to the naturalist Louis Agassiz, who had written a book on marine creatures, that the jellyfish he described seemed to be 'little more than organised water'. Cameron's finger of water is like an abstract, unmuscular version of the horror-film tentacle, classic trope of the invasive Other.

I took this theme further in a piece for *Prospect*.

'Being and Viscousness' (2017)

Science fiction is a genre doomed to profundity, unable to avoid banging its head or stubbing its toes against philosophical dilemmas as it goes about telling its stories. It doesn't seem likely that well-thumbed copies of Sartre's *Being and Nothingness* show up on the sets of many space operas, though you never know. Existentialism is always likely to put in an appearance when the theme is our aloneness in the universe or else the encounter, feared and desired, with otherness and the alien. Being alone in the universe and not being alone in the universe – two inexhaustible subjects.

A pair of mainstream American films released in the last few weeks, neither any sort of masterpiece but full of enjoyable elements, obligingly highlight these themes. In *Passengers* Jim Preston (Chris Pratt), an engineer travelling in suspended animation, one of thousands heading for a colonised planet, is woken nearly a century ahead of schedule. In the first third of the film, its most successful part, he learns that to be the only wakeful person in a world of sleepers is a living nightmare. This is solitude in its hyperparadoxical modern form, full of empty interaction. A smiling hologram was leaning over him with reassurance when he was woken, and then he received an upbeat briefing by a simulated speaker addressing a whole room full of passengers, unaware that she had an audience of one. When the audience-of-one tried to point this out, she sweetly raised a phantom finger and asked for the courtesy of questions being left until the end of the session.

In *Passengers* the void resounds to the non-existent engine noise of the *Avalon* as it heads towards the colony planet of Homestead. How quiet is deep space? 'Quiet' even seems the wrong word to denote the impossibility of sound. Stanley Kubrick's *2001* (1968) is one of the few films set outside the Earth's atmosphere to respect its silence on the soundtrack. Even *Alien*, despite the famous tagline of 'In space no one can hear you scream', made sure the throb of the *Nostromo*'s engines was audible from the first sequence. Already those sounds tell us that the reality of nothingness has been blotted out – perhaps because a deep sound gives a powerful cue to our visual imagination, making it less likely that we will see the special effects in front of us as unreal. In fact, the next film after *2001* to dispense with impossible sounds may have been *Gravity*, more than four decades on.

2001 had the vision to predict a future that was one-part cosmic awe to a thousand parts of stultified travel, but underestimated our compulsive need for distraction from our own company while we wait to arrive wherever it is that we're going. Kubrick didn't foresee the enclosure in recorded sound and image that has been part of everyday life for most people since long before 2001 (the year, not the film). The voyage of the space ship towards a rendezvous with the alien monolith beyond Jupiter in *2001* is still astonishing, but some of that astonishment is down to the iPod – not-so-alien monolith in many million pockets – not having been invented yet, in this supposed future. So far from home and not a playlist to be had! No wonder Bowman (Keir Dullea) looks so glum.

The writer and director of *Passengers* (Jon Spaihts, Morten Tyldum) understand that nowadays we don't take our solitude neat. We dilute it constantly. Jim can whip digitised spectators into frantic applause with the excellence of his basketball. He can make stunning progress in dance-offs with a programmed opponent. It's just that he is robbed of the company who would witness, and give value to, either victory or defeat. Without other people there is nothing. There isn't even loss.

When Jim comes across a working bar aboard the *Avalon*, whose android bartender is programmed with a higher level of interactivity, able to engage convincingly in hostelry-level banter and philosophising, the audience is cued to pick up an echo from a rather different Kubrick film: the sinister bartender Grady (played by Philip Stone) in *The Shining*, suavely inciting the hero to murder. The unsettling android in *Passengers* is played by Michael Sheen, a good fit for an actor who is hard to cast, with his sly sparkle and clever ferrety face.

Films about existential solitude don't need to be set in space, but the ones set on Earth tend to be moralised, addressing the consequences of selfishness rather than the brute fact of being alone in the way of, say, Duncan Jones's *Moon*, or Ridley Scott's *The Martian* – the plight of poor stranded Matt Damon making a customer in a spaceship cocktail bar, however lonely, seem pretty spoiled.

The Shining is a film about aloneness of a particular kind, aloneness within the family, with a narcissist placing more value on his imagination and the unreal than the people he shares his life with. The cinematic tour de force in this line is a film whose hero deals again and again with interactive holograms, though they have the odd extra characteristic that they possess substance and weight. His task is to accept them as they see themselves, as fully individual people. Yes, *Groundhog Day* (1993), in which Phil Connors, someone who has behaved as if he was the only real person in the world, is cosmically punished by having his delusion come true. Everyone else wakes up on February the 2nd for the first time, but he keeps going round and round, starting again from scratch, and he knows what will happen every moment of the day. The paradox is that having more information than other people hollows out your own existence. You become not more real than them but less. Knowledge in solitude is a torment compared to the bliss of ignorance held in common.

In the film Bill Murray, who has played Scrooge just the once explicitly (in *Scrooged*, 1988) but based a whole career around variations on the archetype, is redeemed – admittedly the exact mechanism is mysterious – into equality with the world only when he treats the people he has formerly despised as being worthy of empathy. It's not a case of Christmas Past, Present and Future with their associated ghosts, rather a whole logjam of tenses that he must somehow break up – the present refusing to become past and blocking him off from any possible future. Does he finally win Andie MacDowell round by murmuring Sartre's formula, 'each Other finds his being in the Other' ('chaque autrui trouve son être dans l'autre')? Sorry, no – that would stick out a bit and likely cause consternation in the multiplex, but it's definitely the gist just the same.

Meanwhile the wakeful engineer in *Passengers* gazes into the hibernation pod of attractive journalist Aurora Lane – a name that could hardly be more hopeful if it was Dawn Future. Watching her lying there in her glass casket like a fairy-tale princess, does he think, 'Sartre got it wrong – hell isn't other people, it's not having other people?' No again, but it's a fair paraphrase of his state of mind. And will he wake this Sleeping Beauty, whether with a kiss or an instruction manual and a screwdriver? Jennifer Lawrence's name and face are on the posters, which certainly shortens the odds of an awakening.

As for films in which our species comes across other intelligences, some of them – *Independence Day* an obvious example – have no interest in the Other, treating extra-terrestrials merely as enemies to be obliterated without any thought for their thoughts, the Geneva Convention not applying to folks from off-world. There's no imagination of what the cosmos might look like through their eyes. If they even have eyes. Equally flat are films like *Close Encounters* or *The Abyss*, in which extra-terrestrial intelligences are benign in some undefined way. It seems a struggle for us to imagine an intermediate reason for aliens to pay a visit between exterminating us and conferring a vague blessing. Might they not have needs of their own?

More satisfying are stories with a moral dimension, involving the risk of establishing a relationship of trust with the non-human. In the recent *Arrival*, directed by Denis Villeneuve, Amy Adams plays Louise Banks, a linguist called in to analyse the language of an alien species, whose craft have appeared at twelve sites across the earth. Already this is a departure from genre norms: what is being offered by the alien visitors is language and therefore culture, culture in its defining manifestation. They may be bringing a message but in the first instance what they offer is a language, written language, ink shapes elegantly sprayed from a tentacle into a liquid medium, not permanent but hanging in suspension until replaced by the next secreted utterance.

The aliens hold audience in their craft at set times and for restricted periods. Humans ascend through a strange field of forces, a corridor of wayward gravity, to find themselves facing, behind glass, giant creatures like octopi, not fully visible, and equipped with seven tentacles rather than eight. The creatures are majestic, their floating language oddly delicate, sharing with the Chinese written character the ability to hold elements in a sort of poetic tension as well as an affinity with Japanese brush painting. Each 'word' is self-contained and circular, a sort of mandala full of fractal curlicues, generated from more than one point simultaneously, so that it's impossible to say that there is a right place to begin or finish reading it.

Arrival acknowledges the forces of unreason – the rioting civilians and paranoiac military wanting action against the invaders – but gives priority to the desire to co-operate. If there's an unsatisfying pious residue here, then what could have been done to sharpen the overall effect? Perhaps the presentation of the Heptapods is too safe – there they are, floating behind their glass, with no possibility of being touched. Ink must be the only organic secretion that doesn't immediately strike us as unclean. Our latent distaste for the soft-bodied, the molluscan, is neutralised – except at one moment when a Heptapod tentacle suddenly presses against the glass, reminding us that this hand is also a mouth and may be an eye.

The films that stay in the memory are the ones where there's an element of the repulsive to be overcome by both character and viewer – a pinch of something disgusting, like asafoetida in Indian cookery, that somehow brings the flavours alive. Empathy that encounters no obstacle can hardly count as empathy. Yet what offends us about imaginary bodies isn't really anything alien but the same things that bother us about our own bodies, softness where we idealise hardness, lack of boundary when we insist on things staying in their proper place – which, in the case of guts and secretions, is out of sight.

The defining alien element in terms of our revulsion, the reflex of disgust that needs to be faced down, is gunge. Goo. Sticky stuff. You wouldn't – for instance – anticipate that it would be worse being savaged to death by a wet set of teeth than by a dry one, but the memorable mucous dentition of the creature in *Alien* suggests otherwise, in its grip on the public imagination.

In the 1999 film *Galaxy Quest*, directed by Dean Parisot, there are brutal, extermination-minded aliens and downtrodden, rather childlike ones, their historic victims, who set the plot in motion by abducting the cast of a television space opera, mistaking the actors for the parts they play and imagining that these rugged heroes will fight as champions of the underdog, as they have so often done on screen. There's a scene in which Mathesar (Enrico Colantoni), leader of the pacifists, is tortured by the arch-sadist Sarris (Robin Sachs) so as to extract information from the commander of the *Galaxy Quest* (Tim Allen) that he doesn't have in the first place. Mathesar has adopted a human guise as a matter of politeness when dealing with the brave humans he admires so much, but the pain makes him revert to his normal form, which resembles a pile of viscera. It's a brilliantly managed effect, with the repellent image and the jolt of sympathy combined in a single moment of complex emotion. There's sophistication, too, in David Howard's screenplay with the trusting agony of the creature under torture, so serenely confident in the power of his chosen allies, twisting the knife in the soul of the commander who is no commander.

By the logic of the plot the impostors must start playing in reality the heroic roles they took on in a cheesy but inexplicably popular television series. By a deeper, stranger logic, the film goes through its own transformation, so that what started out as a spoof (bad-faith genre par excellence, having its cake and spitting on it) first turns into a *hommage* and then escalates into a non-parasitic excellence, trouncing anything in the *Star Trek* archive, obviously the original satirical target, in entertainment value and poignancy. Existentialism again, in the form of 'good faith' – the decision to behave, in a meaningless cosmos, as if your choices actually mattered.

Computer-generated imagery has something stubbornly untactile and dry about it – pre-digital effects, making resourceful use of hydraulic bladders and other before-the-camera devices, were on better terms with the viscosity that does so much to boost the yuck factor, the lubricious slurp and squelch of alien tissue. The Pandorans in James Cameron's 2009 *Avatar*, for instance, with their big eyes and athletic physiques, mobile ears and expressive tails, seem utterly synthetic. Their lithe blue flesh looks as if it was grown in a tank of pixels. The film's hero Jake Sully (Sam Worthington) is a paraplegic who discovers a new life when technology miraculously implants him in a fully functioning alien body. It just feels too easy – the film functions more like a video game in a New Age-y pastoral setting than a humanly (or alienly) engaging drama. Why not at least give the situation a bit of texture, by putting Jake inside a creature less immediately appealing than a bounding steroidal Smurf? A millipede, for instance. The love scenes would certainly be less insipid, even if you kept the scenic flourishes of luminous thistledown and magic carpets of moss.

Human gender arrangements and roles are normally taken for granted in science fiction films – Pandoran foreplay, for instance, starts with a non-intrusive kiss before escalating, as if there was an intergalactic rulebook. True, there's a fairly startling plot development in *Enemy Mine*, released in 1985, when the scaly alien played by Louis Gossett Jr (best known for his role as the tough gunnery sergeant in *An Officer and a Gentleman*) dies in childbirth. His species reproduces asexually. *Enemy Mine* is a sort of partial remake of *Hell in the Pacific* in deep space, sharing its theme of two survivors from opposing armies brokering some sort of truce so as to endure a hostile environment. Clearly, given the realistic genre and setting of the original film, it would be more shocking if either of its stars, Lee Marvin or Toshiro Mifune, were to go into labour, with or without complications. But actually the disruption of gender stereotypes in *Enemy Mine* is minimal, with Dennis Quaid's human character Davidge nobly bringing up and protecting the orphaned Zammis – sample dialogue 'Uncle, what did my parent look like?'/ 'Your parent looked like . . . my friend'.

The film ends with Davidge keeping a promise to his dead frenemy (admittedly a word not in existence in 1985) by reciting Zammis's lineage to the Holy Council on the home planet – though why a species that reproduces asexually would be fussed about family trees is anybody's guess.

Neill Blomkamp's *District 9*, released the same year as *Avatar* and also successful at the box office, though at a humbler level, addresses issues of alienness in a much more impressive way. The alien 'prawns' in the film are refugees rehoused after their damaged spaceship arrived on Earth, or actually above it, suspended above Johannesburg. The 'prawns' are physically disgusting, though resembling insects as well as shellfish – both sets of creatures being arthropods – and most of them are low-functioning, tinned cat food being their idea of fine dining. Their arrangements for incubating their young are particularly unsightly, involving the suspended carcasses of slaughtered cattle. In the course of the film its hero Wikus (Sharlto Copley) metamorphoses into a prawn after exposure to an alien chemical, and comes to understand their reality by the involuntary empathy of inhabiting a body like theirs. In a South African film racial allegory is bound to be part of a mix, though *District 9*'s portrayal of Nigerians as gangsters got the film banned in that country. Wikus must come to terms with . . . slime. And there it is, the word I've been tiptoeing around, subject of some famous passages towards the end of *Being and Nothingness* (Sartre's original term being *le visqueux*): 'To touch the slimy is to risk being dissolved in sliminess . . . A consciousness that became slimy would be transformed by the thick stickiness of its ideas.'

In the original 1984 *Ghostbusters*, 'slime' became a verb ('he got slimed'). Being spattered with non-human juices was a sort of rite of passage ('I feel so *funky*'), an ectoplasmic blooding that gives access to what Sartre calls 'the great ontological region of sliminess'. When *Ghostbusters* concurs with *Being and Nothingness*, who among us dare dissent? The confrontation with slime in *District 9* is powerfully managed – and yet there's a limit fixed to the evolution of its hero. Wikus doesn't start to find other prawns arousing but remains devoted to his wife, humbly leaving tokens of love outside the house he once shared with her. Blomkamp's follow-up to *District 9* (though there will eventually be a sequel), the dystopian fantasy *Elysium*, seemed anaemic by comparison, its categories of narcissistic rich and squalid poor not grounded in a bodily dialectic of revulsion and acceptance.

What must be the supreme moment of openness to slime in the movies comes in Nic Roeg's *The Man Who Fell To Earth*, released in 1976. Mary-Lou (Candy Clark, in a great performance) has been living for years with the alien Thomas Jerome Newton (David Bowie), who has adopted human form. They seem to have been lovers in some satisfactory way without him expressing himself in the way that comes naturally to his species. At various points in the film we have seen visions of alien bodies spinning gracefully in space and shedding a pearly liquid, presumably a product of arousal.

Now, after a quarrel, Newton decides to show himself in his true form. In the bathroom he reaches down to his genitals (just off-screen), as if minded to unplug them, and pinches the nipples that are likewise prosthetic. He removes his humanoid contact lenses to reveal the eyes beneath, yellow with a vertical slit. When Mary-Lou knocks on the door he reaches for the lock with a hand that lacks fingernails. In his true form he's also bald. He emerges from the bathroom and walks past Mary-Lou to lie down on the bed. She's terrified – she wets herself. And then with astounding courage she enters the bedroom, undresses and lies down beside him. His hand on her body leaves a snail trail. It's too much for her, and she runs away with a scream.

In the moment before her nerve fails does she say to herself, in tones of wonder, 'It is a soft, yielding action, a moist and feminine sucking, it lives obscurely under my fingers, and I sense it like a dizziness; it draws me to it as the bottom of a precipice might draw me to it'? No she does not. As I say, it doesn't seem likely that well-thumbed copies of Sartre's *Being and Nothingness* show up on the sets of many space operas. But you never know.

There's no sign yet of a slowing down in the cultural change identified in that piece for *Prospect* – in fact there are ominous indications of declining empathy levels in a director who once seemed to have a pleasingly skewed sense of the beauty in ugliness, Guillermo del Toro, one of the two major directors working today who started off making special effects (the other being Peter Jackson). Del Toro has tried to alternate personal and blockbuster projects, though his tenderness towards the character and world of Hellboy makes the two films he made starring Ron Perlman in the role fall somewhere in the middle. By his standards – or what used to be his standards – *Mimic*, starring Mira Sorvino and Jeremy Northam, was a commercial compromise, but the giant mutant insects in the film still produced a shiver of awe rather than simple disgust. (They have developed camouflaged markings so that from a distance in dim light they look vaguely, though not reassuringly, human, right up to the moment they open their wing-cases.) Presumably *Crimson Peak* (2015) was closer to being a personal project than *Pacific Rim* (2013), despite being set in a very under-imagined England, but it was hard to tell, and hard to care, since they were both such frustrating misfires, neither poetic nor mechanically sound.

Del Toro's near-masterpiece *Pan's Labyrinth* (2006) was both. It borrows from Terry Gilliam's *Brazil* the structural idea of two oppressive realities intersected by the central character, each unbearable in itself but providing visual and textural relief from the other. (Had anyone thought of this device before Terry Gilliam?) In *Brazil* they're both fantasies, a parallel present where all the technology is retro and a dream world of angels and giant samurai warriors – except that in both of them actions have consequences that can't be dodged (generally fantasy worlds have a looser, reversible logic, but here they are both parts of the same infernal machine). The same is true of *Pan's Labyrinth*, with the young heroine Ofelia moving back and forth between the world she shares with others, a world of tension and violence (cruel stepfather, Spanish Civil War in its late stages) and a private domain of supernatural beings and imposed magical tasks.

In the first real-world scene of the film, Ofelia is travelling with her pregnant mother to live with the man she is supposed to call Father (she never will). When the chauffeur-driven car stops because her mother has morning sickness, Ofelia idly picks up a fragment of stone lying on the ground near an ancient column. Then she sees that it corresponds to a missing part of something resembling a face on the column, where an eye should be, and fits it in place. There's an exhaling sound from the mouth of the face, and a sort of metallic stick insect or praying mantis emerges, making a noise like a woodpecker or cicada. She tells her mother she has seen a fairy. Her mother dismisses the idea, as she dismisses virtually everything Ofelia says or does in the course of the film. We see that the 'fairy' follows the car, and installs itself in the farmhouse where Ofelia's stepfather, the Captain, is stationed, his job being to carry out mopping-up operations against the rebels, with no upper limit of brutality.

That night the insect approaches Ofelia. It's sinister, scrabbling and scuttling across the floor, and she doesn't seem anything like as frightened of it as she should. She asks it if it is in fact a fairy, and shows it a picture in one of her fairy-tale books to show what she means. Taking the picture as a template, the creature metamorphoses into something less insectiform, an interpretation of fairy shape that retains something hard and potentially cruel. There's an underlying sinister quality to its obligingness – the transformation is like the eerie moment in the first *Gremlins* when the benign Gizmo corrects the hero's playing on his keyboard, reaching over to press the desired note. In *Pan's Labyrinth* the 'fairy' continues to communicate with a metallic chirruping. It never becomes unthreatening as nineteenth-century fairies became (Shakespeare's fairies precede this neutralising process). It isn't clear whether the underworld creatures who set tasks for Ofelia really recognise her as their princess, as they claim, or are manipulating her for their own ends, and the ambiguity of the insect-fairy's transformation underpins the whole film.

The fairies (there are others, camouflaged in the same way to meet Ofelia's expectations) are under the authority of the Faun, played by Doug Jones, though he seems less like an actor playing a part than a human armature around which a characterisation is built. The seductive Spanish vocal intonations, with their under-current of coercive pressure, are certainly not Jones's, though perhaps he is responsible for the vividly Hispanic gestures of the creature's impossibly extended hands. The whole creation is balanced between the fearful and the enchanting – the Faun's ears beneath his horns cock expressively downwards as he talks.

Ofelia's first task is to find a giant toad that is squatting under a tree, draining its vitality, and to feed it three magic stones, which will kill it. Then she must retrieve a golden key from inside the monster. A special-effects expert like del Toro must have had reasons for the dismayingly crude style in which the toad under the tree is rendered. The whole scene is executed without flair. The toad is a retro gross-out creature, wet and slimy to a cartoonish degree, vomiting up a tongue bigger than its body as it dies. It's disgusting without being at all scary, and lacks the homeopathic dose of beauty needed to make screen monsters memorable. It has no suggestion of the practical effect, no aura of presence, and no tangibility even when the creature's tongue slaps stickily against Ofelia's face from many yards away.

Not a complaint that could be made against the 'Pale Man', another guy-in-a-monster-suit built on Doug Jones's armature, an eyeless, emaciated and bleached figure with sagging pleats of skin, first seen in a state of suspended animation sitting at a table laden with food. The predominant colour of the foods on display is dark red. A fire crackles behind him. He lacks a nose, unless two flat holes in his face count. In front of him, stretched out, are his hands, fingers tapering to dark points. Between them, on a plate, are his eyes. Somebody's eyes, anyway. It's like a literal staging of a common excuse for drowsiness – I wasn't asleep; I was just resting my eyes. Ofelia enters the chamber by way of a portal she has made herself, drawing it with a piece of enchanted chalk given her by the Faun. She must take the key from the toad's body with her, and use it to conquer the next stage of this infernal treasure hunt. There's only one rule – don't eat or drink anything in the chamber.

Of course she breaks it. It wouldn't be a folktale if she obeyed the rules. It's in this sequence that the oral culture of traditional storytelling marries most richly with the high technology of the twenty-first century special effect. Ofelia uses the golden key to open a little locked cabinet on a wall. There are three cabinets, and the 'fairies' direct her to the middle one, but she ignores them and chooses the one on the left – so she's more than a runner of errands. She intervenes actively in the quest and uses her own initiative. She reaches in and with some difficulty extracts what turns out to be a ceremonial knife.

On the way out, though, she picks two ripe grapes from a bunch and eats them. The fairies try to stop her, but she flaps her hand to drive them away. We see the Pale Man in the back of the shot come to life as she bites into the fruit. He reaches down to pick up his eyes from the table top, first one and then the other, but instead of installing them directly on his face he fits them into the palms of his hands. Each one slips into some sort of socket, and a lid that can open and close. Then when he raises those hands to his face, the backs of them against his cheeks – an image of appalling beauty – somehow the eyes can see. They swivel right and left in unison, though set apart slightly wider than the monster's head. He moves towards Ofelia, who is too preoccupied with her stolen snack to understand that she is in danger. Two fairies sacrifice themselves to buy her time, flying at the Pale Man's face to distract him. He grasps them (necessarily losing his sight as he does so) and bites their heads off, in an image that echoes Goya's painting of *Saturn Devouring His Son*, much as the chest-burster sequence in *Alien* echoed the distorted excrescent head in Bacon's studies for figures attending a crucifixion.

It's an effective sequence of suspense, with the Pale Man bearing down on Ofelia as she struggles to reach an escape hatch that will disappear when the last of the sand runs through the hourglass she has been given, but it's the patterning of the folktale elements that gives the scene its haunting poetry. Three pairs of objects similar in size, with horrible overlaps and contrasts in texture. Eyes, grapes, fairies' heads. Perhaps a moral equation is involved – Ofelia punished for eating the grapes by her protectors' heads being eaten in their turn. Except that she doesn't seem sentimental about them, and their service to her was likewise unsentimental. They seem to have a kinship with the fairies in Sylvia Townsend Warner's late story collection, *Kingdoms of Elfin*, long-lived but not immortal and not possessing souls, living by an etiquette rather than a morality. Or perhaps it's a more brutally simple equilibrium being maintained in the Pale Man's chamber. Two grapes leave in Ofelia's stomach, and two fairies' heads must stay behind in his.

The weakness of *Pan's Labyrinth* lay in the characterisation of the stepfather, so much a fascist-by-numbers that he might have been basing his behaviour on an actual instruction book. Polish own jackboots fetishistically despite having plenty of underlings, check. Wear tight leather gloves even when tinkering with watch inherited from father, check. Shave with cut-throat razor, check. Indicate self-loathing by pausing to draw blade across image of own throat in mirror, check. Sew own mouth back together after being slashed with a knife, check. The world he inhabited was also corrupt, if less resolutely vile. Fascist sympathisers stuffed their faces while saying that the poor could manage on the rations available if they only exercised some self-control, and the priest pointed out that God cared for the souls of the poor, not their bodies. That was where there was room for improvement, in the understanding that evil too has an interior. People live with themselves somehow, not usually by turning into cartoon monsters. If he could manage that, there seemed no reason why Guillermo del Toro shouldn't make a classic of fantasy with the realistic underpinning that makes such things last.

Instead we have *The Shape of Water*. Otherness in the film could hardly be more timid than an aquatic biped mod-elled on *The Creature from the Black Lagoon* from the 1950s, which wasn't scary in the first place, here reconfigured as the answer to a maiden's prayer. Why would an aquatic creature have legs? Because Doug Jones is going to be the guy-in-a-monster-suit one more time. The creature has been snatched away from its environment and from others of its kind, then tortured over a long period. Luckily, though, its bits are com-patible with a human female, so it can get its end away and Elisa

(Sally Hawkins) can be given the fulfilment a heartless world has denied her.

The battle lines drawn up in the film between the oppressed (women, gay men, those with disabilities, racial minorities) and those who oppress them, namely studiously nasty car-obsessed militarised businessmen who are bad in bed – they're insultingly shallow and anachronistic. An alliance that would have been avant-garde and even inflammatory in a film of the 1950s, when the story is set, is limp as a microwaved lettuce leaf in 2018. Del Toro has lost any sense of the otherness of the past, the aware-ness that emotional landscapes change over time. It's a rare film that captures that, though Todd Haynes's *Far from Heaven* showed it could be done, particularly in the scene where the Dennis Quaid character, a man realising his homosexuality, cries in front of his children. In the twenty-first century this would be a certificate of sincerity, proof that his pain matches theirs. Instead his children recoil in horror and disgust, his tears showing that he's not a man, or certainly not a father.

The baddy in the film is the Captain from *Pan's Labyrinth* all over again, but in a business suit. Same nihilistic narcissism, same faith in cruelty, same refusal to feel anything, least of all pain. He goes around for most of the film developing gangrene, but you know what? It makes no difference. A society like the supposed 1950s America in *The Shape of Water*, whose cardinal points were violence, harsh perfunctory sex and the love of a new Cadillac with teal paintwork, couldn't have sustained itself for ten minutes, let alone a substantial chunk of the twentieth century. It takes a lot to make me feel compassion for the mis-representation and unacknowledged suffering of straight white men, but *The Shape of Water* might tip the balance. For heaven's sake! If del Toro's father was like that, he should make a properly personal film, get it out of his system and start engaging with the world on a less blinkered basis.

Any director who wanted to film special effects without the use of computers these days would have to be pretty wilful, since special effects are so strongly nourished by technological developments, and there are certainly directors, Tim Burton for example, whose digital effects are usually characterful and even idiosyncratic. To embrace an agenda that resisted being led by technology – as the Dogme 95 'movement' did, doing without camera movement and editing within scenes, added lighting or post-production sound – would make special effects unachievable. Just the same, the last time I was actually excited by screen special effects was when a very wayward film-maker, Francis Ford Coppola, decided to film *Dracula* using 'optical' effects, based on techniques used in the nineteenth-century theatre. Yes, period special effects – like a performance of Brahms or Debussy on period instruments. It's just a shame that the other elements of the film were so out of balance.

Bram Stoker's Dracula (1992)

Success in the genre of the Gothic depends on a partial transformation of terror into beauty, and by that standard Francis Ford Coppola's *Bram Stoker's Dracula* is a failure, but for an unusual reason: the transformation of terror into beauty is absolute, leaving no ghost of a shudder behind. Why should we pretend to be frightened, when in fact we are looking forward to the next astonishing manifestation of what is only notionally evil? How can we be in suspense when we know that our appetite for lurid visual truffles will be fed without a moment's stinting? Even at the film's few sanguinary moments, there is no temptation to look away, since violence too is swallowed up – along with the plot – by the ravishments of design.

Coppola has often seemed both too large and too small for any genre he chose to work in. The triumph of the first two *Godfather*s lay mainly in the resonant inappropriateness of an operatic tone and a squalid story, while the weakness of *Apocalypse Now* was that the director's addiction to spectacle, to making a statement at all costs, made it absurd that he imagined he was diagnosing the same ailment in his country's foreign policy.

At one point in his career Coppola filmed two very similar novels for teenagers by the same author, S. E. Hinton, at the same time and with an overlapping cast, but going with the grain of the genre on one, *The Outsiders* (naturalism, colour, Stevie Wonder title song), and against the grain on the other, *Rumble Fish* (expressionism, black-and-white, jazzy soundtrack). Of that pairing, it was the 'sincere' film that felt hollow, while the one where Coppola seemed to have no confidence in the material, and compensated by embroidering it almost continuously with experiments and aesthetic wonders, was the one that was perversely unforgettable.

The new *Dracula*, for at least its first ninety minutes, surpasses the seductive extravagance of *Rumble Fish*. With his last film, *The Godfather III*, Coppola looked like an artist in decline. With *Dracula*, he is rejuvenated. It may only be a transfusion of fake blood, but it has perked him up no end.

James Hart's screenplay may put Bram Stoker's name up there in the title, but there's no certainty that the author would recognise the result. (As his strikingly inept screenplay for the Peter Pan sequel *Hook* demonstrated, Hart wouldn't recognise an author's intention if it flew up and bit him in the neck.) Hart's strongest idea is that Dracula is not a pagan but an apostate, a Christian warlord (the historical Vlad the Impaler) who fights the Muslim Turks, but curses the God he has served when he is told that his wife, a suicide, has thereby damned her soul to hell. This is a provocative twist on the formula, but gets lost in the confusions of the story.

The Cross – or indeed, a sacramental wafer applied to the forehead as a metaphysical poultice – sometimes seems effective against evil, sometimes not. Silver bullets are never mentioned, but garlic puts in an occasional appearance. Dracula seems at one point, when luring Jonathan Harker (Keanu Reeves) to his castle, to need to have hospitality freely accepted before he can gain spiritual ascendancy, but at other times there are no such limitations on his power. He appears as a werewolf as well as a bat, though a werewolf with an attractively bat-influenced nose. These details don't necessarily matter, but no one watching the film would have any idea why Dracula chooses to relocate to London in the first place, buying ten carefully chosen properties for his purpose, whatever it is, and bringing along many crates of the ancestral earth that he needs to sleep in.

Coppola revisits the late nineteenth century as a period of technological turmoil, which makes a change from the costume-drama pieties, though it may reflect primarily the interests of the director. The camera dwells lovingly on type-writers and phonographs. London seems to have thriving porn cinemas in 1897, which is a bit sudden, bearing in mind that the cinematograph made its debut in Paris in December 1895. Van Helsing (Anthony Hopkins) attempts a blood transfusion, which seems anachronistic but isn't – transfusion needed the discovery of blood groups to be reliable, but it could be done.

Although the press kit includes a bibliography for 'Further Reading', what the film shows us is unmistakably the nine-teenth century of a parallel universe. Eiko Ishioka, originally a graphic designer but responsible for the astonishing look of Paul Schrader's *Mishima*, plays almost as important a part here, though her credit is restricted to costume design, and the pro-duction designer (Thomas Sanders) and director of photography

(Michael Ballhaus) must share in the honours. Vampire movies traditionally go a bundle on reds, and Dracula certainly doesn't skimp in that department: the count has a scarlet train about a mile long, which looks particularly good when he is on all fours, and the screen is sometimes flooded with swirling platelets. But Ishioka hasn't neglected green – bottle green, even bluebottle green, for the count's gloves at one point.

Every stock element of the story has been re-thought or re-seen. This Dracula has no patent leather hair and widow's peak, but a towering grey wig reminiscent of Lewis Carroll's Queen of Hearts, in which, if you look at the back of the neck, his flesh is somehow implicated. Lightning leaves a stylised after-image, long enough for us to see that it is made up of curves – art nouveau lightning in neon blue. Coppola has made the unfashionable choice of doing most of the special effects inside or in front of the camera, rather than later on. It is appropriate that many of these techniques derive from Victorian stage magic, and they have the supreme virtue of seeming to flow, with the onward progress of a story that, actually, never materialises.

The main thing missing from this parallel-universe nineteenth century is, simply, repression. Lucy (Sadie Frost) is not merely fast but Concorde-fast, making penis jokes that her social circle seems to find only mildly daring, while even demure Mina (Winona Ryder) looks at the explicit illustrations in her *Arabian Nights* with fascination as well as disgust. There seem to be no parents, disapproving or otherwise. No one in Victorian London is much over thirty, except the count, who admittedly, at four hundred plus, somewhat raises the average.

Without repression, of course, there can be no return of the repressed, and therefore no 'Bram Stoker's Dracula' worthy of the name. Gary Oldman would probably make a good count if he didn't appear in ten or so different guises. The other actors make equally little impression in this gorgeous phantasma-goria, whether they are good (Richard E. Grant), indifferent (Winona Ryder) or plain bad (Keanu Reeves, speaking as if English vowels had been injected into his gums during a painful session at the dentist's).

The splendours and limitations of this *Dracula* can be summed up by one tableau in particular. Renfield (Tom Waits) is eating flies in an asylum, but all the audience will be thinking is, 'Where can I get a *beautiful* straitjacket like that one?' It's so subtly ribbed. A straitjacket like that would cost £2,000 on South Molton Street. But perhaps it should repel us just a bit that he's eating bugs and worms. Instead we're disappointed that Ishioka hasn't done a design job on the creepy-crawlies, which would certainly make us want to keep them as pets.

One other film, chronologically both preceding and following Coppola's *Dracula* – filmed in 1964 but only recently possible to see even in fragments – seemed to indicate an entirely new approach to cinematic special effects. This was the unfinished film *L'Enfer* (Hell), footage from which was included in the 2009 documentary *Henri-Georges Clouzot's Inferno* (directed by Serge Bromberg and Ruxandra Medrea Annonier), along with interviews with people involved in the disastrous shoot and some scenes from the script newly staged.

Henri-Georges Clouzot's Inferno (2009)

Film is an art form in which an unlimited budget can wreak more havoc than an inadequate one. The 1960s was a period, at least until *Easy Rider* rewrote the rules of the system, in which studios would offer almost unlimited resources to directors with a track record of making money. Stanley Kubrick (indulged by Warner Bros) was one beneficiary of this high-risk approach to the financing of cinema, and Clouzot, who had found large audiences internationally with *The Wages of Fear* and *Les Diaboliques*, was another, with Columbia Pictures paying the bills. Studio supervision was remarkably loose, and eccentricities (such as Kubrick's refusal to film outside the British Isles) were accommodated without much question. These were geese who had laid golden eggs. Why wouldn't they increase their yield of bullion if they were made comfortable on the nest?

Even in literature, that economical art, being emancipated from the need to be frugal can be counterproductive, as witness William Golding, struggling to create after his publishers put him on salary. Clouzot, like Kubrick, had started off with tight genre projects – his masterly and very misanthropic thriller *Le Corbeau* (The Raven), filmed under the Occupation, was unacceptable both to the regime of the time, since it portrayed a world of denunciations and secret shame, and to the reconstituted French authorities, thanks to the compromised circumstances of its making. His scenario for *L'Enfer* was potentially simple ('un tout petit film' as he says himself in an interview), certainly as compared with *The Wages of Fear*, with its exotic locations and scenes of action. A married couple – the wife more attractive and younger than the husband – runs a hotel next to a lake, a beauty spot and leisure destination. He becomes obsessed with the idea that she is being unfaithful, with women as well as men, and has some sort of psychotic breakdown. The hero is called Marcel, the wife is Odette, names chosen to make the connection with Proust almost embarrassingly clear (even if it is Swann who is tormented by Odette's possible infidelity, and Marcel's obsessive jealousy focuses on Albertine later in the book).

As the project developed, this slender drama became the framework for an expressionistic exploration of the hero's psyche, using experimental techniques both in terms of image and soundtrack. The attention given to audio is something that might have sounded alarm bells at the American studio backing the film, since subtitles would struggle to capture nuances of French, and it seems likely that speech-fragments bordering on unintelligibility would have frustrated domestic audiences, too. Clouzot described the soundtrack as the mainspring of the film, its motor, and encouraged the experimental composer Gilbert Amy to go far beyond conventional practice. It's almost an index of *folie de grandeur* among film-makers to customise a soundtrack so that it is viable in state-of-the-art facilities, then releasing it on a circuit with lower technical standards where it becomes hard to make out – think of Coppola blurring the voices on *Rumble Fish* for the less than cogent reason that one of the characters (it's not even the hero) is partially deaf.

It was chance that made Serge Bromberg aware of the footage that survives, when he was trapped in a lift with the director's widow. What else was Madame Clouzot going to talk about, with a *cinéaste* for captive audience, but the masterpiece that never was? Some of the shots her husband worked to create were almost unthinkably elaborate, in their search to realise effects that nowadays could be done on a computer in moments. At one point in the film, for instance, the hero needed to be in a precise position overlooking the lake, synchronised with both a train and a speedboat on the lake towing a water-skier. The skier falls, and at that exact moment Clouzot wanted the water to turn blood red. What this meant in those pre-digital days was that he used a filter on the camera to alter the apparent colour of the lake, but in order for the shot as a whole to match with the preceding footage every other element in the image needed to be chromatically shifted. Extras had to wear new costumes, identical except for the fact of compensating for the effects of the red filter, and they also needed meticulous make-up (grey-green) to ensure that their skin tone looked the same approximation of pink as it did before.

Clouzot drove himself and his actors obsessively on, refusing any short cut. It didn't help that he was an insomniac, of the type that doesn't see why other people should have the benefits of the rest he himself is denied. He'd call crew members at all hours. He seemed to be in a state of megalomaniac denial, unwilling or unable to impose discipline on location shooting that had a definite cut-off point. The lake by the hotel, actually a reservoir, was scheduled to be drained on a set date, and after that there would be no water, not of any colour. This was a time when film directors, perhaps particularly in France with its adulation of 'the seventh art', were encouraged to feel all-powerful – in 1967 Jacques Tati was disappointed and even hurt that he was expected to vacate the site where he had built the vast sets for his film *Playtime*, which was hopelessly late and over budget, simply because builders needed to start work on the construction of an apartment block. Did people really not understand what was important?

In the end, the filming of *L'Enfer* was stopped after Clouzot had a heart attack, though one of the technicians interviewed for *Inferno* suggests that this was a 'maladie diplomatique', the only way that the producers could get their money back. The director's health being known to be poor, it was heavily and comprehensively insured. It was a desperate move on Clouzot's part, if so, since he would never be insurable for a large project again. He lived until 1977, but there were no major films after that.

Some of the visual effects are relatively simple, compared to the red-filter madness of the scene at the lake. For instance, Clouzot had an immense sheet of glass (roughly 3 × 9 metres, or 10 × 30 ft) made by the manufacturer Saint-Gobain, with precisely prescribed areas of blurring and sharpness of image. When refracting discs of glass were stuck on in precisely chosen places, this allowed Clouzot in effect to edit and change focus within the frame, while filming a sequence of a busy market, and giving a strong sense of being alone within a crowd, isolated despite the surrounding bustle. The images melt into each other but without any softness. Although the logistical challenge of getting the actors and the prop – transparent, custom-made – into exactly the right positions for the glass to become emotionally eloquent was fairly formidable, it was in essence no different from the way that expressiveness in film had been managed since the beginnings of the medium, a matter of catching the exact angle that brings the shot to life, and in the finished film (if the film had ever been finished) it would have to be counted as a worthwhile use of resources.

The test footage of Romy Schneider is something else again. Just as Kubrick saw a documentary about space travel – *To the Moon and Beyond*, made for the New York World's Fair in 1964 – and hired one of the team who had worked on it for *2001* (not Douglas Trumbull in the first instance, though he soon followed), so Clouzot hired Éric Duvivier after seeing his film *Images du monde visionnaire* (1963), which attempted to render visible Henri Michaux's subjective experience of drugs (mescaline in the first half of the 35-minute film, hashish in the second). Since *Images du monde visionnaire* amounts to a visual poem trying to capture an experience on the far side of rationality, accompanied by disorienting music, it might just as easily have been Kubrick as Clouzot who hired Duvivier – he might have been put to work on the 'Star Gate' sequence in *2001*. The equation between drug experience and abnormal mental states didn't originate with Clouzot but appears in Duvivier's film: 'The similarity or identity of these experimental states, which can be produced and then subside over a few hours, with certain states of mental alienation, is the basis of current research on the bio-chemical pathogenesis of psychoses.' Perhaps this claim was intended to defuse any accusation that the reconstruction of a home movie filmed without equipment inside a drug-taker's head was self-indulgent, without any possible social benefit.

The imagery of *Images du monde visionnaire* seems tired and unevocative today, but Clouzot and Duvivier took the idea many stages on, arriving at genuinely extraordinary results. Their final design was of a spinning array behind the camera, a wheel of lights that cast a shifting arc of light and shadow, seemingly three-dimensional, on an object. When the object is Romy Schneider's face and presence, the effect is startling. Schneider had been if not a child star (fifteen when she made her first film) then certainly a young actress with a wholesome image, best known for playing 'Sissi', the Empress Elisabeth of Austria, as a young woman. It's an indication of how keen she was for the part that Schneider, who had never learned to swim, acquired the skill in water-skiing the part demanded, and even gave a reasonable impression of enjoying it. For the key sequences of Marcel's delusion special make-up was used on her face and body, incorporating particles of glitter. Expressions of seductiveness, mischief, complicity, scheming, malice, balefulness and flinty indifference seem to chase each other across her face, but it's always clear that these ghost emotions are projected from outside, nothing to do with the personality of the woman we are watching. When she lights a cigarette, the interference patterns created by the smoke add an extra layer of suggestive distortion. In close-ups, the texture of her flesh as the lighting moulds it becomes non-human and at times even faintly repellent – it seems to heave like a quicksand.

The devising of a new type of shot is a rare event in cinema, almost as rare as the invention of a new motive for murder in a detective story (something Ruth Rendell managed in *An Unkindness of Ravens*). Hitchcock came up with two novelties for *Vertigo*, the 360° cyclorama tracking shot gliding between competing realities (or fantasies) and what is usually known as the '*Vertigo* shot' proper or 'dolly zoom', as deployed in films as different as *Jaws* and the Jim Carrey vehicle *The Mask*. You could make a case for the novelty of a famous shot, nearly eight minutes long, at the end of Antonioni's *The Passenger* – I'd call it the *passe-muraille* shot, after the Marcel Aymé character who can pass through walls – in which the camera slowly moves from the near side of a barred window out into the space beyond, then turns to inspect the room from outside. Nowadays you could manage to fake such a shot in a matter of moments, or use a bloody drone, but in 1975 it boggled the minds of a whole generation of arty film lovers.

A better candidate might be the extraordinary shots in Raúl Ruiz's *Time Regained* from 1999 in which sections of scenery or set – a line of seats, even a stand of trees – move sideways in and out of position, like flats in a toy theatre being slid in and out by a dreaming child. The theatre of memory, perhaps? Certainly the effect of relativising the parts of the composition, giving its elements their independence, was wildly exciting whatever the intellectual rationale for it, if any.

Clouzot's new shot is a different case, being a self-sabotaging breakthrough. *Henri-Georges Clouzot's Inferno* details the external conflicts that scuppered *L'Enfer* – the endless tests using different lenses drawn from an apparently endless supply (the range went all the way from 9.5mm to 1,000), the three big film crews, each with a director of photography, either idling or getting in each other's way (the film was made in both colour and black-and-white). So many people were working that they couldn't sit down to eat together. Two sittings were required for lunch. There were preparations that sound ambitious but not necessarily excessive, like cutting down the trees on an island in the reservoir (which took a month), or arranging for a working steam train to run over the viaduct, though the actual location, the Garabit viaduct, formed part of the first electrified railway in France. Some ideas were relatively economical, such as the importing of slinky toys from America – those cylinders of coiled wire that slowly climbed down the stairs, head over single heel, living special effects as they seemed to the children of the period – for Schneider saucily to disport herself, so as to leave Sissi the young Empress Elisabeth of Austria, however lively and appealing, behind once and for all. Slinkies were even filmed in reverse, climbing the stairs for once, toys with a will of their own, inaudibly snuffling inquisitive gastropods of coiled metal.

There must have been a probationary period of some sort, but after the first screening of rushes, Columbia signed off on an unlimited budget. Yet Clouzot never stopped authorising test sequences, and being dissatisfied with them. He wanted, for instance, the effect of a nameplate hung in the window of a business premises dissolving to correspond with the hero's disordered emotional state. So a chocolate nameplate was commissioned, and blowtorches were played on it from behind so as to achieve the right effect of melting. No good, said Clouzot. Start again. Find another way. Everything was equally important, and nothing got finished.

There are exquisite games of scale in the footage that survives. In one shot Romy Schneider holds in front of her a little model of the hotel and its surroundings – but there's a tiny model train chugging across the miniature viaduct. Another shot shows an image of the hotel in black-and-white, with a mysterious angled blue line running across it. The mystery is solved when the image is revealed as a postcard, and the blue line as part of the display stand holding it in place.

The film-in-progress that contained these delicious touches, however, lost all sense of its own true scale.

Scenes might be shot any number of times, without Clouzot getting exactly what he wanted, unless what he wanted was to infuriate his actors. A scene in which Dany Carrel's bottom was playfully slapped was filmed ten or fifteen times, until the bruise started to show. Make-up was used to conceal the contusion, but the marks were still visible. Eventually she hit the actor who had been doing the slapping, something the written scene stipulated, but using the heel of her mule, not the toe as she was meant to, and blood gushed out like something in a cartoon. Serge Reggiani, the actor chosen by Clouzot to play Marcel, didn't flourish under Clouzot's relentless regime, which seemed to involve breaking the spirit of the performers, and quit the production, citing health reasons of his own. Jean-Louis Trintignant visited the shoot with a view to taking over the role, but nothing was shot and the production ground to a halt.

There's plenty of detail about the production's logistical problems in *Henri-Georges Clouzot's Inferno*, but the documentary pays no attention to the internal contradictions involved. The shots of Romy Schneider are astonishing as anatomies of the workings of male fantasy, but they wouldn't have worked in the completed film, not because they lack power but because they have too much. They overwhelm the anecdote. In *2001* too there was a mismatch between dazzling special effects and uninvolving human drama, but this could become part of the point of the film – it may even have been there from the start, the cosmic vistas expanding while the human dimensions shrink. Clouzot's shots don't so much express the human drama of a marriage under strain as replace it. If Proust had found a way of distilling jealousy into a paragraph so eloquent that it made the previous five hundred pages redundant, would he feel elation or despair at having gone so far with a novel and then creating a prose poem of greater weight? There's any amount of other thematic material in Proust, social chronicle of extraordinary reach, meditation on art, but the slow revelation of the oppressiveness of romantic love (which consecrates a pedestal for the object of adoration, but one surrounded with barbed wire) is hardly a dispensable element. In *L'Enfer* as Clouzot conceived it there seems to be nothing else on offer, nothing that could survive the disastrous triumph of a breakthrough in lighting design.

If Clouzot had somehow managed to get every shot he wanted, every effect to the standard he demanded, *L'Enfer* would not have fulfilled the hopes he and his producers had invested in it, but it would certainly have had an impact on the evolution of special effects. There would be pretentious books galore by now about Images of the Eye in *L'Enfer*, since, if it had stayed as the 'un tout petit film' that was originally envisaged, it could have ended up as a minor classic, perhaps on a double bill with Roman Polanski's *Repulsion*, released in 1965, and also exploring extreme states of mind, the psychotic breakdown of a woman terrified of sex rather than a man obsessed with his wife's infidelity. There are memorable special effects in *Repulsion* too, but they're remarkably economical, taking place almost on a Cocteau level of directness and physicality – disembodied hands reaching through the wall in a famous sequence to fondle Catherine Deneuve, as if this was a nightmare in the sleep of a frigid Belle, transported from a haunted castle to a Battersea flat where the only Beast is her own id.

Computer-generated imagery means that nowadays special effects tend not to fall below a certain technical standard. An army of obsessives examining every frame on their computers are likely to spot every little botch. Yet even now the old-fashioned reaction shot is a necessary component for the success of most effect-heavy films – though in comedies it can be turned against itself, with an actor registering not astonishment but a feeling of ho-hum, is-that-the-best-you-can-do? – Bill Murray in the first *Ghostbusters*, not all that impressed by a possessed Sigourney Weaver doing a flip clean over his head ('Nimble little minx, isn't she?'), or Tommy Lee Jones standing his ground in *Men in Black* as an alien ship crash-lands, uncannily confident that the spill of debris will stop just short of his feet. In a thriller whose keynote is not comedy we need a stand-in to show us the proper response, a face or faces expressing awe or horror at the giant ape, the avalanche, the volcano, the alien, the explosion, the twister.

Twister (1996)

In the first sequence of *Twister* comes a moment characteristic not of the director, Jan de Bont (*Speed*), nor of its writer/producer Michael Crichton, but of Steven Spielberg, who acted as executive producer. A Midwestern family is cowering in a storm cellar. The skylight shatters. Savage winds are tearing at the hatch. But while her father struggles to keep it closed in a desperate tug of war with the storm, the little girl is bathed in golden light. She stands up, more curious than afraid, while nature flexes her mighty muscles. It's pure *Close Encounters*. Is the tornado going to take her and play tender games with her? Read her bedtime stories and return her to her mother?

Not quite. The tempest takes her dad. But this sequence gives fair warning of how the film is put together. On the one hand, elaborate special effects will show us the weather at its most astoundingly destructive, on the other the script will relentlessly humanise the storm. There's no aspect of nature that we don't immediately turn into an aspect of ourselves.

The major characters of the film are storm chasers, driven partly by scientific curiosity and partly by love of adrenaline. Bill (Bill Paxton) thinks he only wants his estranged wife Jo (Helen Hunt) to sign the divorce papers, but he is like a veteran cop unable to resist one last case, or an alcoholic accepting one last drink. He's brought his nice new girlfriend along, but then Jo outmanoeuvres him by unveiling the ultimate other woman: Dorothy. After that, he has no will of his own.

Any film about tornadoes is likely to have *Wizard of Oz* references – in *Twister*, Jo's Aunt Meg (Lois Smith) is a mixture of Aunty M and one of the witches (a good one, even if she does have a house on top of her at one point). Dorothy, though, actually has a picture of Judy Garland stencilled on her side. Dorothy is a device designed to release hundreds of sensors into a tornado, to track its internal structure. All Bill and Jo have to do is put it right in the path of a twister.

The film tries to keep a straight face about the terrible damage done by tornadoes, the need to give people more warning, but joy in mayhem is just too strong. The script was originated by Michael Crichton's wife, Anne-Marie Martin, but it's typical of his cardboard psychology that Jo should turn out to have been the girl in the storm cellar whose dad was taken back in 1969. She's a perky Ahab, and the tornado is her great white whale. Aunt Meg has dealt with the tragedy, not by doing anything silly like moving to Kent but by staying right where she is and making sculptures influenced by the twister, huge wind chimes and mobiles.

The film's selling line, 'The Dark Side of Nature', makes twisters sound like manifestations of a meteorological id, and that's how it seems at first. We hear the first thunder when Bill admits he's going to remarry. The first twister appears as

Bill and Jo quarrel, as if it were a poltergeist conjured up by a bad marriage. But in the course of the movie, id gives way to libido. What's up there in the sky is, basically, great sex, a roving multiple orgasm. We keep seeing Jo and Bill clinging together, sweaty and dirty, after an encounter with a twister. It's pretty clear that the Earth has moved for them, along with everything else.

These days, hurricanes are given boys' and girls' names in alternation, but in *Twister* a tornado is only ever 'she'. Bill knows when they're going to change direction, capricious as they are. He's intuitive, and Jo is fearless in her desire. Melissa (Jami Gertz), on the other hand, the new girlfriend, is so out of touch with herself that when it rains torrentially, she puts an umbrella up! Talk about frigid. No wonder she's afraid of that ruthless spiral of excitement in the sky. Melissa wears white, and doesn't like to get her clothes soiled. She refuses Aunt Meg's steak-and-eggs breakfast – she's embarrassed by appetite. And what does she do for a living? She's a reproductive therapist. She helps people to have babies. As if that was what sex is about! At one point, she's counselling a client who's giving birth, saying 'Breathe' and 'Push' into her mobile phone, while right in front of her a twister splits in two ('We've got sisters!' shouts Bill). The tempest goes into labour.

Her counterpart is Jonas (Cary Elwes), a rival meteorologist who has sold out to business interests, thus enabling Crichton to portray his hero as ruggedly individualistic despite the usual encrustation of technology. Jonas has all the hardware, but no understanding of twister psychology. He can't find a storm's G-spot to save his life. With a name like that, what are the odds of his ending up inside the whale? If he trespasses into what Bill's team calls 'the suck zone', he may find something closer to *vagina dentata*.

Jonas has a Dorothy of his own, a cheeky rip-off called Dot, except that the eggs in his pod are cubes. Is that any way to pleasure a tornado? Admittedly, there are technical problems with the original Dorothy until Jo, in a moment of inspiration, realises that the sensors must have something to give them a bit more lift. There is an aerodynamic argument here, but also, surely, a symbolic consideration. At short notice, her team cross-dress the eggs as spermatozoa. If they had time, perhaps they'd fit them with individual wiggling tails. Under the gun, they come up with little propellers made from soft drink cans. Now, when Dorothy shoots her load, the storm will be properly seeded.

Twister isn't strictly speaking a disaster movie, since the characters actively seek out danger. It relies for its structure on a succession of ever more severe tornadoes, each of which moves on or blows out. All the film leaves behind is a few last flurries of aroused air, a few wisps of smoke from the massive destruction. The sky, briefly satisfied, enjoying a post-coital cigarette.

I'm not sure how conscious I was at the time of writing (while I filled my sheet of A4 with tiny script over two large coffees in the branch of Café Pasta on Theberton Street, assuming I was following my usual routine) that I was returning to the dementedly analytical style of the high-class journalism I had enjoyed so much in the 1970s (though I didn't know how seriously to take it), knowingly preposterous readings of mainstream productions like *Marathon Man* and *Jaws*. Now it was my turn to practise annihilation by subtext, turning a film inside out and reviewing the lining. I had space to fill, and a thousand words on *Twister* without any flights of fancy would have been unbearable for both writer and reader.

There are things that CGI special effects can do that outrank any other means of achieving a particular illusion, and

one of them is exactly the area in which I'm most conflicted by
their excellence, namely the simulation of anatomical damage,
particularly as it affects a limb (the *Forrest Gump* template,
or perhaps syndrome). The scarred stump where a hand or
foot once was – something that people turn their eyes away
from in real life, from a mixture of motives, from tact combined with squeamishness. Two films from 2017 featured this
sort of effects work, and in the reviews of them I try to wrestle
with my reactions, not wanting to turn into the film-reviewing
equivalent of a single-issue politician. I'd rather not be ruled by
my prejudices, as a matter of professional hygiene.

Logan Lucky (2017)

At one point in Steven Soderbergh's *Logan Lucky* news reports
refer to a robbery at a North Carolina racetrack as 'Ocean's
7-Eleven' (other nicknames for the robbery being 'Hillbilly
Heist' and 'Redneck Robbery'), the phrase mashing up the
names of a basic supermarket chain and the crime caper remade
by Soderbergh in 2001 with George Clooney and Brad Pitt.
There's some token self-mockery here, though it could be read
in either direction, either at the expense of the new film, with
its blue-collar characters, not all of them bright, or the old one,
borderline vacuous in its suavity even before the dreary sequels.

The script is credited to Rebecca Blunt, a writer with no
track record and no media presence, but since the film's director of photography Peter Andrews and its editor, Mary Ann
Bernard, are pseudonyms of Soderbergh's, the mystery may not
be impenetrable. As a script it shows every sign of expertise,
from the first extended scene, in which young Sadie Logan
(Farrah Mackenzie) – the actress is eleven but looks younger –
helps her father Jimmy (Channing Tatum) to work on his car,

asking knowledgeably whether it's the needle-nosed pliers he wants, the Philips screwdriver or the slot. The film is both plot- and dialogue-driven, and if the character-drawing is sometimes unsubtle then the crisp pace leaves little time to notice or complain. You can afford some broad touches as long as you keep things moving.

As a piece of entertainment *Logan Lucky* leaves the *Ocean* films in the dust, and it makes Edgar Wright's *Baby Driver*, a well-reviewed recent release also dealing with crime and cars, look distinctly underpowered. The films that made Wright's name (*Shaun of the Dead*, *Hot Fuzz*, *The World's End*) were written with Simon Pegg, who also starred in them. All three started in one genre and ended in another, exactly the sort of cleverness that gets scripts turned down, and each of them played fantasy off intimately known settings – respectively Crouch End, Wells and the garden cities of Hertfordshire. Setting a film in Atlanta was a much less comfortable exercise for Wright, one that he tackled by stylising the visuals from beginning to end and turning the soundtrack into one long mixtape. The conventions of fairy-tale romance and bloody violence didn't cohere, but neither did they lend one another vitality, and the action sequences, on which the success of the film depended, couldn't decide whether they were entirely fantastical or needed to have some connection with the way objects behave in the real world. Though the assumptions behind *Logan Lucky* (innocent criminality, underclass redistribution of wealth) can get a little too close for comfort to *The Dukes of Hazzard*, they do at least mesh.

When Steven Soderbergh won the grand prize at Cannes for his first film, *Sex, Lies, and Videotape* in 1989, he seemed a rather earnest film-maker, preoccupied with truthfulness in relationships – but then he was 26 at the time. By 2000, when he was nominated as Best Director at the Oscars for two films in the same year (for *Traffic* and *Erin Brockovich*) his profile seemed clearer. He was a highly accomplished crafter of mainstream entertainments, with just a little bit of political edge. *Traffic* dramatised the human cost of the drugs trade, and *Erin Brockovich* combined a personal-redemption character arc with an emphasis on the importance of holding public bodies to account.

This too now seems an inadequate account of Soderbergh's priorities. Social issues come and go in his films, making him a contrast with a maverick of an earlier generation like John Sayles, who would write genre scripts for money, and earned well as a script doctor, but had a consistent engagement with political issues, both hard (a mining strike in *Matewan*) and soft – the racism that is central to his 1984 fantasy *The Brother from Another Planet*, the restrictions on women's lives in *Lianna* and *Passion Fish*. Soderbergh's taste for working fast and cheaply would have made him a terrific director of B-movies – but that job description no longer exists. Well-managed genre films of his like *Out of Sight* or *Side Effects* are effectively B-plus or A-minus movies, just a little short of delivering full satisfaction.

Soderbergh likes to work independently, but independence in film-making no longer means what it once did. At a time when the equipment and materials required were extremely expensive, those who tried to work outside the studio system struggled to get access to cameras, film, lighting rigs and editing suites, and the resulting films, however successful (as *Carnival of Souls* and *Night of the Living Dead* were in the 1960s) had a visual texture that couldn't be mistaken for the features people were used to seeing. Now technology has brought the price right down, and audiences are used to big-budget films that mimic no-budget ones to create authenticity, an idea that would once have seemed insane. Superficially Soderbergh's idea of independence is close to Robert Altman's but the results are much less distinctive. He's a lot less erratic than Altman was, admittedly, but what he wants is not the freedom to experiment so much as the right to control his own product.

For a director to be his own cinematographer can suggest a mania for control, but there's a strong argument running the other way, that his physical closeness to the performers allows Soderbergh to give cues during the filming itself. He has always been a strong director of actors, good at balancing ensembles. He made Julia Roberts find some rough edges as Erin Brockovich, and though Michael Douglas wasn't stretched by his role in *Traffic*, Liberace in *Behind the Candelabra* was a different matter.

The cast of *Lucky Logan* is full of pleasingly clashing notes. Soderbergh's *Magic Mike* gave Channing Tatum a major career boost – now he can keep his clothes on in a film and even pretend to look a little chunky as he cruises towards forty. In *Foxcatcher* he played the vulnerable younger brother to Mark Ruffalo's character, but here he must be the strong one. Adam Driver, playing Jimmy's younger brother Clyde, has a mysteriously wide range despite his apparently impassive face, and an ability to change the tone of a scene. Elsewhere there are some rather self-indulgent games with accents, so that the British mogul Max Chilblain is played by Seth MacFarlane, who was born in Kent (Kent, Connecticut), while one of a pair of dimwit brothers is played by Brian Gleeson, his Irish accent showing through every few lines.

Even with characters like those brothers, Soderbergh's camera is adept at finding grotesquely convincing details, such as a West Virginia county fair at which sideshows include horseshoe throwing, except that the flung horseshoes are replaced by toilet seats, and bobbing for apples, only with pig's trotters standing in for the apples. Perhaps the country fair was staged for the film, but there's certainly a documentary element in footage of the crowds at the racing track. The great discovery of *Easy Rider* was that anything you point the camera at, not just a few hallowed locations (Monument Valley, New York skyline), becomes Americana, and it helps if you bring along on the trip an eye that was formed elsewhere (László Kovács, the cinematographer, was from Hungary). In last year's *American Honey* the British director Andrea Arnold threw herself into a similar adventure, but it's understandable that most directors from outside the States should shrink from the challenge.

The wildest card in *Logan Lucky*'s pack of wild cards is Daniel Craig as explosives expert Joe Bang. Craig seems to be enjoying himself on his holiday from Bond, particularly in a scene corresponding to the 'science bit' in a shampoo commercial, where he explains, using chalk on a wall, that his purchase of two bleach pens and some gummy bears, combined with the low-sodium salt he is prescribed for his high blood pressure, amounts to a recipe for unleashing serious destruction.

Logan Lucky builds to a scene of pathos bordering on sentiment, played entirely straight, in which Sadie, appearing in a talent show, makes the ultimate sacrifice of not performing Rihanna's 'Umbrella' but instead singing her Dad's favourite song, 'Take Me Home, Country Roads', made famous by John Denver. It's important to her to make the gesture since her mother is planning to move out of state with her new husband, making paternal visitation harder. Farrah Mackenzie resists the temptations of moppetry, despite being done up as a mini beauty queen, tiara, teased hair and all – perhaps she's just relieved no longer to be playing the young Dolly Parton's kid sister in the TV movie *Christmas of Many Colors: Circle of Love*.

The scene is saved from excessive sweetness by Jimmy Logan's earlier discussion of the song – which has since become one of West Virginia's official anthems – when he mentioned that its writer had never visited the state at the time that he wrote it ('Massachusetts' was another option he was considering, since it had the right number of syllables). Soderbergh seems to be signalling the phoniness of populist feeling even while he channels it. It helps, too, that Mackenzie hardly hits a note even approximately, so that her performance is supported if not entirely created by her audience, helplessly singing along in a murmur that gradually builds with her confidence.

Logan Lucky isn't exactly a conflicted film in terms of its cultural politics, it's more that its liberal and conservative sides are coded differently in terms of how they manifest themselves. A conservative value system, the conviction that all is essentially right in America, in presented visually and with musical reinforcement, in Sadie's song and also when the camera shows stern and transfigured faces, military and civilian, at the opening ceremony of the NASCAR race meeting, while the chosen singer warbles the hell out of 'O Say Can You See . . .'.

Social concerns appear indirectly, in the guise of plot points, so that contamination of the water supply (the explicit subject of *Erin Brockovich*) here merely provides a mechanism for a prison inmate who needs to make himself sick at short notice. The inadequacy of medical provision in West Virginia, the second-poorest state in America – to the point where voluntary organisations must step in to provide such fripperies as tetanus shots – becomes an occasion for Jimmy Logan to meet cute with a woman (winningly played by Katherine Waterston) who had a crush on him in high school, now dispensing basic services from a van. Clyde Logan lost his lower arm while on active service in Iraq, and it seems that all a veteran qualifies for in the way of replacement is a clumsy lump of approximately contoured plastic – a 7-Eleven prosthetic if ever there was one, a replacement body part from the Economy range. At one point the police, seeking to arrest Clyde, come up against the difficulties of handcuffing someone who has lost a hand,

and seem very disconcerted, though I'm pretty sure they're trained for that.

It used to be the case that you needed actual disabled people to represent disability on film, as Harold Russell did in *The Best Years of Our Lives* (1946), though he didn't lose his arms in combat but in an accident during training. He won two Oscars for the role, since the Academy had created a special award in case he didn't win it for his acting – even so, he had to wait a third of a century for his next role in a film. By the time of Fred Zinnemann's *The Men* (1950), 'Forty Five of The Men of Birmingham Veterans Administration Hospital' got a group credit for playing 'Themselves' but all eyes were on Marlon Brando, in his screen debut, since he could get better, not really being damaged in the first place.

Finally, in the 1990s, digital special effects enabled able-bodied actors to play disabled convincingly, which every-body prefers because it separates the correct attitudes, so easily struck, from the troubling reality, just as people prefer to process the proper response to fat people while watching a slim actress in a fat suit (such as Gwyneth Paltrow in *Shallow Hal*). Gary Sinise as Dan Taylor in *Forrest Gump* had lost a leg, or rather had been digitally furnished in post-production with a sort of reverse prosthesis. The absence was convincingly rendered, but the missing limb wasn't in all that many shots. Clyde Logan's amputation, of the forearm, is required to appear in a much higher proportion of the footage. The darned flesh looks impressively angry. It's a technical advance. The question is whether it's better not to represent disability at all, or to represent it in the absence of disabled people. It's a bit of a toss-up, isn't it?

That piece was written for the *Times Literary Supplement*, where I have a little more space and the possibility of more time for reflection, though it sometimes happens that I can only manage to see the relevant film in the cinema when it's on general release, as happened in the case of *Logan Lucky*, so that my review is likely to appear a fortnight after anyone else's. That's quite a disadvantage – on those occasions I really have to go deeper and broader, as well as longer, to justify a reader's time and attention. I'm sure there are differences between the approach of my *Independent* pieces and my work for the TLS, but I couldn't put my finger on it or explain the reasons. Perhaps it's just that I've got more films under my belt as a viewer. Reviewing any work of art requires a strange mixture of resistance and surrender. With any luck my surrendering skills are stronger now.

Downsizing (2017)

For the first half-century of cinema's existence, seeing a film was an experience of scale. Susan Sontag gives the example of the shot in *Double Indemnity* that shows Phyllis Dietrichson's (or Barbara Stanwyck's) lower legs and feet in somewhat tarty shoes – she's also wearing an anklet – as she comes downstairs in her first scene with the insurance agent Walter Neff (Fred McMurray). On a big screen those feet are transgressive hooves the size of buses, while on a standard television set they're smaller than the real thing. Since the time of Sontag's observation screen size has fluctuated in ways that corroborate Norma Desmond's desperate boast in *Sunset Boulevard* – 'I *am* big. It's the pictures that got small.' – while also making nonsense of it. Cinema screen size has shrunk while domestic screen size has enormously expanded, so that they seem almost to be meeting in the middle, but commuters also watch films, or make valiant attempts, on their mobile phones.

Cinema may have lost its monopoly on absolute size, but relative size is an inexhaustible source of surprise and strangeness. There's a typically sly shot in Alexander Payne's new film *Downsizing* in which residents of a rundown apartment building get their entertainment from a gigantic screen in its central public space ('atrium' would be too grand a word). Except that it isn't the television that is exceptional but its spectators, who have been shrunk to five inches tall as part of an initiative that has environmental credentials (when your stature has been so drastically reduced, your carbon footprint inevitably follows) as well as any number of other implications.

The 1957 sci-fi classic *The Incredible Shrinking Man*, celebrated in its time for special effects but more durably distinguished by the adventurousness of its ending, was able to establish its premise fairly simply. You're out in your boat, a radioactive mist sweeps across the water, soon your trousers are mysteriously loose, then you're dwarfed by your chair in the doctor's office and before long you're fighting off a spider with a pin for a sword. *Downsizing* (credited to the director and his long-time writing partner Jim Taylor) needs to trace a set of technological and social developments unfolding over a number of years rather than an individual catastrophe, and must lay the groundwork in a more leisurely way. First a laboratory in Norway, and a scientist's eyes widening in wonder at the results of an experiment, before he races through the corridors to bring the good news to his superior. Then a press conference, at which the same scientist is brought in to address the startled audience – brought in inside a small box, since he has himself undergone the miniaturising procedure he discovered and weighs 18 grams. He introduces the first community of the Small, which includes Little Ronni, the first child to be born of Small parents.

Ten more years pass in a flash before we even get to the title sequence. The audience needs time to absorb the ramifications of Small settlements like Leisureland, protected from insects and birds by a net. The square footage is so modest, and the cost of living so low, that a cash-strapped couple like Paul and Audrey Safranek (Matt Damon and Kristen Wiig) can become virtual plutocrats in Leisureland. 'Transitioning' to Small combines elements of retirement, emigration, winning the lottery and euthanasia – the last demanding to be included because the process is irreversible. This section of the film is a slow extended preamble, not helped by the casting. As a leading man Matt Damon is as drearily nutritious and flavour-free as a block of tofu. It seems uncoincidental that in his signature role, Jason Bourne, he played an operative whose identity has been taken from him. Damon's durability is explained by the fact that he has learned, like tofu, to absorb or at least not be overwhelmed by strong flavours. In *The Talented Mr Ripley*, admittedly, where he played a predatory chameleon, taking on identities he covets, he was overwhelmed by Jude Law, a performer with exactly opposite characteristics, able to steal a film but not to carry one, as his subsequent career has shown. Damon has learned some craft since then.

Alexander Payne seems to be one of the many directors who regard a film's music score as a sort of assistance dog, there to lick your hand in every sequence to make sure you know exactly what to feel. It's easy to imagine the composer on *Downsizing*, Rolfe Kent (another regular collaborator) saying, 'I'd rate this sequence as about 70 per cent perky, 30 per cent uneasy – does that sound roughly right? And I was thinking shepherd's pipes as a change from clarinet. What do you think?' And Payne saying, 'You're the music man. Go for it.'

The result is a relentless musical shadowing of the action, so that when Paul and Audrey fall silent, after being told just before consenting to the procedure that there is a risk (one in 250,000) of something going badly wrong, the score goes to troubled pizzicato strings, in case we imagined they were thinking of something other than the imminent possibility of dying. Transitioning isn't untraumatic in any case, since dental work and any other inorganic modification must be removed (and reinstalled later on the appropriate scale) – which gives the saleslady a reason not to undergo herself the process she so warmly recommends, since her husband has a replacement hip.

Transitioners' hair, eyebrows and body must also be shaved, though the technical logic isn't clear. The visual logic is obvious – that the newly Small (the process isn't shown directly) resemble tiny babies in their hairlessness, lying stranded in the middle of the beds they filled so fully a matter of hours ago, to be tenderly scooped up by nurses with something resembling a fish slice. This isn't really rebirth, though, but a variation in a fantasy register of Alexander Payne's primary subject, at least since *Election*, the midlife crisis (latelife crisis, actually, in *Nebraska*) and the travails of the beta male generally.

The naked forms of newly Small males are shown without euphemistic camera angles or editing, while female transitions aren't shown, which makes *Downsizing* one of the very few films (by design, it's reasonable to hope), whether American or otherwise, mainstream or otherwise, that addresses male bodies more frankly than female ones.

It's easy to pick holes in the scenario of the film – if Small people need loudhailers to communicate with people of the size they used to be, then they would be deafened by the roaring speech that issues from those giant throats – but Payne builds up just enough reality with cunning peripheral detail. The rings that Paul and Audrey used to wear are delivered as part of a Keepsake package, the size of hula-hoops and so heavy the delivery man shouldn't really be trying to carry them both at the same time. Paul is warned to be careful with dairy products to begin with, since his miniaturised system will need time to adjust. He can't find chervil in the Leisureland supermarkets and must settle for dill.

One of the attractions of Leisureland is a zero crime rate, a fortunate statistic since there is no police force on hand to deal with any wrongdoing that does arise, in fact no government of any sort. Despite the implied cues, though, this is not the sort of film in which an engineered perfection (as in, say, *Westworld*, *The Stepford Wives* or *Seconds*) turns out to be hell on Earth – and much the better for it. Paul keeps to the limits he knows, until after a failed romantic dinner he goes to a party held by his Serbian upstairs neighbour Dušan (Christoph Waltz) carrying a single yellow rose the size of a microwave oven – apparently you can buy such things at an outlet called Full-size Flower Mart. Waltz is enormously more powerful as an actor than Damon, and Dušan is as colourful as Paul is bland, making a good living by trading between the two worlds and satisfying needs no one else has spotted yet, by (for instance) shredding down a single full-size Cohiba into two thousand not-quite-Cuban small cigars. Waltz reins himself in admirably while continuing to shine, not taking more actorly oxygen than his entitlement, leaving space not only for Paul but for Udo Kier's Konrad, a sort of Eurotrash fixer who takes cruises all over the world, sending his miniaturised motor yacht ahead by FedEx to the appropriate port. Late on in the film we see the ship heading towards the original Norwegian settlement, pulling a barge laden with supplies, notably colossal (though actually only full-sized) bottles of vodka. There's also Dušan's angry Vietnamese cleaning lady Ngoc Lan Tran, played by Hong Chau, who provides the film's slow-burning surprises.

Tran is angry for a reason. Back in Vietnam she was punished for her activism, campaigning against a dam that would drown her native valley, by being shrunk and deported – though dumped would be a more accurate word – loaded with a group of other dissidents inside the packaging of a television being exported to the States. All the others died in the TV box, including Tran's sister, and she lost part of a leg as a result of her maltreatment. When Paul, who was a physiotherapist in full-sized life, suggests making adjustments to her prosthesis she dragoons him into coming to the shantytown where she lives to help her neighbours. The bus drives through an overflow drain in the wall of Leisureland.

Chau's is a great, uningratiating performance, uncomfortable even when extremely funny. Cinema is not ordinarily a welcoming environment for pushy women, and this character is beyond pushy. Her goals are charitable, taking out-of-date medication from the bathroom cabinets of the well-off and left-over food from their fridges, all for the benefit of her underclass neighbours, but virtue as she practises it is so abrasive it could take your skin off. When an Indian woman for whom she cleans doubtfully offers her some days-old sag paneer she prises up the foil, inhales with rapture and says, 'In prison we die for such food.'

The suggestion that Americans are children, having no idea what life is like, when set beside a European like Dušan, who sees Leisureland as an opportunity for exploitation ('Baby, this is the Wild West') and an Asian like Tran, who turns herself into a one-woman social services network, isn't exactly profound, but it's an unusual thing to appear in an American film. Despite the foregrounding of environmental fears and apocalypse being imminent by the end of the film, *Downsizing* pulls back from the brink of black comedy and retains a certain wholesomeness.

Ngoc Lan Tran would be a distinctive enough role as a character part, what with her scorching directness and her evangelical Christianity – when we see her attending a prayer meeting a huge tambourine, reaching almost to the ceiling, has pride of place. As the film develops she is revealed as its female lead. Personally I have difficulty with the cinema of the digitised prosthesis (as seen in *Forrest Gump* and *Logan Lucky*), and the contorted messages that are sent when physically unimpaired actors occupy non-standard bodies thanks to the magic of special effects. Disability gains visibility at the cost of presence, in a sort of filtered inclusion, with issues being admitted but separated from the people who must live through them. But the gain to *Downsizing* of putting this multiply marginal existence close to its centre can't be argued with. This angry woman becomes something infinitely rarer in films than a sexual object – a sexual subject, whose desire rather than her desirability takes charge of events.

The extra space allowed by the *Times Literary Supplement* makes possible a leisurely and sidelong approach to films that are leisurely and sidelong in their own right, such as Alfonso Cuarón's recent *Roma*.

Roma (2018)

There's a curious scene in the middle stretch of Alfonso Cuarón's fascinating *Roma*. The central character Cleo (Yalitza Aparicio) – despite its title, the film is set in Mexico – is directed to a martial arts training camp in the open air. She's looking for the boyfriend who has left her without a word. In charge of the drills, rather surprisingly, is 'Profesor Zovek', a physical performer from a different tradition, in fact a showman wrestler in the Mexican style. The part is played by Latin Lover, just such a showman in real life, and a household name in Mexico. Even audiences unfamiliar with Latin Lover as a celebrity on their own screens will recognise the Profesor from an earlier appearance in the film, when he was shown in a television programme pulling a car with his teeth. Either way there is a brief shifting of formal ground, a change of register, in what is otherwise a meticulous realist portrait of domestic life in the early 1970s.

A call goes out for a volunteer, but all that is required of him is that he use a scarf to blindfold the Profesor's eyes. With an air of concentration the Profesor raises his hands above his head, brings them together palm to palm, and stands on one leg. After a few seconds of him holding this pose there's a murmur of discontent – that's it? That's all he's going to do? And the Profesor asks, what did you expect me to do – fly? Pull an aircraft out of the sky? Try doing what I'm doing, then you'll see how hard it is. Eventually the trainees try to emulate his solid balance on one leg without their eyes to help them. None of them can manage it.

By way of this interlude in the film's action Cuarón seems to be addressing his audience at a slight angle, slyly commenting on the startling contrast between *Roma* and his last film, *Gravity* (2013), starring Sandra Bullock and George Clooney, in which people did indeed fly, or at least float in zero-gravity conditions, and a craft was indeed pulled out of the sky, out of orbit and into a desperate descent towards the surface of the earth. To put it in more general terms: the real challenge in cinema is not to do the spectacular but to do the unspectacular spectacularly well. As a manifesto, this fits *Roma* very snugly.

There are stylistic preferences that Cuarón has retained despite the sharp change of direction. He's still abstemious, even puritan, when it comes to the aural aspect of cinema – *Gravity* may have been the first film since *2001* to be set in space without supplying sound in contexts where the ear would receive no signal. *2001* was full of music that was somehow free-standing, contradicting the images as much as supporting them (the *Blue Danube, Also sprach*), but though the composer on *Gravity*, Steven Price, won an Oscar for his work the music was there to build emotion self-effacingly, prominent only towards the end to celebrate the triumph of survival against the odds. If you didn't notice the music in *Gravity* it meant that the film had achieved its goals. If you didn't notice the music in *2001* it meant you had been asleep. On *Roma* there is no composer listed, just a music supervisor and a music editor. What we hear is what the characters hear. The sound design is remarkably elaborate, with a wide aural ambiance, so that viewers in cinemas may imagine from time to time that there's someone chatting in Spanish at the end of the row.

Cuarón still loves long takes, and excels in the composition and execution of travelling shots. The first take of *Roma* is long but hardly dramatic, perhaps as a warning that the film's dynamism will be held-in rather than florid: the camera is fixed, showing an area of tiled floor for the duration of the opening credits. When water is abruptly sloshed over the tiles, it's not just a small shock but an opening up of visual space, since there is now a glass roof reflected in the puddle. The tiles are part of the area between the front door of a spacious family flat, spread over two floors, and the street entrance. This area functions as a rather narrow garage, into which vehicles must be driven with great care if they're not to scrape the sides, but also divides the family's residence from the stairs leading up to the maids' quarters, where Cleo, currently cleaning up after the family dog Borras, goes upon finishing her day's duties – when she has put her employer's four children to bed and ushered them into sleep.

The camera tracks Cleo from a central vantage point as she goes about her work in the flat, rising when she climbs the stairs then back down as she descends. It would be hard to say whether the camera is leading or following her, and the subtle interplay between character action and camera movement is a continuing pleasure to watch. When Cleo takes the washing up to the roof it becomes clear that there are many similar households, many similar maids, many other dogs barking at intruders at the street entrance of properties, but the film doesn't seem to be telling a generic story.

One sort of film about masters and servants takes a hard line about the impossibility of real human contact in any such alienating hierarchy. Cleo is racially different from her employers and her first language isn't Spanish, meaning that her culture diverges significantly from theirs, but in emergencies the family she works for functions as if it was her own. This isn't a narrative of oppression as such. In a more mysterious tradition, exemplified by the films of Robert Bresson, the underdog has special access to grace, so that the power relations of everyday life count for nothing. *Roma* doesn't fit that pattern either.

This is the second highly accomplished film of 2018 to be made in black and white. Paweł Pawlikowski's *Cold War* exploited the formal elegance of monochrome to give his story of untidy, conflicted lives a crispness it might otherwise lack, and the refusal of colour rhymed with the restrictiveness of life under communism. Mexico in popular awareness, though, is virtually synonymous with colour, garish or vibrant according to taste. At Christmas the family goes to stay in the country with friends, in an overdecorated house full to the brim with knick-knacks and stuffed animals – only black and white has a chance of keeping the images on the right side of a visual riot.

Take away the colour from Mexico and what's left? That seems to be the question Alfonso Cuarón sets out to answer with *Roma*. Black and white is an asset to him in staging intricate shots because nothing can 'pop', as designers like to say, from the back of a monochrome image in the way that, say, an area or even a small patch of red can demand attention in a colour film – Hitchcock was fond of saying that he shot *Psycho* in black and white because it enabled him to get away with so much more blood. Cuarón could make a similar claim about the dog-logs deposited in the garage-entrance hall by Borras and cleaned up, when nagged to do so, by Cleo. In a colour film these images would need to be much more discreet to avoid disgusting viewers. No one seems to take Borras for a walk. He's a guard dog, guaranteed to bark and jump wildly when strangers approach the street door, rather than a family pet.

It's not just literal colour that has been subtracted from *Roma*, it's everything melodramatic and unsubtle. Cuarón's storyline – the maid and her employer both betrayed by men they trusted – could easily be the basis of a telenovela, full of shouted confrontations, false climaxes, cliffhangers and twists of fate. In fact the collapse of Señora Sofia's marriage is under-played almost as much for the film's audience as it is for the couple's children, who are told that Daddy is away on business, his return repeatedly delayed by the pressure of work. When the children run into their father with an unfamiliar woman coming out of a cinema (his new life is being played out very close to his old one) the moment of drama is whisked away the instant it happens, swallowed up in the rich realisation of 1970s street life. The actress playing Sofia, Marina de Tavira, has herself appeared in telenovelas such as *sos: Sex and Other Secrets* (2007–8), so that her presence in the film may emphasise the contrast in style for domestic audiences. Her desperation is conveyed peripherally, in a snatch of phone conversation, by a few lines of dialogue Cleo overhears in a hospital.

Cleo's own involvement with Fermin (Jorge Antonio Guerrero), the cousin of the man her fellow maid Adela is dating, ends abruptly but also without drama. The two of them are watching a film together when Cleo mentions she's missed her period. He doesn't respond except to say that he needs to pee. Can he bring her back an ice cream? He doesn't return. Obviously he hasn't done a runner, since he's left his jacket with her. She's reassured by that. As it turns out, he's left his jacket behind in the same way that lizards shed their tails when cornered, so as to buy time and delay their pursuers. The men in the film break their word in pretty much every case. Even the doctor who says he would accompany a frightened woman into surgery if only he was allowed makes excuses when it turns out there is no objection.

Character-drawing has fallen away along with conventional drama. The four children are particularised only in terms of the sibling dynamic, their unawareness of the larger picture not played for pathos but simply accepted as a fact of life. The two older boys fight over everything, the girl alternates between trying to join their games and running to Cleo to intervene between them. There's something slightly odd about the youngest boy, though it's lightly passed over. Twice in the film he says, 'When I was older . . .', and Cleo corrects him, thinking he's got the words mixed up and means 'younger'. But he persists with his framing of the thought, and says he was a pilot. Humouring the fantasy, she says that it must have been exciting, but he says no. He was terrified. The moment isn't dwelt on, like every other moment in the whole extraordinary film, but there is a similar exchange near the end. This time they're by the sea and the boy remembers, when he was older, being a fisherman.

Cleo's mother is mentioned in passing, and at one point her ownership of land is under threat, but Cleo doesn't visit (she has her reasons) and the mother never appears. Señora Sofia seems similarly isolated, though more by authorial decree than her likely circumstances, and naturally she has more resources than a maid. When she tells the children that she has quit her job as a biochemist and will be working full time for a publisher to support the family, she says it's no sacrifice. She never enjoyed biochemistry. The children contradict her – she loved being a biochemist! They seem to be well informed, but until this moment their mother's career has not been something the audience has had any inkling about.

Mexico is in social turmoil though none of the characters seems to notice. This is humanly plausible, and certainly preferable to Cuarón researching the political background and making it obtrusive. He would have been nine or so at the time the film is set. Is the uniformed troop that regularly marches outside on the street ominous or reassuring? No one pays attention either way. There is just one moment when the public and private realms overlap, perhaps even collide. Cleo and Sofia's mother go shopping. Outside the department store, so that they can see what's happening through the windows, a student demonstration is brutally put down by police and thugs along for the ride. Not only that – the violence reaches into the shop, even into the department where the women are, and Cleo recognises one of the perpetrators. He's someone she knows. This is the Corpus Christi Massacre, a black day in Mexican history, but that's as far as the situation goes in the film. There's no plot development beyond that point.

It's forces of nature rather than narrative shape that divide the film into sections. First there's an earthquake, as meticulously staged as everything else in the film, shown as it affects the maternity ward in a hospital. The final image of the sequence, nudging sentimentality, is of a premature baby in an incubator covered in rubble, the machine still doing its job, the tiny body still breathing. Then there's a forest fire that the Christmas house party does its best to extinguish, a scene that provokes not exactly awe but a sort of secondary wonder – how many times can you shoot a scene like that? How is it possible to control long takes so completely and still leave so much life in them?

Finally there's an encounter with rough sea at Veracruz. Earth, fire, water – if there was an ordeal by air to complete the set I'm afraid I missed it.

In the absence of dramatic tension the film depends on Yalitza Aparicio's performance as Cleo for its overall impact. She is tipped for Best Actress nominations and it seems wrong to question her eligibility, though such awards weren't devised to reward amateurs. There's footage of Bresson directing Nadine Nortier, the untrained young woman who played Mouchette for him, another great performance that isn't quite a piece of acting. (Nortier had been working in a bank, and didn't act again.) He gets her to repeat a simple sequence of actions – getting out of bed, say – again and again until he's satisfied, and that's it. Amateurs have more patience, or less ego – maybe that's all it is. They don't advance their opinions. In a different style of film production, Alfred Hitchcock was supremely aware of every nuance of his stars' personas, and that was a vital part of why he cast them, but after that all he really wanted was for them to hit their marks. The audience would do the rest.

Aparicio, like the other members of the cast – many of them first-timers like herself – wasn't given the whole script to read, so that there could be no question of her shaping her performance organically as a professional would seek to do. Mind you, Ken Loach withheld the full script in the same way on *I, Daniel Blake* (2016) and it didn't affect Dave Johns's chances of winning prizes.

Certainly without Aparicio's face to look at audiences wouldn't have any great reason to become emotionally involved in the film, as opposed to following it with detached fascination. There's always a risk of throwing out the baby with the bathwater, the human interest with the gaudy melodrama. Melodrama as a cinematic form always allowed for an element of critique in Sirk and in Ophüls, something that was taken up by Fassbinder.

More recently Almodóvar has shown that the embrace of strong colour can co-exist with a sense of emotional truth.

It's possible to admire every single aspect of *Roma* and still be puzzled by the film as a whole. There must be a strong impulse behind the project, set as it is in the world the writer-director knew as a child, but an enormous amount of discipline has been devoted to neutralising its urgency – and nobody ever rushed to see a film because it was a masterpiece of balance.

Something happens to a review at about the 2,000-word mark. It stops being enough for the writer to make a case as strongly as possible. It becomes more rewarding to engage with the reader less predictably. The focus can widen, so as to include not just obviously similar films, or even whole acting or directing careers, but national traditions and competing philosophies of cinema. At this point a film review acquires a sort of generic dual nationality as a proud and independent essay, while still performing the service of telling you whether the film that provides its starting point is one you will actually want to see.

Sauvage (2019)

Camille Vidal-Naquet's *Sauvage* shares its name with a fragrance by Christian Dior, currently marketed with images of Johnny Depp wearing black clothes and stalking moodily through the desert with a spade, but in a cinematic context the word resonates most deeply with Truffaut's *L'Enfant Sauvage* from 1969, about a boy supposedly raised by wolves, able to function socially only thanks to the devoted attentions of a doctor (played in the film by Truffaut himself). The hero of

Vidal-Naquet's film, a sex worker played by Félix Maritaud, might indeed have been raised by wolves for all his awareness of anything beyond the primal drive of sex. Sex is how he earns his living but that's almost incidental, and he doesn't compartmentalise things as his fellow hustlers do – he identifies as gay, and doesn't regard kissing a client as unprofessional, though he only does it when he wants to. He has a crush on Ahd (Éric Bernard), who is protective and affectionate but insists on regarding himself as straight, having sex with men only for money.

The writer-director withholds his hero's name from the film's audience but hasn't been able to prevail against the website IMDb's appetite for information, according to which it is Léo. Anonymity is an existential threat to an omniscient database, even one that has in the past allowed Joan Fontaine's character in *Rebecca* (1940) to be named merely as 'Mrs de Winter', and Paul McGann's in *Withnail & I* (1987) as '& I'. 'Léo' it is, then, for convenience of reference.

Maritaud's performance is fearless, in the gendered way in which the adjective is used in film reviews – a fearless performance by a woman is one in which she makes a sacrifice of her glamour (Charlize Theron in *Monster*, Nicole Kidman in *Destroyer*), a fearless one by a man is one in which you see him naked, and *Sauvage* is explicit even by the standards of films like Michael Winterbottom's *Nine Songs* (2005) or Andrew Haigh's *Weekend* (2011). Of course explicitness is no guarantee of truthfulness.

Sauvage starts with Léo being given an examination by a doctor – at least that's what seems to be happening until the mask of professional jargon drops, and the 'doctor' (who has really only borrowed a doctor friend's premises to make the role-play more convincing) starts urging his patient to 'squirt it out, kitten' rather than to cough, please, or breathe in and say 'ninety-nine'. It's a funny, disconcerting opening, particularly when Léo voices some real concern about his health after the session – he has a cough, and life on the street is no joke – as if the 'doctor' might actually know something about medicine, despite working in a tax office.

The film makes no concessions to the dignity of the sex workers but is intermittently tender towards Léo's clients. One of them, in a wheelchair, is obviously making the best of very limited opportunities. Another, elderly, wants a little intimacy and someone to talk to about the wife he still misses. Léo offers more than is required of him, though somehow it's clear that this is a spontaneous gesture, not be relied on a second time or confused with virtue, yet also not the cynical action of someone who simply wants to sleep in a comfortable bed for once. The lighting in this scene creates a warm harmony of browns out of the bedhead and the flesh tones of the two very different bodies, though elsewhere it can be pitiless, notably in a scene where Léo is used by a gay couple with brutal matter-of-factness, degraded without even being acknowledged. (In the closing credits of the film they are identified as 'Client Plug' #1 and #2, but IMDb has been spared this sordid detail.)

There's no equivalent of a pimp in these sex workers' lives, though they're capable of turning into a posse of unlikely vigilantes, ready to use violence against a newcomer (Mihal, played by Nicolas Dibla) when he dares to charge less than the going rate for his services. Léo doesn't see the logic of this retaliation, but then he's not primarily driven by economics. Sex is his hobby and his obsession as well as his livelihood. Yet despite all the grim details, the subject of *Sauvage* isn't really sex but life at the social margins, approached in a philosophically tinged way that makes the film seem almost preposterously French. It's not that Léo has somehow slipped through the safety net that society pretends to offer, more that he doesn't recognise the authority, and hardly the existence, of the forces that would label him as marginal.

In the British cinematic tradition of social engagement (Ken Loach its figurehead) the marginalised are a standing reproach to their more fortunate fellow-citizens. Even a highly distinctive venture like Carol Morley's *Dreams of a Life* from 2011, as close to cinema-poem or cinema-essay as dramatised documentary, still rings with the anguish of failed connection. Morley's film broods over the life of Joyce Vincent, whose body was found in her flat two years after she died (of natural causes), surrounded by Christmas presents that had been wrapped but never delivered, next to a television that had never been turned off. Direct debits provided the bureaucratic equivalent of a life-support system – she paid, therefore she was. Vincent had withdrawn from family and friends, to the point where she named her bank manager as her next of kin when hospitalised after an asthma attack. She had somehow not been missed, with friends imagining her enjoying herself somewhere, upwardly mobile beyond their reach. Vincent was played on screen by Zawe Ashton with barely a word of dialogue, not speaking on her behalf but embodying an elusive presence. It's a device of remarkable effectiveness, particularly when Ashton plays Joyce Vincent in her flat watching the television as if from the future, while it relays the testimony of her friends, friends who describe her in utterly incompatible ways, passive, ambitious, manipulative, straightforward. Then she uses the remote to turn them off, knowing her secrets are beyond their reach.

In American culture the figure of the citizen abandoned by the state has much less reproachful force, trumped by the myth of the rugged individualist who owes nothing to anyone, and certainly nothing to any institution. The extreme version of this position is the survivalist's, a refusal to be taken in by any of the soft promises that civilisation makes. In this context the problem is not that 'they' care too little but that they know too much, and the danger isn't slipping through the cracks but being trapped in the coils. Directed by Debra Granik, *Leave No Trace* (2018) offered a variation on this theme with its story of traumatised army veteran Will (Ben Foster) bringing up his 13-year-old daughter Tom (Thomasin McKenzie) off-grid in a public park in Oregon, a municipal Arden, teaching her how to cover her tracks in the most literal sense. On occasional visits to the city the father picks up the medication he's prescribed, which he then sells on for the benefit of addicts.

Nature heals, humanity contaminates, that seems to be Will's attitude, but the film doesn't leave his views uncontested – if anything there's too much balance on offer, which isn't exactly a common critical complaint. The latent oppressiveness of social services never quite manifests itself. Enforced belonging brings benefits to Tom, in the shape of access to education and a peer group, even if for Will the experience of supervision is atrocious in itself. There's a lack of drama, perhaps because the tensions are so easily soluble, with Tom taking her place in society while Will becomes a sort of honorary Bigfoot, a wild creature avoiding being seen but willing to make use of supplies left in its habitat. The way the plot works itself out, so low-key and neat, is especially surprising after the same director's supremely powerful *Winter's Bone* (2010), where the heroine had to choose between two intolerable actions: either she abandoned responsibility for her siblings or she located her father's body and brought back legal proof – an identifiable body part – of his death. The cost of being part of society and of refusing its demands seemed equally ruinous.

Sauvage is extreme in its fascination with a character who scorns any stake in society, but not unprecedented in French cinema. Agnès Varda's 1985 film *Vagabond* followed the last months of Mona, a drifter played by Sandrine Bonnaire. Mona doesn't abide by the social contract even as it might be expressed in its simplest terms – she complains, for instance, to a driver about the absence of a radio after accepting a lift in his truck. She encounters coldness and exploitation, acceptance and even intimacy (to which her response is ungracious). A graduate student turned goatherd offers her a patch of land on which to grow potatoes, after she says that's what she would like, but it turns out she was only telling him what he wanted to hear and can't really be bothered. A Tunisian vineyard worker takes her in over the holidays, but when his Moroccan co-workers come back they object to her presence. His minority national identity weakens his hand. She gripes about being let down, though she herself shows no sign of solidarity or fellow feeling at any point.

Vagabond comes midway through a remarkably long directorial career – *La Pointe Courte* dates from 1956, *Faces Places* from 2017. It's Agnès Varda's most substantial achievement, free of the oddly cutesy formalism that can be her weakness. Though the film seems episodic, it shows signs of careful construction – a sub-theme involves 'canker stain', a parasitic disease of the plane tree, of all things, to demonstrate that rootedness too has its drawbacks. One recurring device is to have the various witnesses to Mona's progress move smoothly from testimony to reflection, addressing the camera directly. There's resentment on display as well as regret, but also a surprising element of envy, of admiration for the integrity of refusal, which acts to distance the film from the secular passion-play it might have become in other hands. *Vagabond* is also an effective oblique portrait of the area around Nîmes, with a high-season population of 90,000 that falls to 3,000 (these are the figures given in the film) when the visitors go home.

Vagabond is a bleak sort of pastoral, a wintry one in which nature is to be endured rather than luxuriated in. It could qualify as a version of the fable of the Ant and the Grasshopper, except that Mona makes such an unlikely grasshopper, dourly wilful rather than spontaneous, definitively at odds with her environment. *Sauvage*, despite its urban setting, is very much a pastoral. Recurrent shots show sunlight filtering through the trees of the woods by which the men tout for trade, with birdsong prominent on the soundtrack. There's a sort of innocence to the way Léo and his fellows watch aircraft taking off and landing, never tiring of the spectacle. Heavy drug use may help.

The heroine of *Vagabond* isn't given much of a history, but she has a full name – she even writes *Mona Bergeron* on a mirror at one point – and a few wisps of education and experience. Left in a car without the radio on, since the owner doesn't trust her enough to leave the key in the ignition, she announces almost cheerfully that she will pass the time reciting English irregular verbs. At one point she refers to having had a secretarial job. That's it, but compared to Léo in *Sauvage* she's as fully substantiated as Leopold Bloom.

Léo has no history of any kind, no family, no revealed memories. He has no possessions and is in no hurry to acquire any. When he and Mihal go home with a client, it turns out that Mihal plans to rob him, and though Léo had no advance warning of the scheme he goes along with it. With the client drugged, they can take anything they want, but Léo selects only an ugly ornament and a stapler. He has nowhere to display the ornament, but at least it fits in a pocket. The apparently mildly deranged choice of the stapler, though, is purposeful – he uses it to carry out primitive repairs on the tears in his jacket. It's as if buying new clothes would require imagining a different version of himself, something that is foreign to him. Mihal offers him a mobile phone, but he doesn't want it. Who would he call? Only Mihal, and they meet when they're working anyway.

One possession he does have is an asthma inhaler, but when Mihal sees him using it he wants to have a go. Léo says that it's to help with his breathing, but the principle that everything exists to furnish immediate sensation is too strong to be resisted. The two men take turns to inhale until the medication is exhausted, and then Léo says, with apparent satisfaction, 'We're breathing well.'

It's obvious that Léo is taking no thought for the future – he's a better temperamental fit for grasshopper status than Varda's Mona. A man in his twenties presumably knows what winter is like for rough sleepers, but he takes no steps to do what straight-identified Ahd does (and recommends), namely finding a nice older man and moving somewhere warm. The narrative difficulty of any film about compulsive behaviour is that the two options for closure, recovery and collapse, are equally unsatisfying. The best decision might be to shift the tone away from a realism that is, to my mind, deceptive in any case. There's a very suave man in *Sauvage*, at the wheel of an expensive car with a sound system that plays nothing but Chopin, who solicits the sex workers every now and then. Léo shows some interest, but is warned never to go with the Pianist. He's into blood and torture. A satisfying finish for the film might be to allow the Pianist to personify Léo's death wish, ending the story with his getting into the car.

It seems likely, though, that the writer-director doesn't see his hero as having such a thing as a death wish. The nice (real) doctor in the film, played by Marie Seux, suggests that he change his style of life, and he responds 'What else would I do?', not despairing at the lack of alternatives but shocked that she can't see the perfect fit between who he is and what he does. It's in this scene that the withholding of the hero's name seems most artificial – medical care may be available in France for someone in his position, but surely a name is required for bureaucratic purposes, if not an address. Even when an attractive man tries to create an intimacy with him, and asks his name, he doesn't say Léo, just

'Call me anything.' What is being denied is the continuity of personality that strings moments together, so as to turn them into a necklace or else a chain, something consequential.

In the scene with the real doctor, 'Léo' gives her a hug when she's examining him at close quarters. She reacts carefully, not breaking the embrace but seeming to assess it, as if it might be some sort of desperate appeal, but that's not how Félix Maritaud plays it. It's just another impulse without a history. Camille Vidal-Naquet certainly seems to think there is something noble about the character's fidelity to impulse, as if all it took to live in the present was erasing the past and the future. But as Michael Frayn put it in *Constructions*, his 1974 book of aphoristic propositions, 'you can't live in the present any more than you can live in the border between Kent and Sussex' – a blast of cold fresh Anglo-Saxon air to disperse the Gauloises fug of dodgy philosophising.

I'm sure it has become obvious by now that I'm interested in the way film music functions, and try to pay real attention to the way it is used from film to film. It's often said about food, and the importance of presentation, that we eat with our eyes. I don't think I've ever heard it said that when it comes to films we watch with our ears, but it's at least as true. A music score can transform an audience's experience of a film, even with a single cue – as when the disastrous borrowing of Elgar's 'Nimrod' turns Christopher Nolan's *Dunkirk* from a remarkable study of men at war into a celebration of plucky old England. Perhaps it was included so as to add some oomph to the film's trailer, but either way it was a disastrous bargain to strike.

Unlike the other elements that can be used to enhance the impact of a film's script and performances, such as camerawork, lighting, set design and costumes, music is already a totality, a self-sufficient aesthetic object – a rival totality, not necessarily willing to accept a subservient role. In 2004 *Granta* let me explore the issue in more general terms than an individual review is likely to allow.

Quiet, Please (2004)

I miss silence in the movies. Not silent movies – the films so called were anything but, since they relied on live music from a piano pit or an orchestra to convey mood, momentum and sound effects. What I miss in films is silence, not only as a neutral medium, or even for its powers of contrast, but for the things from which music is debarred. There are things that only silence can express.

Music in films can be as carefully chosen from sequence to sequence as wines to match the courses of a banquet – or it can be sloshed about as casually as syrup or custard over institutional pudding. Film music can be stained glass or wallpaper. The classic directors in the past who are most associated with appreciating the power of music also had a complementary understanding of silence. Music best retains its power by being rationed.

When music is everywhere in a film, audiences feel less rather than more. A case in point would be a mildly successful, mildly fizzling blockbuster from 2000, *The Perfect Storm* (directed by Wolfgang *'Das Boot'* Petersen), a story of fishermen's ordeals in extreme conditions at sea. It's sometimes hard to hear the roaring of the winds over the lachrymose raging of the orchestra. The composer is James Horner, whose most famous score was also for a marine disaster – but at least *Titanic*, in James Cameron's vision, was a romance (a romance with 1,517 real deaths used as the backdrop for a single fictional one, but a romance all the same). *The Perfect Storm* is based on a true story and aspires to tragedy, but Horner's score in its lushness and sweep is jarringly wrong. Petersen doesn't even have the excuse that the music is there to hide the weakness of the special effects – the special effects are the most impressive parts of the film. So why have music there at all? The presence of music on a soundtrack always tells us we're at a distance from the natural world (which is why music accompanying wildlife documentaries feels so tacky and suspect). Every dollar spent on the music neutralizes a thousand spent on the visual effects, the digitized mountains of water which would be awe-inspiring if they were only let alone.

The omnipresence of music in films is part of a general cultural pattern of obliterating silence, in lifts, airports, shopping centres, lobbies and restaurants. For film-makers there is the additional temptation to fill a soundtrack with pop classics and sell the film that way – but that hardly applies to a piece of product like *The Perfect Storm*. Hollywood always assumes that the young are the prime market for almost every film, which becomes true when films rival music television in the relentlessness of hit placement. Despite regular waves of prediction, film as an art form has survived the onslaught of television and even MTV. Demographically it would be sensible (more sensible every year) to chase a senior market, for whom saturation with music becomes a deterrent. Older people may have a degree of hearing loss that is hardly noticeable in daily life but makes it hard to extract film dialogue from its inanely seething background.

When music is a constant feature of a film, the director forfeits the possibility that a moment of music will provide a pivot around which the whole film swings in a new direction. For his 1956 film *A Man Escaped*, for instance, Robert Bresson keeps music reined in, concentrating instead on patterns of significant sound inside the prison where the hero is confined – tappings on the walls, a spoon being scraped into sharpness on a stone floor, the gamelan-jangle of keys against metal railings. Roughly every ten minutes Bresson gives us the same sombre burst of a Mozart *Mass*, always when the hero is mixing with others in the confines of the prison. There is some talk about God among the inmates, but still the music in its organised sorrow is pitched far higher, spiritually, than the action can justify. Those few sombrely blazing bars of orchestra and chorus are more than enough to furnish the soundtrack, since when they aren't being played they are likely to be replayed in the audience's memory. Then when his hero escapes, Bresson lets loose with Mozart in the major. The blaze of organised joy at this point shifts the plane of the story from physical release to transfiguration. Bresson has made us wait ninety minutes to experience one of the simplest effects in classical music, the move from minor to major, as if we had never heard it before, and the music at this point tells us that we are witnessing not good fortune but grace.

The word 'dialectic' was quite properly pensioned off years ago, after decades of overuse, but perhaps it could be brought out of retirement to convey the way silence and music can act on each other as elements of the aural design of a film. Bresson is inescapably a director of 'art films', but much more limited craftsmen in film can achieve modestly overwhelming results. Michael Anderson, for instance, who directed *The Dam Busters* in 1954, is no one's idea of an auteur, but his use of music is highly sophisticated. Eric Coates's 'The Dam Busters March' is a classic of film music but it isn't played to death in the film, and the incidental score is carefully modulated. Passages of tension usually rely on natural sound and dialogue, with music being reserved for moments of release. Then at the end of the film the camera shows, in silence, the rooms of men who didn't come back from the raid on the Ruhr. As an account of a dazzling wartime exploit, the apotheosis of boffinry, *The Dam*

Busters isn't above a certain amount of tub-thumping, but the director also knows that there are moments when it's the silent tub that makes the most noise.

Silence in this short sequence performs the function that the Mozart *Mass* does for Bresson – it takes the film into new territory. The camera doesn't stand in for a person, Barnes Wallis (Michael Redgrave) say, or Guy Gibson (Richard Todd), though that too would be a legitimate sequence – the victors should acknowledge the cost of their triumph to others. What is being registered here is absence. The approach is impersonal, almost documentary, though there's little enough to document in the bare quarters of these servicemen: just a travelling clock ticking on, outliving the man whose wrist-turns wound its spring. Music is absent also. Music is the sign that something has become part of culture, whereas this little sequence documents bare absence before it can be tamed into grief. Music takes the edge off, and here we need to feel the edge. The *Dam Busters* Silence deserves to be as well-known as 'The Dam Busters March'.

There are several current directors who could have imagined the visual side of the sequence, Steven Spielberg among them, but none of them would have dared to abstain from the stock musical cues for feeling. Spielberg took over from Stanley Kubrick a typically slow-brewing project, only partly prepared when he died – *AI*. If Kubrick had made it, the music score would certainly have been less saccharine. Kubrick enjoyed using pre-existing pieces of music (at least once cancelling a commissioned score during editing), and used them in longer extracts than has ever been the fashion. Whether it's Bartók's *Music for Strings, Percussion and Celesta* in *The Shining* or Ligeti's *Musica Ricercata* in *Eyes Wide Shut*, Kubrick used substantial stretches. It's as if he set himself the challenge of absorbing the energy of the music into his visuals without cheating by chopping it up.

During the editing of *2001*, Kubrick received an advance pressing of a record by the Berlin Philharmonic from his friend Herbert von Karajan. It included music by both Johann (*Blue Danube*) and Richard (*Also sprach Zarathustra*) Strauss. He started playing it in the editing suite with no thought – to start with – of its bizarre appropriateness. If this story is true, then it seems that music was an area where the great control freak could allow himself to be seduced into spontaneity. After excluding chance so single-mindedly from his project Kubrick could let it back in at the last moment, and even enjoy playing with it.

2001 is remarkable for Kubrick's use of the present that Karajan sent. Johann Strauss's magnificently insipid waltz loses all its sentiment when it's made to accompany a sequence of docking with a space station. Richard Strauss's grand gestures seem quite modest, really, when configured as a fanfare to eternity. But the film is also remarkable for its fidelity to silence. For once in the movies, engines roaring in a vacuum make no sound. Infinity isn't given an echo just because we're more comfortable with that illusion. Music and silence, bland actors and overwhelming sets – everything contributes to Kubrick's vision of a cosmos full of grandeur and devoid of personality, full of emptiness and waiting. A dozen years later, the advertising campaign for *Alien* warned that 'In space no one can hear you scream'. But every engine-note and explosion in the film was helpfully relayed to the audience's ears through a conducting medium that didn't exist.

Sometimes music can enter a film even later than it did in the case of *2001*. It can happen that a commissioned score fails to find favour, and must be replaced at the last minute or even later. Music shares this never-too-late property with another element of film language, the voice-over, but voice-overs are inherently suspect. They've been used so often as sticking-plasters for a bleeding narrative that their very presence makes critics narrow their eyes. It's the cheapest way to cover up defects that can't be remedied, orange pancake make-up in spoken form.

Music doesn't give the game away like that. No one watching Alfred Hitchcock's *Torn Curtain* on its first release in 1966 could have known from internal evidence that the original score was composed by Bernard Herrmann, before John Addison was called in. Hitchcock had a profound understanding of the possibilities of sound design in films, and could boast at least two technical firsts – first British sound film for *Blackmail* (1929), where the soundtrack is as inventively expressionistic as the visuals, and first electronic score, with *The Birds* (1963). His partnership with Herrmann is one of the great pairings in cinema history, up there with Greenaway and Nyman, Lynch and Badalamenti. The high point of their collaboration was certainly *Vertigo*, but Herrmann had a credit (as 'sound consultant') even on *The Birds*, where there isn't anything that could really be described as music.

There was no obvious reason why *Torn Curtain* should have led to rupture, though Hitchcock did have a complex attitude to artistic sharing, and a certain amount of history in terms of driving his most talented collaborators away (such as the brilliant screenwriter on *North by Northwest*, Ernest Lehman). It's true that Herrmann's music for the new film (which you can hear on the DVD) was dark and ominous, and Hitchcock was under pressure from Universal to come up with something more varied and entertaining. But the question of the relative power of music and silence is in there somewhere too.

The most famous scene in *Torn Curtain* – really the only sequence which is even grudgingly admired – is where the hero kills the agent who has been detailed to keep an eye on him in a farmhouse. The killing is slow, ugly and desperately hard work. Other Iron Curtain agents are only a few yards away, so there can be no question of using a gun – it's all down to saucepans, kitchen knives, spades and finally the (gas) oven.

Bernard Herrmann wrote music for the scene. If there is one 'cue' he is famous for, it's the screeching violins that accompany the shower-bath murder in *Psycho*. He had come up with an extreme score before, so why not now? Hitchcock didn't use it, not because it failed as music, but because it was music. The scene as released plays in silence (the characters, after all, are desperate not to be heard at their grisly work). Hitchcock understood that music, even when it seems inflammatory of the emotions, is actually a lubricant. Certainly the scene is much harder to watch without the orchestral score. Hitchcock and Herrmann never worked together again.

That's the myth, even if it doesn't quite add up. After all, if Hitchcock was so adamant that the farmhouse killing should be shown without music, why did he get Herrmann's replacement John Addison to score it all over again, before he finally decided? But it's a necessary myth, now that music has so largely vanquished silence.

Still, there are tiny signs of a silent backlash, and not just in art movies like Gus Van Sant's *Elephant*, where music and silence, speech and ambient noise were woven with astonishing subtlety into an aural design. For me, much of the tension of watching Peter Weir's splendid *Master and Commander* came from waiting, as a master film-maker set his story in motion, with dialogue, sound, set design and special effects all making their mark, for the moment when he remembered to underestimate his audience, and dropped in some of the sea music that has been a celluloid plague at least since Erich Wolfgang Korngold wrote the score for *The Sea Hawk* in 1940. It didn't happen. When music was eventually used it was familiar (Vaughan Williams) or more or less in period (the fiddle and cello duets between Russell Crowe and Paul Bettany). But the first forty minutes played without music. These days we have to be grateful when at least one mainstream director trusts the visual and dramatic language of film to stay afloat, without an orchestra below deck constantly pumping out bilge. Silence and music have coexisted in films in a thousand different ways in the past, and music is the loser when silence dies.

These aren't new objections to crass film music. Among directors Michelangelo Antonioni was unusually categorical in his objections:

> in certain films from Hollywood, a battle scene is accompanied with violent symphonic crescendos from a full orchestra; a sad scene is always accompanied with violin music because it is felt that violins create an atmosphere of sadness. But this seems to me to be a completely wrong way to use music, and has nothing to do with cinematography . . . I am personally very reluctant to use music in my films, for the simple reason that I prefer to work in a dry manner, to say things with the least means possible. And music is an additional means. I have too much faith in the efficacy, the value, the force, the suggestiveness of the image to believe that the image cannot do without music.

Most directors would take less hard a line, and this is an area (like any other) where there are rich choices available as well as impoverished ones.

Even the simplest methods of marrying sound and image – overlaying a celebrated existing piece of music onto your footage, hoping for a transfer of qualities the classic score is agreed to possess – isn't a predictable business. Just plonking a famous tune on top of a big scene can be an act of daring, as witness that weirdly frictionless collision in *2001* between a nineteenth-century Viennese dance form, topped with whipped cream, and a hi-tech rendezvous in space.

Most such splicings of music and image are cruder, closer to shotgun weddings than love matches. Take the history of Samuel Barber's *Adagio for Strings*, first in the concert hall and then as a part of a broader culture of emotion and finally on screen, endorsing a range of images and genres with hardly any overlap. The *Adagio* is a part which has become a whole – that is, it was the slow movement of a string quartet (composed in 1936) that was later arranged for larger forces and now stands alone. The other movements have receded, leaving the adagio as both orphan and sole inheritor. Being arranged for larger forces increases the impact of the piece without adulterating its anguished eloquence. This new whole, though, comes to represent something that is only wholeness in a certain sense – loss, and a reluctant dealing with loss. Toscanini performed the piece in America (North and South) and in Europe, the performances being both recorded and widely broadcast.

The piece's association with bereavement, and national mourning, was slow but steady. The *Adagio* was played on the radio to accompany the announcement of FDR's death in 1945, played at Einstein's funeral in 1955. A radio transmission accompanied the announcement of President Kennedy's death, giving the piece a further lurch of shock and sorrow. The association was made more personal when his widow Jackie (who claimed it as one of his favourite pieces of music) staged a performance of the piece the next Monday, played by the National Symphony Orchestra, which was broadcast though performed in an empty hall, a brilliantly stage-managed projection of private feeling. Barber himself grumbled a little about the popularity of this one piece, wishing the vogue extended to the rest of his output, though many composers (Rachmaninoff, Sinding) have suffered more from the fetishisation of a single early piece, and it didn't stop Barber from arranging the *Adagio* for chorus in 1967, using the words of the *Agnus Dei*, not a sensible move for someone who wanted to scrape off the work's accretion of a sacramental aura.

Full consecration of the piece in popular culture came later, with the release of David Lynch's *The Elephant Man* (1980) and Oliver Stone's *Platoon* (1986), two caricaturally different films that both use the *Adagio* in their closing stages. This music, with its slow melody winding upwards, both faltering and unstoppable, its acknowledgement of pain that moves to the edge of despair and then finds a way back without a break in its continuity, must be the only point of contact between Lynch's tenderly estranged vision of ugliness, physical and moral, and Stone's loud, righteous war movie with its unsubtle conflicts between good and bad father figure. But though the music's associations are complex, in both of these films it is actually being used in a simple way, the piece's emotional history poured over the footage in the form of a syrup conferring transcendent value.

Supposedly Oliver Stone used Barber's *Adagio* as the 'temp track' while editing his film, just as Stanley Kubrick had used Karajan's new long player for his while working on *2001*. The difference was in the subsequent decision: Kubrick shelved the score Alex North had already written in favour of the two Strauss cues – two Strausses as well as two cues – while Stone just wanted his designated composer, Georges Delerue, to turn out pastiche Barber. Not a flattering assignment for a composer who had worked with Truffaut (many times over), Resnais and Godard, but he did as he was asked. Then Stone rejected much of the material, and used the passages that were closest to the *Adagio* – at one point in the film, Willem Dafoe's character seems committed to going on dying, perforated with gunfire, for the whole length of the cue, though in the end it's too much for his powers of endurance. But Stone also used the *Adagio* itself, just as he tried to summon up its ghost for the soundtrack of *JFK*, with John Williams as his medium. It's as if this was the Ur-cue for Oliver Stone, the most intense possible distillation in sound of the contradictory emotions he feels, not a thing that could be outdone or superseded.

A famous cue doesn't need to be used as an endorsement of what is on screen – it can be set at an angle to the action, in a way that implies a critique that can even be mutual. Terrence Malick in particular seems to enjoy setting a stereotypically European piece of classical music against a visual image that screams Americana – a *Gymnopédie* by Satie in *Badlands*, perhaps, or the siciliano piano concerto movement (from Mozart's number 23) for *The New World*. Dynamics can also be fruitfully manipulated: in *The New World* the music was mixed far down in the soundtrack, outranked by the noises of nature, not controlling the mood but subordinated to it. It advertised its own irrelevance to this unforeseen continent, while helplessly bearing witness to another notion of order.

The primary music cue in Lars von Trier's 2011 *Melancholia* is at last as famous as Barber's *Adagio* – the prelude to *Tristan und Isolde* – though he uses it more strategically. *Tristan* is itself both a beginning and an ending, the foundation stone of modern music according to Debussy, but also a drama that pushes towards extinction. The first time von Trier uses the prelude the effect of disproportion is almost comic – this infinitely extended moment, saturated in morbid longing, being used to accompany the doings of a spoiled family.

There are other pieces of music on the soundtrack, mainly middle-of-the-road ballads, undemanding wedding-reception fare (Charles Aznavour's 'She', 'Strangers in the Night', 'Fly Me To The Moon'), but the *Tristan* prelude keeps coming back. Perhaps Lars von Trier is an admirer of Bresson's *A Man Escaped*

– he certainly plays the same trick of leaving plenty of silence in the film, plenty of air in which that overcharged music can resonate, so that its return seems predestined, a cued response to sounds that were already playing out in the viewer's head. The subject of *Melancholia* turns out to be the end of the world, no less, though the apocalypse is approached with some subtlety, and there's a striking shift of point of view, halfway through the film, between the sisters played by Kirsten Dunst and Charlotte Gainsbourg. Each time the *Tristan* music comes back it becomes less jarring, and by the end of the film it seems as obviously right as it had originally seemed wrong. The visual and musical rhetoric are perhaps not functioning as a unit but are certainly of equal weight. They seem to belong together, like the *Blue Danube* in 2001 exchanging particles of sprightly grandeur with the waltzing manoeuvres of the Pan Am spaceplane that docks with Space Station V.

One of the consequences of having written film reviews for over a third of a century is that my timeline as a critic coincides with the heydays of particular directors in a way that creates an odd feeling of affinity. There's a sensation, illusory but having a certain power, of being directly addressed, squarely part of the target audience. It comes down to a sense that a director's next film might achieve some sort of absolute quality, hit a cosmic bull's-eye, however childish the idea might be. The resurgence of a banal masterpiece-ism, the list-making, pantheon-filling hyperbolising that flattens out any actual response to individual works made by an individual. Technically my adult film-going years overlap with a number of veteran practitioners – Hitchcock was still making films in the 1970s. A meticulous review of *Frenzy* was lurking as part of a consignment (even a sort of care package)

of back numbers of *Sight and Sound* that my parents brought out with them when they paid a visit to me in Perugia, and there was still *Family Plot* to come, with its flickers of mastery. But Hitchcock's work was already an infinitely rich archive to be explored rather than a bulletin from the present.

I feel connected to those directors who got their start or established their distinctiveness in the 1970s and '80s, not because of any overlap of subject-matter (there's usually none) but because the present tense of their development was something I happened to share. It's the difference between assessing (for example) Schubert's development almost two centuries after the fact and hearing a new Beatles song as a teenager – *Hello Goodbye*, say, or *Lady Madonna* – and registering viscerally the shift in your understanding of what pop singles, or Lennon and McCartney, were capable of. These directors aren't necessarily my contemporaries in any real sense, not sharers of any particular or even general experience, since the oldest was Robert Altman, born in 1925, closer to my parents' age than mine – and Nicolas Roeg, born in 1928, falls into the same category. Each director's breakthrough film, as it happens, either passed me by or left me cold. I disliked the phony rebelliousness of the lead characters in Altman's MASH, with 1960s attitudes projected onto the 1950s as if they were actually universal, and a definite meanness in the portrayal of women. Roeg's *Performance* (co-directed with Donald Cammell) came pre-encrusted with devotees and exegetes. Its intellectualised low-lifery didn't particularly appeal to me. But with *McCabe and Mrs Miller* and *The Long Goodbye* I was hooked on Altman, and though I had reservations about *Walkabout* I found *Don't Look Now* overwhelming. *The Man Who Fell to Earth* was more baffling, though I didn't grudge the time and expense of seeing it again. It was worth a little effort to consolidate my bafflement.

I wasn't the only family member to be enthusiastic about Roeg. My brothers were equally keen to catch his next film, *Bad Timing*, as soon as we could. In fact, the three of us travelled by Land Rover against the clock from Ruabon to Liverpool to catch an evening showing, somehow finding a parking place and reaching the cinema with seconds to spare. This was a high point of our film-going in terms of adventurousness – cinema attendance almost as an extreme sport. We were disappointed by the film, deflated, even feeling obscurely betrayed by badly judged performances and an uninvolving story. Did we mutter, 'Bad timing? More like bad taste and bad faith'? Not in so many words.

It certainly seemed as if Roeg, casting a pop star in a film for the third time – Art Garfunkel was the star of *Bad Timing*, following in the footsteps of Jagger (*Performance*) and Bowie (*The Man Who Fell to Earth*) – had badly miscalculated, even though Garfunkel was more experienced as a screen actor than his predecessors had been when Roeg had cast them (Jagger filmed *Ned Kelly* after *Performance*, whose release was delayed). He had held his own on screen against Jack Nicholson in *Carnal Knowledge*. Still, on screen for Roeg, Jagger had been ambiguous and Bowie ethereal, while Garfunkel was just not very present. Turner in *Performance* and Thomas Jerome Newton in *The Man Who Fell to Earth* were roles that had been tailored to their respective performers, approximating to personas that were already well established, but if Garfunkel even had a persona he hadn't been told about it. Sensitive student of literature, perhaps, but hardly psychology professor, the part he was called on to play as Alex Linden in *Bad Timing*. Harvey Keitel, cast as a Viennese policeman in the film (Inspector Netusil, no less), wouldn't have been much more natural casting as the psychology professor, but he would have been more at home than Garfunkel with the other side of Linden's character, the obsessed lover.

Bad Timing wasn't quite the act of self-harm that *Peeping Tom* was in Michael Powell's career (Roeg has gone on to make many more, widely distributed films), but it has some uncomfortable things in common with the earlier *film maudit*. Powell seemed not to notice that *Peeping Tom* was a horror film – one in which a psychopath stabbed women with a sharpened strut attached to the tripod of his movie camera, and filmed their agonies as they died – so taken was he by the metaphorical element in the screenplay, the idea of the artist doomed to kill reality in the act of recording it. Roeg for his part seemed not to notice the repellence of *Bad Timing*'s screenplay, in which Alex, finding his lover's unconscious body after an overdose, has sex with it (you can't really say 'her', since Theresa Russell's Milena, being unconscious, is by definition absent) before calling an ambulance. What can it have been, the metaphor that blinded Roeg in this case? Hard to say. He certainly seems to have convinced himself that his actors, far from floundering, trapped in a squalid psychodrama, were baring their souls as they explored the outer limits of behaviour, revealing in the process profound truths about (what else?) the human condition.

Above all Roeg's editing, which had once been so elegant and suggestive, now seemed not far from crassly confrontational, juxtaposing for instance Theresa Russell's body convulsing in orgasm with the same body subjected to defibrillation after a suicide attempt. The montages that began and ended *Don't Look Now* had been saturated with significance, bringing any number of charged patterns into play. The plot was fatalistic but the director's freedom to edit, staying barely within the confines of the thriller genre was intoxicating, able to offer a rich compensation in texture. Now exploration had been replaced with something calculated and even coldly gimmicky. If the storyline of *Bad Timing* had been less tawdry, Garfunkel might have made something of the part – though (looking at it the other way round) if the lead character had been played with more conviction the result would have been even more unsavoury. After that Nicolas Roeg's aura dissipated, at least as far as I was concerned (my brothers likely concurring), and he was just a film-maker who did more or less good work from project to project. He was no longer someone who could transform his medium as he went along.

The Draughtsman's Contract was another film that made a huge impact on me, though not an emotional one, emotion not being part of the territory it staked out. It wasn't just an extra-ordinary film but one that seemed to strike out confidently in a number of new directions. I didn't review the film on first release but interviewed the director, whose avoidance of eye contact and lack of small talk made him hard going. He spoke at length about a suitcase left in a locker by a fictional figure called Tulse Luper. The director seemed much smaller than his film, and though this is exactly the way art is supposed to work it wasn't convenient when I had a deadline to meet and an obligation to deliver insights that passed muster.

The absence of human interest in his next film, *A Zed & Two Noughts*, was close to shocking, and set a pattern. Greenaway's compulsion to stylise every element in his work cast less of a spell in a modern setting, seeming less like a vision than a refusal of vitality. I was disillusioned, though it had probably been a case of mistaken identity in the first place. The Peter Greenaway I fell in love with wasn't the director that Greenaway himself wanted to be.

Prospero's Books (1991)

Who is the great British film-maker? Peter Greenaway, alas. Why Peter Greenaway? Because every frame of his films is fraught with imaginative learning. No director has ever spread out so glittering a treasure of images. Every sequence is an adventure in aesthetics and a whispering gallery of art references. Wherever the eye moves in these astonishing compositions, it has been anticipated, is both teased and rewarded. Compared to Greenaway, his rivals seem to be finger-painting.

Why 'alas'? Because Greenaway's visual obsessiveness, so triumphantly un-English, can seem like a more flamboyant mask for the same English blankness and fear of feeling; because he treats his actors as set-dressing with lines to speak – Greenaway would as soon expect to find truth in topiary as in an actor's performance. And after a while, the lack of psychological space for the viewer to occupy crowds out the fierce pleasures of looking.

The screenplays of Greenaway's previous feature films, all rather hermetic, have been written by him. Now with *Prospero's Books* he has based a film on an existing text – *The Tempest* – but the result is not so much a collaboration as a meticulous cancellation of Shakespeare's imaginative world. Shakespeare doesn't turn Greenaway into a humanist; Greenaway turns Shakespeare into a cold manipulator of images.

The books of the title are referred to in the play but not described (the faithful Gonzalo selects them from Prospero's library in Milan to sweeten the overthrown duke's exile). Greenaway lists them rather in the manner of Borges, and visualises representative pages with the help of a new piece of computer technology, the Graphic Paintbox. The books – Greenaway imagines 24 – form a little *summum* of Renaissance learning, but are also paradoxical or impossible objects: *A Book of Motion*, for instance, or so we are told, drums against the bookshelf and must be held down with a brass weight.

The listing of the books sometimes complements, more often interrupts, the unfolding of the drama. Even when Greenaway illustrates events referred to in *The Tempest*, he can twist them out of shape. The Neapolitan court shipwrecked on Prospero's island is returning from the wedding of Claribel to the King of Tunis. Greenaway shows Claribel after the wedding night, as if in a genre painting of the seraglio, but bleeding from the groin: a woman not so much married as raped. Could anything be more out of place, in a play that contains courtship but no consummation? To show Claribel at all is to sacrifice the starkness of Miranda's position as the sole representative of her gender.

More important than Greenaway's additions and distortions are his subtractions. No comedy survives in this version of the play. His chosen style, pursued unwaveringly through his career, sets itself against the mechanics of audience identification. The tracking shots that are his trademark, moving parallel to the scene rather than advancing into it, 'minimises', as he puts it in his introduction to the published screenplay, 'the camera becoming a subjective eye'.

This makes sense only for a moment. The camera can't be anything but an eye, and an eye can't be anything but subjective. What would an objective eye be like? Certainly not like Greenaway's camera, smoothly rolling on rails past vistas gorgeously prepared for it. Greenaway's cinema is as subjective as anyone else's, but weakly subjective, making no attempt to involve the viewer in its vision. He is rightly contemptuous of film-making that foists second-rate emotions on audiences that wearily play along, wrong to think he has come up with a solution by digging a trench of style between his imagination and its audience.

How is it that 120 minutes spent in the company of pictorial genius at full stretch can also be two hours of awed indifference? The viewer of a Greenaway film is both glutted and starved, glutted with visual glory and starved of something as simple as feeling displayed on a face. Just as Greenaway's favoured literary form is the list, his favourite unit of composition is the tableau.

A tableau in movement becomes a procession, and *Prospero's Books* is full of them. The viewer scans these majestic march-pasts in something like desperation, looking not for a wink or a smirk but for some evidence of a world that behaves organically, that interacts with itself. What becomes of the theme of sundering and reconciliation (none more basic to *The Tempest*) when the audience is scrupulously estranged throughout from what it sees?

The Tempest, like a number of Shakespeare's plays, ends with a masque in which the themes of the drama are turned into ritual, recapitulated as allegory. The complaint against *Prospero's Books* is not exactly that it is all Greenaway and no Shakespeare, but that it is all masque and no play.

Derek Jarman's *Tempest* of ten years ago, for all its quirks, caught much of the Shakespearean spirit. You could watch *Prospero's Books* over and over again, and never learn the basic human truths about the characters – Ariel is bored, Miranda is lonely and doesn't know it, Prospero is lonely and knows it all too well.

John Gielgud, wearing a stunning embroidered cloak and a Doge's hat out of a Bellini painting, gives an exemplary performance as Prospero, but one that Greenaway constantly intercepts with distractions and embellishments. A line like 'this thing of darkness I acknowledge mine', or the half-line after Miranda's exclamation at a brave new world – ''tis new to thee' – count for nothing, however well delivered, if they don't have room to breathe. Gielgud's performance, for all its wintry force, remains a snowstorm under glass.

Even if Greenaway went in for identification as a general thing, he wouldn't have much in common, surrounded by his aesthetic technologies, with a marooned duke. Greenaway narrows the gap, not by imagining Prospero's isolation, but by neutralising it, furnishing him with an ideal city and a huge retinue. (Peter Greenaway's other literary adaptation, *A TV*

Dante, works much better than this one, perhaps because his mental habits come closer to late-medieval pattern-making than Renaissance humanism.)

Prospero in the film voices all the characters up to the point where they are released from enchantment – a bright idea that further dims the actors' expressiveness. Ariel is played by four performers of different ages and sexes, a brilliant stroke that makes his particular loneliness altogether unreal (he could play tennis doubles with himself, or a rubber of bridge). Caliban is played by Michael Clark, who wears his usual uniform of corset and red-painted penis. Only close personal friends have seen him in trousers. This is a daring piece of casting, since Clark looks like a naughty Ariel, but would need work before it became an interpretation.

One of the oddities of *Prospero's Books* is a credit for 'Actors' Coach'. There used to be a word for someone who worked with cast members, helping them to shape their performances. The word was *director*.

The re-release of *The Draughtsman's Contract* in 1994 gave me a chance to explore my ambivalence more fully, going beyond the reluctant dismissal that was becoming my pained response to Greenaway's films as they appeared.

The Draughtsman's Contract (1982, re-released 1994)

The Draughtsman's Contract proclaimed the arrival of Peter Greenaway with a blast on the Baroque trumpet. Few directors can have contrived so piercing an annunciation of their talent. Twelve years on, what is striking about the film is not the presence of Greenaway's trademarks – mannerist beauty, emotional aloofness, love of lists and puzzles, Nyman pulsations on the soundtrack – but the persistence of elements eliminated from later Greenaway, and much missed. *The Draughtsman's Contract* is a formal garden less strict than memory makes it. Even the palette of black and white and green allows for modulation – from the green of August grass, for instance, through green apples, to the duckweed of stagnation, and the pewter-green of encrusted statuary. Growth-greens are shadowed by greens of decay.

At this stage of his career, Greenaway's skill as an extinguisher of acting talent had yet to manifest itself. Anthony Higgins's exasperated reaction to a film of which he had supposed himself the star is well-known, but the director's world was still one where wigs and their wearers, strict compositions and nuanced performances could peacefully co-exist. The human furniture of the fable still had some attention lavished on it. There was no real sign of the Greenaway who could squash Bernard Hill flat on the screen (*Drowning by Numbers*), or draw from Chloe Webb, who had just given one of the best performances of the decade, in *Sid and Nancy,* and one of the worst (in *The Belly of an Architect*).

Hitchcock notoriously compared actors to cattle, but at least he wanted living, breathing cattle, while later Greenaway seemed to prefer holograms. Even Gielgud's performance in *Prospero's Books* was less a contribution to the film than the pretext for it. Yet, watching *The Draughtsman's Contract*, you could almost feel that Greenaway valued what his performers were doing. When Mr and Mrs Talmann (Hugh Fraser and Anne-Louise Lambert) have a bitter marital squabble, it comes across as a bitter marital squabble. There are no allusions to art history, compulsive allegories or counting games for minutes on end.

The cast of *The Draughtsman's Contract* had two great advantages over their successors. First, they were in period costume

– and if there is one thing that we in this country do better than anyone in the world, it's walking around with a wig block or a monogrammed chamber pot as if we'd done it every day of our lives. The actors used their costume-drama instincts to produce the right impression of mannered ease. The way Higgins throws his hat aside and flicks apart his coat-skirts while sitting down reminds us that we're not in the present, without being preciously alien.

There is just enough social texture in the script to justify this approach. When Mr Neville (Higgins) calls out to his servant not to trot, it is because, whatever else he is doing, he is trying to make an impression. When Mrs Herbert (Janet Suzman) kisses a child goodnight, it is his hand she kisses, since childhood has not yet been fully invented. When she burns her hand on the heating block beneath the teapot, she flinches but suppresses the reaction, since, whatever else is in her mind, she is also a hostess, with a hostess's obligations.

Greenaway's cabalistic obsessions were there in the script, but not yet dominant. They were like the tics of a sufferer from Tourette's Syndrome not yet diagnosed, and still socially functional. The actors are likely to have noticed the script's insistent listing of fruit (apples, pears and oranges have been mentioned even before the credits are over), but inventories had not yet supplanted human narrative as ways of structuring a film.

For someone who will be remembered for his images, Greenaway is an unrelentingly verbal director. But, in *The Draughtsman's Contract*, Greenaway's wordiness masquerades successfully as period speech, and the tendency of all his speakers to sound the same does no damage. The best moments, in a script larded with wit and artificially brilliant observation, are actually those when rhetoric implodes: when Mr Talmann is so elaborately insulted that he can only say, 'What?', or when

Neville, finally realising that he has overplayed his hand, says merely, 'Ah.' What? Ah. If only Peter Greenaway had remembered how to write speeches like that.

It may be that Greenaway wanted to stylise the grounds of the Herberts' house, as much as Alain Resnais stylised the grounds of the hotel for *Last Year at Marienbad*. If so, a tight shooting schedule and English weather conspired to thwart him, and nature is still a presence in the film. In one scene there is a mist of voluptuous thickness, though the sun is high in the sky and, in one outdoor conversation in particular, the level of light fluctuates wildly. The sun refuses to be enlisted as a source of mannered light.

The Draughtsman's Contract has an undeserved reputation as an incomprehensible film, when it is really only an insoluble puzzle. In any case, the first half of the film is lucid enough, because the audience is likely to see things from the point of view of the outsider, the draughtsman, to whom the world that he deals with is necessarily mysterious. The screenplay only takes a perverse turn when Neville's contract is over and he leaves the house. He has another commission elsewhere, but the film doesn't follow him. The audience has to relinquish its tentative identification with him, without being any more in the know than before. When Neville reappears, he is already chastened and vulnerable, as if knowing that the centre of gravity of the film has moved ominously away from him.

The curious construction of the story could almost be an allegory of Greenaway's artistic development. He casts himself first as the artistic outsider, trying to break into the circles of power with only flair and charm to help him. But his high estimate of himself won't allow Greenaway to dramatise his situation this way for long. Soon he sides with the powerful rather than the conspired-against, with an elite against a parvenu. Before our eyes he metamorphoses from apprentice, hungry for appreciation, to mandarin, disdainful of acclaim (the Greenaway we know). *The Draughtsman's Contract* is Peter Greenaway's masterpiece, because he was still learning while he made it, and when he had nothing more to learn about the process, his product lost a vital dimension.

A 'masterpiece' used to signify not a high point in an artist's career but the end of a craftsman's apprenticeship, refer-ring to the object accepted by the guild when it granted him membership (the Royal Academy continues this practice, though the term 'diploma work' is used). Perhaps I should pre-tend that I knew that when I wrote that last paragraph. If Peter Greenaway's output of films showed a narrowing of the aesthetic arteries, a progressive enclosure in self, another film-maker who built a reputation in the 1980s somehow learned to step outside the constriction that had originally seemed inseparable from his talent. When I reviewed Terence Davies's *Distant Voices, Still Lives* it seemed only fair to emphasise what was absent from the film, the things it didn't do as well as the things it did.

Distant Voices, Still Lives (1988)

There are two main reasons for recreating the personal past in a work of art, one of them respectable: to understand it and so be free of its power. The other reason is to retreat into it, and so become a curator of memories. The British film-maker Terence Davies, though, somehow manages to combine both approaches. He shows all the signs of loving the past – in his case, working-class Liverpool of the 1950s – without being able at all to recommend it.

Distant Voices, Still Lives, Davies's new film, is an extra-ordinary and even a wonderful piece of work, but its potential audience deserves to be told what to expect, and what not. This is a family saga with its narrative present only in fragments, or removed altogether. The effect, combined with Davies's scrupulous technique and fetishistic attention to period detail, is a strange magnification of the people and their emotions.

Posing for photographs on special occasions, the Davies family (so called in the film, though there is no actual stand-in for Terence) brace themselves against the camera. The film shows weddings and funerals, but the attendant emotions are not as different as they might be. With the death of Dad (Pete Postlethwaite) his wife and children are at least free of physical fear, while wedding days seem to provoke despairing tears, not in those who traditionally weep at weddings but in the people actually being joined.

Marriage in *Distant Voices, Still Lives* is not seen as a breaking free, much less as a physical union (the film is curiously innocent of sexual tension) but as a dwindling of possibility like the menopause, a change that cannot be put off for ever. These are, if anything, the emotions of a mother losing a child to another household, though also plausible in an invisible little brother of the bride or groom (Terence is the youngest of seven children), who cannot appreciate the advantages – or even the reality – of leaving home.

The father of the family is seen with an eye unblurred by hindsight, the edges of his brutality not sharpened by adult attempts at understanding. During an air raid in the Second World War (in what must be a family story rather than an actual memory of the director, born in 1945) Dad slaps his eldest daughter's face when the children arrive late in the shelter, and then tells her to sing. The phenomenon of male love and fear finding expression only in anger is not an uncommon one, but Davies is interested in its impact, not its psychology. He cuts between incidents so as to emphasise discontinuities of behaviour – Dad hanging up Christmas stockings and murmuring, 'God bless, kids,' Dad yanking the tablecloth then summoning Mother to clear up the mess. Even when Dad's actions express something that the family understands, Davies withholds the meaning. Dad discharges himself from hospital and walks all the way home, perhaps as a way of denying the reality of illness, perhaps on the contrary because he wants to die at home, perhaps even so as to be present at Eileen's marriage. Davies shows him as an apparition, not a person with an interior.

Davies adopts a style of filming that is formal without being stiff, and has room in it for warmth and occasionally even humour. The images, though, could hardly work as well as they do without the artfulness of the soundtrack. The characters sing for celebration, for consolation and for distraction, often all at the same time. Davies regularly does without direct sound, exploiting the paradox that people often seem most eloquent when we do not know exactly what they are saying. The first appearance of the children is done, by contrast, with direct sound and not image, the camera showing only the empty staircase as they come down for breakfast. The effect is not of desolation – memory effortlessly supplies the fullness.

Songs on the soundtrack are used with a wondering irony. There is an extraordinary sequence of one of the girls looking up as Mother (Freda Dowie) cleans the windows, and praying that she does not fall. The camera cuts to the inside of the house and advances slowly towards Mother as she works – Dowie's face, expressing eagerness and defeat in equal measure, is a perfect representative of the film as a whole. On the soundtrack, Mother is asked why she married Dad, and she says something about him being nice and a good dancer, while Ella Fitzgerald starts singing 'Taking a Chance on Love'. She goes on singing as the camera cuts to one of Dad's explosions of violence. The mood of the song remains mysteriously unbroken.

Distant Voices, Still Lives is actually two films made two years apart. The first part uses dissolves between scenes, while the second part prefers white-outs, something which slightly interferes with the film's careful choice of colours, pale shades made to look somehow sombre. The earlier part, too, is less linear in structure, full of flashbacks and circlings, so that the absence of narrative momentum does not feel like a lack. But the film's combination of great directness and great obliquity continues to make an impact.

The film's final song is 'O Waly, Waly', sung by Peter Pears, with Benjamin Britten's piano accompaniment undermining the song's lyricism with dissonance, while also somehow intensifying it. With its artful drawing of almost abstract emotion from a jaggedly particular personal history, *Distant Voices, Still Lives* achieves something remarkably similar.

Davies's next film stayed on home ground but organised itself differently.

The Long Day Closes (1992)

In the most characteristic moment of Terence Davies's new film *The Long Day Closes*, the camera pans over the floor in a Liverpool terraced house, giving it the sort of sustained attention normally reserved in Hollywood movies for an actress's face. If Davies was von Sternberg then his Dietrich, fascinating in every calculated mood, would be the carpet in his childhood home. We watch its irregular pattern of red and ochre bars at different times of day, under different conditions of re-enacted weather.

There are three British directors now working who are visual poets by even the most rigorous EU standards – of these Davies is the most consistent in his waywardness. Peter Greenaway uses a precise, perverse dialect of film language, but he starts from scratch with each project. Derek Jarman is more intuitive and more mischievous. Both have produced versions of classic texts (*A TV Dante*, *Edward II*), each in fact has a *Tempest* to his credit. But Terence Davies is fixed by his subject matter, his working-class Catholic family's history in the decade or so after the Second World War. You could almost say he is fixed in it. He might be tempted to make a religious film if only he could cast his mother as the Virgin Mary (as Pasolini did in *The Gospel According to Saint Matthew*), except that for him the Holy Land could only be post-war Liverpool.

The Long Day Closes is cut from the same cloth as Davies's previous film *Distant Voices, Still Lives*, the same darkly shining bolt of family memories. The films share a distinctive texture of sound and image. On the soundtrack, scraps of radio pro- gramme, popular songs, English traditional music both sacred and secular. On screen, static compositions and ceremonial camera movements, an alternation of celebrations and ordeals with moments of transfigured dailiness, producing an effect of emotional syncopation that makes it impossible to tell if any individual memory, let alone the whole skein, is bleak or infinitely rich.

The actress who plays the mother in the new film, Marjorie Yates, doesn't particularly resemble her counterpart in its pre- decessor, Freda Dowie, but Davies endows her with the same domestic holiness. In *Distant Voices, Still Lives* the point of view sometimes seemed to be an unseen child. In *The Long Day*

Closes the child is visible and called Bud (Leigh McCormack). Bud watches and listens from halfway up the stairs, a commanding position that is also a retreat from full participation in family life.

The Long Day Closes takes place after the death of the father whose unpredictable violence overshadowed *Distant Voices, Still Lives*. You would think his absence would make all the difference to a child growing up in the house, and consequently to the tone of the sequel. Certainly the director seems to think he has made a film about happiness to offset the misery of *Distant Voices, Still Lives*, but you would never guess it from simply seeing the two films, one after the other. Terence Davies works his effects in a realm somehow beyond 'happy' or 'unhappy'. He pursues epiphanies like the ones in Joyce's early fiction, which can be triggered by the sight of, say, the worn heels of a woman's shoes as she kneels during Mass. The shoes can be made to represent something (poverty, self-oppressive submission to the Church) but they mean more than they represent.

If Davies is a sort of Joyce, he is a Joyce who may never move beyond this portrait of the artist as a pre-adolescent. Already as a young boy, Bud is experiencing events as sacred memories almost the moment they have happened. We see him, by the effect of superimposition, contemplating recent happenings from a distance that is somehow unbridgeable.

We hear Bud's mother ritually asking her older sons to lock the doors, but it is Bud who locks himself in with a premature sense of pastness, as if nothing new could ever happen. He stays mainly at home, while his siblings socialise. When his brothers bring dates back, he is expected to withdraw upstairs. When in warm weather the family picnics on the front steps, it feels like an expedition. In his fantasy of Christmas, the gleaming table is set in the winter street, but the real miracle is that the outside world has been brought safely into the house.

Davies's peculiar gift is for images of abstract intensity. The supreme moment of this order in *Distant Voices, Still Lives* was a shot of two men falling in slow motion through glass. It so happened that such an event had occurred in the Davies family, but the shot did not primarily record an event. In *The Long Day Closes* there are three such heightened passages: a vision of a ship, a vision of Christ crucified, and a vision of coal being poured down a chute into the cellar.

The image of the ship, appearing to Bud during class, is the least successful. The film has not by this stage established its way of doing things, and there seems no reason for the ship to visit this boy in particular, misting his face with spray from another world. When Christ appears to the boy, though, the power of the vision derives in large part from the soundtrack's being of a ship's rigging creaking, as well as from the way camera and Christ alike are dizzyingly free of a precise orientation with gravity.

Catholicism, though, is sacred to the director not because it is true but because it is part of his childhood. Religion as such occupies only a side-chapel in the cathedral of remembrance (films occupy another). The school nurse, intoning her liturgy of 'Lice. Lice. Clean. Lice. Lice' as she examines schoolboys' heads, is as pontifical a figure as any in this private cult of memory.

The third image, of coal slack cascading in slow motion into a cellar, is the most inexplicably overwhelming. Bud, who is descending the cellar steps at the time, has been temporarily deserted by his best friend, but that is hardly enough to account for it. Childhood emotion is always out of proportion, as proportion is assessed by adults, but behind the camera Terence Davies knows how to fix that disproportion in the highest aesthetic degree.

The Long Day Closes is full of artistic risks, not all of which come off, but contains only a single actual mistake, the use of dialogue from other films on the soundtrack as an editorialising device. Bud's experience in the cellar is overlaid with Orson Welles's voice-over from *The Magnificent Ambersons* and Miss Havisham from *Great Expectations*. These quotations appeal to the part of Davies able to see, for instance, that other carpets are objectively preferable to the one in his mother's house. That is not the part of him that makes the films. Fetishists don't have anything as ordinary as an opinion about the object that they have chosen, or has chosen them.

I make rather a meal of those 'heightened passages' – by the time I wrote the review I seem to have forgotten that at the end of the vision of Christ, the Saviour shouts 'Boo!'. On seeing the film again, I'm not even sure the coal is filmed in slow motion. And it seems odd that I didn't mention the series of slowly moving shots observed from above, going from the area steps of the house to the cinema, then church and school, that are a high-water mark of Terence Davies's formalised naturalism, staged almost as documentary but filmed with a ceremonial majesty and consistency of point of view. The constituent elements of Bud's experience, home life, leisure (the shared dream world of the movies), worship and education are all elevated and unified. When a list of the Best British films was circulated some years later, and *The Times* asked me for my top choice, it was *The Long Day Closes* that I nominated, a film where nothing 'happens' but nothing is missing. I'm not a fan of lists, but I was the paper's film critic at the time and I couldn't really refuse – and it's not that I'm retracting an endorsement the film hardly needs.

I'm embarrassed, though, by my comment about Terence Davies's likely inability to 'move beyond this portrait of the artist as a pre-adolescent'. Davies had already made a sexually autobiographical film, *Madonna and Child*, the second part of his trilogy, it's just that I put it out of my mind, finding its self-pity and guilt-wallowing unbearable. There is a high-minded way of accounting for my distaste, by saying that I was emotionally formed both before and after the decriminalisation of homosexuality in 1967 while Davies, nine years older, was an adult of 21 by the time his desires were given any sort of legitimacy. Politically I was impatient with the persistence of old patterns of self-oppression, the only change brought about by the new openness, apparently, being that they circulated more widely. Dogmatic negativity didn't particularly appeal to my temperament, but I was actually more tolerant of straight miserabilism *à la* Larkin than of its gay equivalent, because it had less connection with my own life. And it's pretty obvious that my revulsion was far from purely political – I objected to being reminded of unbearable parts of myself.

The limitation I suggested in Terence Davies's responses to a wider world hasn't held him back. In fact he hasn't returned to autobiographical expression, unless you count the voice-over to his archive compilation *Of Time and the City*, in the last quarter-century.

A Quiet Passion (2016)

With the release of *The Long Day Closes* in 1992, it seemed that Terence Davies had both worked out and perfected the auto-biographical vein that had originally brought him to attention. In interview he mentioned an idea for a murder mystery inspired by Otto Preminger's *Laura* and set in the gay underworld of New York, but his completed films in the quarter-century since *The Long Day Closes* have all been literary adaptations. Not that they have been safe choices – Davies has shown the special boldness of the meek temperament (E. M. Forster might be a point of comparison). *The Neon Bible* (1995), for instance, from a novel that John Kennedy Toole wrote in his teens, had a strong atmosphere of Southern Gothic, with a sectarian context and a flavour of deprivation very different from the director's own underprivileged Catholic childhood in Liverpool.

The idea that art purges emotion, whether in its creator or its audience, is mostly fantasy, but it does seem as if the themes of Davies's early trilogy (the first segment completed in 1976, the last in 1983) burnt themselves out in the making of the work. Sexual self-loathing, mother fixation, terror of death – hard to imagine them being more intensely evoked than in Davies's early films, but there's not much sign of them later on. Mother figures become more equivocal, and the emphasis falls on women who are held back from fulfilment. It used to be assumed that gay directors were expressing their own thwarted longings in their preoccupation with female fates, but that's hardly the case when same-sex feeling can be addressed directly. Davies's feminism, like Todd Haynes's or Almodóvar's, is anything but tokenistic.

Lily Bart, as played by Gillian Anderson in Davies's adaptation of *The House of Mirth*, has a sense of her own value that is part of her attractiveness in a world of restricted choices for women, but shades into a spiritual pride when it leads her to overplay her hand and to imagine herself as above the struggle. In one magnificent scene Davies conveys an almost physical sense of social danger, when a few words spoken by her hostess at the dinner table ('Miss Bart will not be returning to the boat') destroys her fragile position. It's an assault as vicious as a mugging, except that the victim of a mugging doesn't have to pretend that nothing is happening.

Davies's films are hardly fast-paced, but often have the far more precious quality of making every moment they contain seem as important as every other, particularly in his full-length autobiographical films (*Distant Voices, Still Lives* and *The Long Day Closes*), where the smallest events can be suffused with rapture. His closest rival in this conveying of immanence is Terrence Malick, in other ways his opposite by virtue of being academically trained (his translation of Heidegger published by a university press) while Davies left school at sixteen. The film that shows this affinity most clearly is Davies's next adaptation of a novel, Lewis Grassic Gibbon's *Sunset Song*, which could almost be *Days of Heaven* transposed to northeast Scotland. Of the two directors, Malick is far more the prisoner of his own manner.

Nevertheless Davies's next film, a version of Terence Rattigan's *The Deep Blue Sea*, was his weakest piece of work despite some astounding moments, the opening-out of the dramatic structure leading to emotional incoherence. It may even be that Davies was more impressed by the heroine's romantic obsession than Rattigan was. Since Rattigan was turning gay experiences of his own into a form acceptable to the time, a more productive approach might have been for Davies to reconstitute the original, as Mike Poulton's *Kenny Morgan* has since successfully done on stage. Terence Davies thinks of himself as a director who happens to be gay, rather than a gay director (as Derek Jarman saw himself being), but in this case the distinction seems hollow. Why open out the play for the screen and go on confining it to the closet?

If Davies has seemed to experience difficulty in finding material that suits his curious constellation of talents, then a biographical film about Emily Dickinson, celebrated recluse and archetype of the neglected genius, hardly seems the answer. Not to mention a title – *A Quiet Passion* – that would seem dangerously insipid even if that word 'passion' hadn't been co-opted by sandwich shops and supermarkets. Never mind. He successfully meshes two sensibilities from different centuries, different classes, different denominations.

The film's first scene, in this hushed context, is one of high and public drama. Young Emily (Emma Bell), a student at Mount Holyoke College, resists pressure to dedicate herself to Christ and doesn't even align herself with less resolute dissidents among her classmates, but provokes a genteel personal confrontation. The exchange between staff member and student is formal, but no less intense for that: 'I fear you are a no-hoper, Miss Dickinson.' 'Yes, Miss Lyon.' This sort of defiance of institutionalised religion amounts to apostasy in Catholic terms, but insisting on the primacy of your own conscience is only to follow Protestant thinking to a logical conclusion.

Emily's father and siblings arrive at Mount Holyoke, not to reproach her or persuade her to change her mind but to escort her to the safety of home. Emily's character, her blend of rebelliousness and ecstatic submission, is a variation on the family type. There's a precedent for reclusion also – Emily's mother spends most of her time upstairs in a state of radiant melancholy, so easily overwhelmed by emotion that she can barely finish a sentence. When Emily's father (played by Keith Carradine) gives her permission to write while the household is asleep he makes her a present of a routine, a cage within a cage that is also a workshop allowing her to manufacture locks and keys to her own eccentric design. In the early parts of the film, the poems are only read on the soundtrack, but when Dickinson gets a tiny amount of encouragement she starts to speak them aloud, to herself at first and then, as if she was improvising, recites 'I'm nobody – who are you?' to a baby.

The surprise of *A Quiet Passion*, to those who remember the dominance of stark image over dour word in his early films, will be the sheer amount of dialogue here, much of it very funny. Some of the talk has a Wildean glitter, particularly

when Emily's sister Virginia (Jennifer Ehle), her closest confidante, is involved in it, as contributor or audience.
Sometimes it darkens, coming to resemble the close-textured
deadly banter that is the only weapon (and the only armour)
of the characters in an Ivy Compton-Burnett novel. Emily's
obsessive attachments, and her mourning when those close
to her moved away or got married, comes to make emotional
sense. Playful catty bickering turns to rancour as the audience dwindles, and a withdrawal among intimates becomes
merely solitude.

On one occasion the dialogue is intensely dramatic rather
than comic. Emily's brother Austin demands to be allowed to
serve the Union in the Civil War, but his father insists on paying
the five-hundred-dollar bond that will enable a surrogate to
fight in his place. Austin is angry, humiliated and then capitu-
lates – and all this happens not only in a short conversation but
on the very day that Fort Sumter is bombarded and the war
can even be said to have started. Compression of emotion and
incident at such a pitch shouldn't have a chance of working, but
the actor playing Austin, Duncan Duff, makes Austin absolutely present. Duff hasn't much of a track record in films, but
Terence Davies has always had a remarkable gift for directing
both individual performers and ensembles.

The script's debt to Wilde becomes explicit later in the
film, when Emily (now played by Cynthia Nixon) bursts into
a room where Austin is having adulterous sex with Mabel
Loomis Todd (Noémie Schellens) and demands that they rise
from their 'semi-recumbent posture'. This scene is impossible,
quite apart from the anachronistic *Earnest* allusion, but the
truth is much stranger. Austin and Mabel did indeed use the
house for their sessions of adultery, but one of the reasons they
could safely do so was that Emily had determined never to
meet Mabel. The first time Mabel saw Emily was when she

was in her coffin, though this didn't stop Mabel from making a posthumous claim on her and editing her poems.

One of Davies's strongest devices as a film-maker is the occasional deployment of a sequence at a higher formal pitch, like the astonishing moment of bodies falling through glass, hardly required by the plot-less plot, in *Distant Voices, Still Lives.* Here he devises a series of shots in which the characters' faces are digitally aged – an effect similar to the morphing used in Michael Jackson's *Black or White* video but here an extraordinary meditation on mortality, as well as an astute way of negotiating the awkward moment when an older actor takes over from a younger one.

The most characteristic element of Davies's film language used to be a tracking shot that moved in parallel to the action (breathtakingly used in *The Long Day Closes*). In those days such things must have taken an enormous amount of organisation, and his admirers may wonder why the camera now holds back from such movements when they would take so much less work – but perhaps the question has answered itself, Davies having such a strong aversion, like Emily Dickinson, to anything easy.

I don't feel I've come close to pinning down the qualities that set Terence Davies's films apart, but perhaps I'll do a better job if he makes more. Only with *Madonna and Child* has he set a film in the present, and it's not easy to explain why this doesn't make him an evader of reality, caught in the sticky web of nostalgia and not even struggling. The films are prepared with precision, but I don't see signs of a dictatorial approach. He can shape a rounded performance when one is called for (Gillian Anderson in *The House of Mirth*, Agyness Deyn in *Sunset Song*) but is content to channel Gena Rowland's radiant presence and persona in *The Neon Bible*. Rowland's character Aunt Mae is a transitional one in Davies's work, partly a woman with her own selfish agenda but still mainly an ideal figure to be adored (the film didn't really resolve this double status). In the autobiographical films it's hard to talk about performances as opposed to acts of incarnation – though maybe Tina Malone as gobby Edna in *The Long Day Closes* has been given some license to shine.

The story goes that when Davies approached Gillian Anderson to play Lily Bart in *The House of Mirth* she accepted immediately, having admired *The Long Day Closes*, while he had no idea about her previous life on the small screen as Dana Scully. He had cast her on the basis of a photograph, as having exactly the right look for the period, and spent his time in a parallel universe where *The X-Files* did not feature. I like this story far too much to want to check it.

There's an assumption, if you've worked as a film critic, that you must have seen every film ever made – which was a stretch even in the days I worked for *The Independent*, when there might only be two or three films released in a given week. I try to resist the temptation of claiming to have seen something when I haven't, let alone to varrick. To 'varrick' is to make such an eloquent contribution to the discussion about a film that you change people's minds about it, without having seen it yourself. This conversational manoeuvre got its name after I convinced a friend when we were both undergraduates, though I had come no closer to the film than reading the reviews, that there were things he hadn't noticed in Don Siegel's *Charley Varrick* (1973). To varrick is to fall back on bluff when film-buffery fails, and of course it could have been named after any other film I had pre-tended I had seen (I owned up about *Charley Varrick* – I wasn't found out) but the word is appropriate in some strange way. There's a spurious etymological connection with *prevaricate*.

To prevaricate is to conceal your knowledge while to varrick is to mask your ignorance.

In any case, to assess a new film I don't think it's necessary to have seen every one of a director's previous efforts, though I've been a reviewer for so long now, on and off, that these days there's often no research to be done. I remember, for instance, seeing a double-bill of David Cronenberg's early films, *Stereo* and *Crimes of the Future*, one Sunday at the ICA soon after their release, after seeing a recommendation in *Time Out*. Canadian experimental cinema, the ICA, even *Time Out* – then more or less an organ of the counterculture – at the time it felt like a very adventurous expedition to the Mall.

Maps to the Stars (2014)

David Cronenberg's new film *Maps to the Stars* is one in a long line of satires on Hollywood (from *Sunset Boulevard* to *Barton Fink*), jaundiced navel-gazing being one of the film world's favourite pastimes. Bruce Wagner, who wrote the screenplay, has put in his hours on the treadmill of fame, from (briefly) attending Beverly Hills High School to being a limousine driver attached to the Beverly Hills Hotel. He had an early script produced by Robert Stigwood but not released, and raised his profile as a writer by self-publishing an updated version of Fitzgerald's Hollywood stories (with Pat Hobby made over as Bud Wiggins). His first writing credit on a film was in 1987, as co-writer of the story (with Wes Craven) of the second *Nightmare on Elm Street* sequel.

The screenplay of *Maps to the Stars* follows two overlapping family dramas. Julianne Moore (who won the best actress award at Cannes for her work) takes the role of Havana Segrand, an actress desperate to resuscitate her career by playing, in a remake, the part that had made her mother a star. Havana has recently revealed, or perhaps merely 'revealed', that she was incestuously abused by her mother Clarice, who died in a fire. Now Clarice has started appearing to her, rejecting her version of events.

The therapist who has brought Havana's painful past into the light, or alternatively encouraged her delusions, is Stafford Weiss (John Cusack), he of the 'Hour of Personal Power' on television. When we first see them he is performing psycho-dynamic bodywork on her, something which looks very much like sexual role play. She lies face down while he leans down onto her, holding her arms from behind and urging her to release her feelings, muttering 'Everything's stored in the thighs.' If it's not cellulite it's trauma. Perhaps they're the same thing.

Stafford has troubles of his own. His son Benjie, thirteen-year-old star of the comedy smash *Bad Babysitter*, is fresh out of rehab and being required to audition for the role, in the sequel, that made *him* a star. In Benjie's first scene he is visiting a terminally ill girl in hospital, doing the celebrity version of social work (handing out iPads to the dying). He has been mis-informed about her diagnosis, though, thinking she has AIDS rather than a lymphoma, which leads to some embarrassment. 'Non-Hodgkins,' he protests afterwards, 'what's that? Either it is or it isn't.' Evan Bird is fairly extraordinary in the part.

Agatha (Mia Wasikowska), a young woman arriving from Florida, turns out to be Benjie's older sister, severely scarred in a fire and recently released from psychiatric confinement, keen to make amends though not on anyone else's terms. The circle of the plot is closed when Agatha starts working for Havana as errand girl/gofer/girl Friday, though the current term in this milieu is 'chore whore'. Havana is an unpredictable employer, her list of errands likely to start urgently pharmaceutical before get-ting side-tracked by special truffles (only available at Neiman's). Then she may decide that the task that absolutely can't wait is dragging the pot plants by the pool into a new position. When Havana gets a phone message telling her she hasn't got the part she coveted so desperately, she's in a yoga pose and listening to wind chimes with a serene arrangement of Japanese tea things nearby, but there isn't enough inner peace in the world to stop her from howling and hurling the phone around.

Carrie Fisher plays herself, though she also discharges a plot function by recommending the disturbed Agatha as a suitable employee. A line delivered by Fisher about putting your mother on screen may have been tailored for her – Wagner rewrote constantly to keep the script current – since after all she put a version of herself and Debbie Reynolds into her novel *Postcards from the Edge*, further refracted in Mike Nichols's film version thanks to performances by Meryl Streep and Shirley MacLaine. There are other in-jokes to do with casting. Clarice, the name of Havana's mother, sounds strange on her lips since Moore took over the role of Clarice Starling from Jodie Foster for the sequel *Hannibal*. The character in *Maps to the Stars* who drives a limousine while writing and doing small bits of acting may be autobiographically based, but having him played by Robert Pattinson raises an echo in Cronenberg's filmography. Pattinson spent the whole of *Cosmopolis* (2012) in a limousine, though in that film he was the passenger, and a billionaire. The script is self-consciously literary as well as film-savvy, with a Paul Eluard poem making obsessive appearances, and Anne Sexton rubbing shoulders with *The Sixth Sense* – a film in which Olivia Williams had a major part. Here she's Cristina Weiss, Stafford's wife, mother to Benjie and Agatha.

Despite such rich bits of byplay, the film doesn't have the referential crackle that gave Robert Altman's *The Player* much of its vitality, perhaps masking there the toothlessness of a rather gentle, insiderly kind of satire – if Julia Roberts and Bruce Willis get to join in the fun about the commercialisation of prestige projects, who is there left on the outside to serve as targets of mockery? Wagner's script may choose easy targets (therapists, divas) but it invests them with an intermittent dignity and pathos. Havana, learning that a tragic accident means she can play her mother after all, experiences a small impulse of concern lost inside a large narcissistic triumph. Stafford the platitudinous shrink shows a certain strength in his dealings with Agatha, refusing to reward her psychopathic behaviour. Perhaps Bruce Wagner's worldview isn't entirely New Age-averse – he became something of a disciple of Carlos Castaneda after interviewing him for a magazine in 1994, and has made promotional videos for Castaneda's organisation Cleargreen Inc.

The element of the supernatural, with ghosts appearing not just to Havana but to Benjie, shifts the genre territory away from simple satire and introduces an element of ominous dreaminess. In other words *Maps to the Stars* begins to align with David Lynch's skewed Hollywood satire *Mulholland Dr.* from 2001 – except that Cronenberg isn't in the same class as a creator of images. In *Mulholland Dr.* the lines between dream and nightmare were fluid and constantly being crossed. A scene in *Maps to the Stars* where Benjie (having abandoned his sobriety) plays around with a gun isn't predictable in the way it ends, but it can't compete with the weird laterality of the botched killing whose chain of grotesque consequences unfolds with such lazy magnificence in *Mulholland Dr.*

The conjunction of Cronenberg and Lynch seems fair because of an overlap in aesthetic, these being the North American directors most attuned to the arbitrariness of our ideas about beauty and ugliness. They also made strong films in the 1980s, breakthroughs in terms of technique and emotion, *The Elephant Man* and *The Fly* – both with Mel Brooks's production company Brooksfilms. It seems unlikely that Brooks should insist on disciplined construction, since it was something he rarely managed himself, except when he held a type of film he loved (above all James Whale's work in Brooks's *Young Frankenstein*) in the bear-hug of parody. If it's true that Cronenberg started production on *Scanners* without a script, needing to meet a deadline if he was going to take advantage of the rules governing tax rebates on Canadian films, then the relatively stable conditions of production may have been enough to improve his focus.

His first films *Stereo* and *Crimes of the Future* (1969, 1970), resembling ambitious student projects, had announced a bleak and cerebral interest in erotic transgression and the corruptible soft power of science. *Stereo* presented itself as the record of a research programme into induced telepathic powers, *Crimes of the Future* posited a world in which adult women had all been killed by a plague passed on by cosmetics. These films, lacking dialogue, had an element of the didactic Godardian avant-garde in their refraction of narrative, and were almost as much fun as that description makes them sound. They were filmed in large deserted institutions where people strolled or lounged singly or in small groups, while a voice-over affectlessly recounted the breakdown of an elaborate experimental project.

Cronenberg's first commercial film, *Shivers*, made in 1975, more or less created the genre of 'body horror' with its story of slug-like erotic parasites infesting the residents of a luxury apartment building, though it was let down by poor acting and lack of conviction in action scenes. The art direction was more effective than the direction itself – the print of Paul Klee's 1922 painting *Senecio*, for instance, hanging on the wall and exercising some sort of presence while a middle-aged doctor kills a contaminated young woman and destroys the (unshown) parasites in her abdominal cavity by pouring acid over them, before killing himself.

Rabid (1977) and *The Brood* (1979) went to town with the metaphorical diseases, but they still seem solemnly trashy rather than exciting or imaginatively realised. In *Rabid*, experimental surgery after an accident leaves a woman with a sort of probe beneath her armpit, with which she feeds on the blood of her partners and infects the whole city with zombie fever, while in *The Brood* 'psychoplasmic therapy' causes a woman having a bitter marital breakup to generate homunculi that attack anyone who has caused her pain. As a divorce film it would certainly make a striking double bill with *Kramer vs. Kramer*, and you could argue that its misogyny is interestingly foregrounded by the genre rather than masked by domestic realism, which pretends not to be a genre at all.

By this stage of his career Cronenberg was using known actors – Oliver Reed on *The Brood*, James Woods on *Videodrome* – but it was only with *The Fly* that performances made a real contribution. Jeff Goldblum and Geena Davis may have been helped by having a rapport, though this was also the first time a Cronenberg screenplay (adapted in collaboration with Charles Edward Pogue from a classic science-fiction story, bypassing the screenplay of the 1950s film version) thought of encouraging audiences to care. The film profited from the topicality of AIDS at the time of its release, but isn't limited by it. Though the scenes in which the genetically undermined hero chronicles his disintegration, setting up a sort of museum of shed body parts, had precedents in Cronenberg as far back as *Shivers*, where a character palps the parasites which infest him (they're like roving tumours), talking to them and apparently wanting to hear their side of things, here the effect was transformed by an unprecedented splicing of revulsion and sympathy.

The strange fact is that of the eleven features Cronenberg has made since then, only two have been original screenplays. Just when he might have been encouraged by the success of *The Fly* to spread his wings as an auteur, he folded them instead. Meanwhile his film-making has gone from ramshackle unevenness, with schlocky excess and philosophical ambition awkwardly yoked, to an immaculate neutrality. It's true that *Dead Ringers*, the immediate follow-up to *The Fly*, was his own invention – a chilly melodrama about twin gynaecologists, benefiting from an eerie turn in the leads by Jeremy Irons. It's an unusual criticism of a film to say that it isn't misogynistic enough, but it's one that applies to *Dead Ringers*. Misogyny is what happens when men project their horror of the flesh (in its capacity for pleasure, in its susceptibility, above all in its mortality) onto the other gender. It's a way of claiming the high ground, ontologically. I'm mind, you're matter. I'm (super)ego, you're id. The twin brothers in the film become obsessed with the idea that more and more of their patients are presenting with mutated vaginas, and they commission special instruments to operate on these malformations. The logic behind the plot demanded that they use these instruments on the lover they couldn't share, played by Geneviève Bujold, but the screen-play went down another, strangely tangential, route. One of them becomes convinced they are in fact conjoined twins, and that what is needed is the severing of the connecting tissue between them. To wrestle a misogynistic premise towards a self-destructive conclusion feels like a failure of nerve. If you're not going to follow through on your premise, choose another.

It's now fifteen years since Cronenberg's last original feature, *eXistenZ*, which revisited the theme of the hybridising of flesh and machine, posited in *Videodrome* (1983), though the flesh-mounted VHS player of the earlier film has been upgraded to a spine-mounted USB port streaming video games directly into the body. Since then he seems to have lost interest in the ideas behind virtual reality, which has after all shaped rich films from *Blade Runner* to *Inception*, just when it was becoming a fact of daily life.

Of the non-original projects since *The Fly*, four have been from novels (*Naked Lunch*, *Crash*, *Spider* and *Cosmopolis*).

Two have been of stage plays – *M. Butterfly* and *A Dangerous Method* – and one from a graphic novel (*A History of Violence*). Two have at least been originally written for the screen, though by others, *Eastern Promises* (the most satisfying film in his recent output, certainly the most red-blooded), written by Steven Knight, and now *Maps to the Stars*.

David Cronenberg has certainly learned how to curb the excesses of his composer Howard Shore since they first collaborated on *The Brood*, whose score was as relentless in its deployment of horror-film clichés as the ones he provided for *The Lord of the Rings* were clichés (in a different, heroic mode) two decades later. There's a plangent piano-based cue used on the soundtrack of *Maps to the Stars*, but it makes its first appearance in the film-within-a-film *Stolen Waters*, only gradually spreading to the larger world, mirroring the structural principle of the film, of things spreading out of their categories, with the past refusing to be over, dead people refusing to stay dead.

The camera glides elegantly, the director of photography being Peter Suschitzky, with whom he has worked consistently since *The Fly*, but Cronenberg's eye isn't one that licks and tastes the light, the way (say) Ridley Scott's does, nor does he have the knack of storyboarding dread the way Brian De Palma can. The production design by Carol Spier (whose association with the director goes back even further) is very telling, particularly in the design of the Weisses' nightmare dream house, minimalist and open-plan, utterly exposed, a place that for him emblematises the absence of secrets, in which she cowers, smoking the old-fashioned way while he inhales more trendily from a vape. Although many of Cronenberg's films have been set in the States, they have usually been filmed in Toronto (the script of *Maps to the Stars* includes a reference to the remade *Stolen Waters* being a Canadian co-production). He has never filmed south of the border before, and even on this project, with Los Angeles being much more than a background, closer to a character in the story, there were only five days of shooting in California. Every palm tree has been made to pull its atmospheric weight.

All that is missing is a strong sense of impulse, something more than the sort of high professionalism that would have held no interest whatever for David Cronenberg when he started making films. Once upon a time his films were powered by unstable tides of revulsion and anger, and now that those have subsided he seems almost excessively well-adjusted. The Buñuel who made *Un Chien Andalou*, if shown *The Phantom of Liberty*, might not have detected that the same impulses were at work, but that isn't quite the test. From the outside a continuity is there, even if the provocation has changed in style away from the confrontational to the suave. Cronenberg's films over the last decade or so give a very different impression, less the culmination of a major career than an exemplary active retirement.

Robert Altman didn't stop working, making seven films after he was seventy. He somehow held on to my loyalty despite a rich catalogue of stinkers because the unpredictability wasn't an affectation but an integral part of the way he worked, the refusal to control everything. In my time as a weekly film reviewer I saw a number of his films, mainly strong ones (including *Vincent and Theo*, *The Player* and *Short Cuts*) but never felt I was able to determine what made them work, when they did.

There was an article in *Sight and Sound* that tried to analyse *The Long Goodbye*, around the time of its release, making a persuasive case for the power of one particular sequence being produced by a reversal of conventional film language. In the scene where the gangster Marty Augustine (Mark Rydell) moves from threats to actual violence, it would be usual to build tension by bringing the camera progressively in, whether in stages or a single movement. Instead Altman pulls the camera away from the building drama as much as he moves it in, creating no fixed expectation, so that the abruptness of the violence becomes more shocking. Though still serving the script, the camera betrays no advance knowledge of how the scene will play out. Elliott Gould's Philip Marlowe, menaced in his own apartment by Augustine and his thugs, does his best to preserve the precarious cool that is his only weapon while trying to get a read on a complex situation, but the camera doesn't represent his point of view any more than it represents Augustine, whose behaviour is alarmingly arbitrary, all the more frightening for being so unpredictable.

Augustine doesn't attack Marlowe but the woman he has brought along with him, though he has just praised her beauty and described her as the most important person in his life. He can't have premeditated the assault (on the face whose perfection he has just made so much of) since the weapon is a Coke bottle from Marlowe's fridge. Augustine tries to justify his deranged actions with a nihilistic wisecrack: 'That's someone I love – you I don't even like.' The psychosis can't be turned back into effective gangster menace, but it hardly needs to be. It's effective menace in its own right.

You could make a similar case for the scene in *Vincent and Theo* in which Tim Roth's Van Gogh paints sunflowers. He's not painting *Sunflowers* – that's the whole point. Altman's camerawork sets out to reverse the typical procedure of biographical films about painters, where we are shown arrangements of form and colour out there in the world that seem to be waiting for anyone with half an eye and the basics of technique to immortalise, so that the artist, far from having unique gifts, is virtually redundant. How could anyone miss this composition? The art of painting is reduced to a knack for easel placement.

Altman's camera shows a whole field of sunflowers, not from Vincent's fixed perspective but as a hyperactive bee might see it, a real glutton for pollen lurching from bloom to bloom. The flowers are agitated by the same wind that whips at the ragged shirt Van Gogh wears and makes his easel totter. These sunflowers aren't meekly waiting to have their likenesses recorded but resist his efforts. Individually they won't stay still. Collectively they're mutinous and even jeering. Van Gogh vandalises first the paint surface and then the canvas itself, using it to give a good beating to the nearest of the sunflowers that have offered him so little co-operation. Some flowers he vindictively tramples and kicks, others he hacks down, taking a handful home with him almost as an afterthought. It's reasonable to assume that he'll have better luck later on, but we're not shown the success, only the frantic failed attempt to make a painting happen. It's as if the camera hasn't been tipped off about the crucial difference between the failed attempt in the field and the indoor session, later on, that fathered a million posters.

There are directors who are known for restricting the privileged access of the camera, but they tend to be European – Bresson, Antonioni – and rather austere in their vision of cinema. They may refuse to offer special insights but they continue to control the viewer, though by less direct means. Both Bresson and Antonioni are perfectionists and planners. Altman differs from them in lightening the existential burden on the camera, freeing it to explore on its own, without too much forced allegiance to the story being told. As his films are more conventional, though, he needs a solid structure to start from. If the director is going to be dancing on the tables, they had better be sturdy pieces of furniture.

The Player, Altman's best-known film from this period, seemed to me slightly bogus, not only in the weakness of its satire but the contrived freedom of the camera – not freedom at all, in other words – during the long opening take. *Short Cuts*, too, as I saw it, had a few problems.

Short Cuts (1994)

Raymond Carver never wrote a novel, but if he had it would have been very unlike the film Robert Altman has made of a handful of his short stories, *Short Cuts*. Carver would certainly have been flattered, but he might also have been horrified at what happens when his scrupulous grey strips of narrative are woven together until they are big enough to carpet a ballroom (*Short Cuts* runs over three hours). By his juxtapositions, both on the level of the screenplay, written with Frank Barhydt, and of editing, Altman superimposes his own meanings to the point where Carver's intentions are pretty much irrelevant.

Altman's eccentric career follows from his eccentric temperament: here is a maverick with a strange streak of parasite, an anti-authoritarian with a powerful need of other people's structures to inhabit and contradict. Most of the successful films of his great period in the 1970s go against the grain of existing stories or genres. He seems to need a ready-made supply of sweet and sour flavours before he can substitute for them his own versions of sweetness and sourness. *MASH* went against the grain of both war movie and hospital movie, *McCabe and Mrs Miller* went against the grain of the Western, and *The Long Goodbye* was a negative revision of the private-eye genre, though not quite a satire.

The shining exception to this pattern, of Altman being a sort of termite with genius, whose depredations yield new value, was *Nashville*, where the sheer scale and ambition of the idea (and of Joan Tewkesbury's script) freed him to create his own meanings from scratch. Choosing a number of easy targets

– country music, bicentennial fever, electioneering – *Nashville* somehow forgot to satirise them, and became an epic poem in praise of dislocation and self-invention.

Altman's attempt at a follow-up, *A Wedding*, proved that he didn't know how to repeat the trick (few major film-makers have made so many terrible films, often in close proximity to masterpieces). Only now, fifteen years later, has he made a return to polyphonic form, and although *Short Cuts* is a fine piece of work, it seems closed-off when compared to *Nashville*'s openness, and it has a sourness and a sneaking sentimentality that can grate in different ways.

Nashville was structured around an election campaign, but we never saw the candidate. There is so little public culture left in the Los Angeles of *Short Cuts* (though LA was not where Carver set his stories) that it has virtually disappeared. One of the major characters is a policeman, but we only ever see him using his authority for his own manipulative ends. He might as well be an impostor for all the service he renders to the community. Television is the only institution that links people in any way. Most personal encounters are bruising and humiliating: men are creeps and women are doormats. There is no contact between strangers. An eight-year-old boy who has just been struck by a car remembers his mother's warnings, and refuses to talk to the driver responsible when she tries to make sure he's all right.

If culture has broken down and left everyone isolated, nature persists, though only in negative ways. If people share nothing else, they share a vulnerable ecology. The city is suffering from infestation by a creature called the medfly. In the gorgeous opening sequence we see a formation of neon-coloured helicopters, themselves looking more like sinister parasites than anything else, spraying insecticide. The film ends with the glib but timely mini-apocalypse of a medium-sized earthquake.

In this artificial city, an insecticidal shower is the closest approach to the communal experience of rain. Bodies of water play an important but ambiguous part in the construction of the film. There's a river full of fish somewhere away from the city, but there's a murder victim's naked corpse in there too, and the urban fishermen who find her resist any claim this ex-person might be making on them. There are swimming pools, of course, and the girl we see in one of them, though naked, is alive and imagining what it is like to drown, while the pool cleaner spies on her and her alcoholic mother flicks ice-cubes down at her from a balcony. There are fish in the city, too, glamorous fish in an aquarium, fish in fact so glamorous that they are given other fish to eat.

Early in his career, Altman's technical innovation was over-lapping dialogue, but that only makes a brief appearance in *Short Cuts*, in one scene at a bakery. The overlapping we see in the film, particularly in a series of early sequences, is of a more sociopathic sort. Public space and private space are mutually sustaining fictions, and when one is eroded so is the other. We see a helicopter pilot making a phone call from a public booth, while filling a specimen bottle with urine. Audience members at a concert seem to forget they're not watching television, and talk among themselves during the music. A devoted mother looks after her children without interrupting the phone-sex rap she is producing so fluently: the timesheet on which she logs times and lengths of call is covered with half-eaten cookies. She can change a nappy while murmuring 'You're making my panties all wet,' without either laughing or crying at the juxta-position. What is disturbing about a scene like this is not the overlap but the absence of overlap, a wilful separation of things that once belonged together.

The phone-sex mother looks forward to the coming of Virtual Reality (which she describes as 'practically totally real, but not') in a crucial speech which makes the point that she already works there. Other characters inhabit the virtual reality of pathological lying or game-playing. They invent family illnesses ('It's a cruel disease') or family members, or important secret business, to cover up the sordidness of actual circumstance. Real family bonds can't compete with these inventions. When an actual father turns up at a hospital to be reunited with his son, he is as insubstantial and fleeting an apparition as a ghost.

A recurring image in the film is of a woman or a pair of women bursting out laughing, usually after a bullshitting male has just left. A pair of sisters seem to have the closest link of anyone, but even they don't tell the truth, it's just that each knows when the other is lying. The film certainly sees women and children as more truthful than men, and in a series of scenes towards the end of the film, women and children insist on the connections that men deny. One woman attends a stranger's funeral to atone for her husband's neglect. Another goes to meet the baker who has been pestering her abusively about an uncollected cake to explain why it was never picked up. A group of children, by their continuing stubborn attachment to a missing dog, force their father to locate it. The phone-sex mother invents a new register of intimacy, in bed with her husband: 'I'm so glad Jo Jo got your eyes,' she says, insisting on the reality of genetic inheritance rather than the fantasy of desire.

Altman swings these stories back towards bleakness, but the problematic issue isn't really sweetness or sourness of tone. It's true that in Carver's original story, for instance, the missing dog refuses to return home, but there is nevertheless sentimentality latent in his work (American taste likes its unsentimentality on the sentimental side). The issue is point of view. When you read a Carver story, by and large you know less than the characters do (never mind that your position of underprivilege is highly artificial). Watching *Short Cuts*, you know much more than the characters. Their lives may be restricted, but your panoramic view of them is rather intoxicating, and your eye (or ear, thanks to the songs on the soundtrack) is always being drawn to the connections they have missed. In this sense *Short Cuts* is a conscious homage that is an unconscious travesty, and connects back to the compulsive revisionism of Altman's earlier adaptations of genre or story.

In one scene, for instance, two people collecting their developed films from a Foto Buster booth drop their little packets and pick up the wrong ones. It only takes a moment for them to realise their mistake, but by then each has been shocked by the images from the other's life. They back off in mutual alarm, and note down each other's licence-plate numbers. Only the viewer knows that the images are not what they seem – that the woman's boyfriend is a horror make-up artist, that the corpse in the river was not put there by the man who photographed her. It's the opposite of a Carver moment, and it's also very uncharacteristic of the Altman who made *Nashville*. Any film that flatters its audience in this way, serving up fractured lives on a platter of omniscience, is in permanent danger of patronising it also.

As if contractually bound to alternate real achievement with feebly going through the motions, Altman followed *Short Cuts* with *Prêt-à-Porter*, one of his weakest efforts. *Short Cuts* stayed in the shadow of *Nashville*, while *Prêt-à-Porter* struggled to outshine even *A Wedding*. *Kansas City*, though, his next film, showed that he could still do extraordinary things.

Kansas City (1996)

Most films are so linear in their construction that it takes a little time to get used to the ones that aren't. Robert Altman's *Kansas City* isn't one of his large-scale ensemble pieces – it's not a *Nashville* or a *Short Cuts*. It's more like a film from his great '70s period, the period of exploration after the overrated (both then and now) MASH. It has the balance of centrifugal and centripetal forces – between magpie detail and underlying unity – that has eluded Altman so often. *Kansas City* harks back to *Thieves Like Us* (1974) in its 1930s setting, and in having at its centre a woman in love with a gangster. But while Shelley Duvall's Keechie in the earlier film was an innocent who showed, in the last sequence, disconcerting powers of survival, Blondie in the new film, as played by Jennifer Jason Leigh, is rather the other way about: a woman with an apparently flinty will, and a self-presentation modelled on her heroine Jean Harlow – ill-looking, defiant, cheap – whose core is her soft, helpless love for Johnny (Dermot Mulroney).

The film has an outstanding jazz soundtrack, and Altman sees the whole film as a kind of jazz, with each character contributing a solo. But it wouldn't be a rewarding workout if there were no fat juicy chords for the soloists to bounce off. The director himself was raised in Kansas City in the period of the film, and admits to a degree of nostalgia, but he has taken care to give nostalgia a bitter taste.

His screenplay (co-written with Frank Barhydt) emphasises dark elements that a pre-teen Altman is unlikely to have noticed: stark political corruption, the miseries and tensions of segregation. At one point, a black woman returning to her seat in a cinema after a visit to the powder room passes two white women behaving oddly. This isn't even a speaking part, but as a fleeting study in the body language of oppression it beats what Hollywood has attempted in whole well-meaning films. She draws her arms in, flinching defensively with the knowledge that her vulnerability is not lessened but actually increased when white people step out of role.

The whole story is one of crossing boundaries: Johnny dons blackface to rob a rich black man who is visiting the city with a fat money-belt to gamble away, and when he is rapidly caught (since this is not a heist of the highest intellectual ambition) his life is forfeit to the club owner – Seldom Seen, played by Harry Belafonte – who is the rightful recipient of the money, as it flows across his gaming tables. Blondie, in her desperation to save her man, kidnaps the wife of a local politician, relying on his extorted influence to arrange a rescue.

As a thriller plot, this isn't exactly perfect. It requires Blondie to come up with an elaborate scheme at a moment's notice, and one that depends on Seldom Seen doing what he in fact does – keeping Johnny alive and unharmed, almost as a form of torture, while Belafonte considers how exactly to punish him, and delivers monologues about black and white in America. It's nice to see Belafonte cast as a heavy – and he bears himself almost like Brando in *The Godfather*. But his speeches rather overstay their welcome, particularly as there's no one in the film to challenge him (Johnny says very little). Jazz is to some extent a competitive art form, as a 'cutting contest' in the film demonstrates.

Nevertheless, Blondie's plot produces the duet between her and her captive, Mrs Stilton, which is the highlight of the film. The two women come from different worlds, and remain separated even when they are hiding together in a car, or dozing on a bench in the railway station. Blondie is preoccupied with Johnny's danger and with defending Jean Harlow against accusations of cheapness, while Mrs Stilton is preoccupied with anything and everything, thanks to her dependence on the laudanum bottle, whose dropper she sucks with genteel need. In Miranda Richardson's superbly disoriented performance, she may ramble on about ghosts and rabbits, or drop into the language of dime magazines ('This is our final ride'), or cut across a tense confrontation with the airy comment that the word nigger is not used in her household.

Altman must know how unlike jazz the negative bonding of this odd couple is, but Richardson's off-key reactions are what keep the film on track. The character's emotions remain ambiguous: when she slyly adds a drop of laudanum to the drinking water of Blondie's pet bird, is it because she identifies with the captive, or is this sort of furtive revenge the way she retaliates inside her empty marriage?

Kansas City has a weary moral centre in Addie Parker, mother of Charlie, who will grow up to be a Bird with a laudanum problem of his own. Addie responds with dignity and without fear to everything life throws at her. But Altman is less interested in people who make good out of bad than in those who make stubborn beauty out of ugliness – Blondie, whose love for a worthless man is absolute and unshareable, and the musicians who are entirely enclosed in a world of exploitation and cruelty except when they play. And they play all the time.

In a number of old reviews I notice that I use Altman as something of a stick to beat other film-makers with. In a generally favourable review of Christopher Guest's *Best in Show*, I ended with a little scolding: 'Love of the loose and the tight (improvisation, sturdy structure), the high and the low, balance of contrasts, great trust in performers – why isn't Guest bidding for Altman's mantle? When is he going to try for a *Nashville*?

All he needs is more ambition and a boost of visual flair.' I did have the grace to mention that *Best in Show* was already as good as minor Altman – and as compared with *Prêt-à-Porter*, it was *Nashville* already.

It seems faintly insane to be urging a film-maker who has marked out a stylistic and tonal territory of his own to emulate another director, one almost better known for unreliability than anything else. But Altman's best work does seem to arrive at a new place, and it doesn't seem fanciful to think that his virtues might be absorbed by another sensibility, his waywardness filtered out.

I'd be fascinated to know how things worked between Altman and his screenwriting collaborators. It's a relationship that can reveal buried conflicts – Hitchcock, for instance, didn't take credit for his contributions to scripts (at least after the early 1930s) though he was an adroit controller of the process, knowing when to break for lunch or tell a joke, yet he seemed to need to keep his writers in their place. He was anxious to defend his monopoly on prestige, which is hardly the way to build a team. John Michael Hayes won a dispute about screen credit with Hitchcock, after four successful collaborations in the 1950s, but that was enough to end their relationship. After that Hitchcock didn't work with the same writer for two films in a row. He moved away from expensive and experienced screen-writers like Ernest Lehman, who devised the sublime confection called *North by Northwest*, preferring to save money by using lesser-known talents, though the result was often a script that needed additional work by others.

The credits for Altman's 33 feature films are revealing in their own way. He wasn't shy about crediting himself as a writer (thirteen times in all), nor about sharing credit. The first time he wrote a script in collaboration (with Brian McKay, adapting Edmund Naughton's novel) the result was *McCabe and Mrs*

Miller (1971), his first film of real richness. He followed it with *Images*, an original screenplay starring Susannah York about a woman's hallucinated breakdown in a remote house in the countryside that proved two things: he didn't write well on his own, and solitude was not his subject. These days, when I give evidence in court, I prefer to swear on IMDb, but for once I have to overrule holy writ. The IMDb page about *Images* makes out that the film is an adaptation of a book by York herself, when in fact it's only that the central character Cathryn is writing a children's book, which forms part of her voice-over. Susannah York's *In Search of Unicorns* was published the year after the film appeared, and though its imagery has some connection with the film, *Images* would be just as good – just as bad – if Cathryn was working on a book of poems or a guide to home butchery. It's not primary source material, though it makes an atmospheric contribution. The various possible genres the film enters – horror movie, exercise in suspense, ghost story – aren't so much deconstructed as not built in the first place.

The reference point is bound to be *Repulsion*, which Polanski shaped with implacable control, establishing a realistic setting (repressed Belgian manicurist living with her tarty sister in London) before he began to enter the disturbed world of the heroine. It's not a Freudian case study but it's certainly a viable sketch for one. In *Images* Altman doesn't bother to portray much in the way of objectivity before it is supplanted by doppelgängers of the heroine, and people visible only to her. The low point of the film must be the scene in which Cathryn runs in terror, John Williams's music doing its best to abet her hysteria, from a spaniel that is, yes, technically chasing her but really just lolloping along in her wake, wagging a happy tail. Altman might at least have located an animal that was less of an advertisement for Battersea Dogs' Home, a pooch capable of delivering some aggro – it doesn't seem a lot to ask.

The next time Altman had full responsibility for a screenplay was *3 Women*, in 1977. The control here was impeccable, in fact he had gone rather to the other extreme, producing something glassy and uninvolving. (He said the film was based on one of his dreams.) What seemed to be missing was the maverick element, the sense of a controlling intelligence tempted towards benign sabotage as much as the satisfactions of craftsmanship. *3 Women* needed a sort of mini-me Altman to do what the director did himself when he wasn't also the only writer, disrupting the rather solemn visual rhythms of the film, enriching it against the grain.

At the start of his career, Altman seemed to be alternating projects with an ensemble cast, like MASH and *McCabe and Mrs Miller*, with (theoretically) more tightly focused ones, like *Brewster McCloud* or indeed *Images*, but tightness of focus seemed not to suit him. Perhaps it simply bored him. It was no secret during his lifetime that Altman enjoyed a joint, and there may be some connection between that habit and the decentred quality of his attention in the films that work best.

Kansas City was also a period film, and such things need a lot of preparation. In fact it's striking how many of Altman's successful films were set in period: *McCabe and Mrs Miller*, *Thieves Like Us* and *Vincent and Theo* before *Kansas City*; *Gosford Park* after it. It seems a fair guess that the meticulousness of production design in these films provided some useful reinforcement of the furniture the director would be dancing on. The sense of a raw frontier in the process of construction in *McCabe and Mrs Miller* is very strong, unrivalled until *Deadwood* came along thirty years later.

I don't include MASH in the list of period films, not only because I don't like the film but because the Korean War setting is so notional. *The Long Goodbye* was almost its opposite, a 1970s story with a 1940s character at its centre, being tested by a different set of rules and found wanting though not worthless.

At the time of *Gosford Park* (whose idea is credited to Altman and Bob Balaban, an odd pairing to have come up with the template for *Downton Abbey*) Altman said in interview that for him the most important presence on a shoot was the continuity person. Altman might film a scene a number of times, and finally be satisfied with its rhythm and texture, but he might very well have lost sight of the scene's expository function – the necessity for a cigarette case, for instance, to pass from one person's possession to another's. The dramatic mechanism was subservient to the sense of flow. Without the vigilance of a professional charged with maintaining the narrative infrastructure, Robert Altman was quite capable of offering his public a film that was mechanically defective in elementary ways – a bus with three wheels.

Altman wasn't particularly loyal to his writers – only one of them, Anne Parr, got to write two films for him solo (*Cookie's Fortune* in 1999 and *Dr T and the Women* the next year). There was an unusually brisk rotation of collaborators – Hitchcock worked with Charles Bennett, for instance, seven times. The name that recurs most often in Altman's catalogue is Frank Barhydt's, but it's an odd trajectory and even a special case.

Barhydt worked with Altman four times, the first two films being *Quintet* (1979), a slow and wintry version, starring Paul Newman, of the mysteriously durable game-become-deadly-entertainment-in-a-dystopia trope (*The Tenth Victim, Rollerball, The Running Man, The Hunger Games* – that's half a century's worth) and *Health* (1980), a frantic satire with Carol Burnett and Glenda Jackson, neither of which found indulgent reviewers or anything much in the way of an audience. Why did Altman, who wasn't conspicuously loyal, stick with him after two failures?

To judge by the dwindling number of other collaborators, though, Barhydt's contribution became more important from film to film, even if his only credit prior to *Quintet*, according to IMDb, had been for writing a short documentary, *Modern Baseball*, made in 1953. A quarter-century's sabbatical doesn't usually have a sharpening effect on talent, but there are always exceptions. After *Health* there was a smaller interruption, but it was still a dozen years before *Short Cuts*, and though Altman worked with other writers during this period, Barhydt worked with no other directors. After the success of *Short Cuts* it would seem to make sense to consolidate the partnership, but perhaps *Prêt-à-Porter*, written by Barbara Shulgasser, was ready to go.

A film in development must be like a glacier that can abruptly become an avalanche. A project that was frozen immovable, time out of mind, must suddenly be realised in an obliterating rush, by the end of the tax year. Or to coincide with Paris fashion week. Or while Julia Roberts is still available.

Then Altman and Barhydt worked together on *Kansas City*, and that was it. They didn't collaborate again, though from most points of view the partnership had finally clicked. Altman made half a dozen more films, but Barhydt didn't write another, either for Altman or anyone else. There's a slightly more nuanced history, though, to be read between the lines. IMDb lists two Frank Barhydts, father and son, and credits Frank Jr with that *Modern Baseball* script, though this seems unlikely since he turned eleven that year. (I really need to find another Bible.) In 2012 an aspiring film-maker called Gary Huggins bought a film at a flea market – it cost him ten dollars – that turned out to be a sports documentary from 1951 called *Modern Football*. The director, working on his first film, was Robert Altman.

After his war service (he flew over fifty bombing missions) Altman had worked in publicity, for a company that had invented a device for tattooing dogs so as to make them traceable. Writing with two different partners, he sold a couple of stories to film studios, which were made as *Christmas Eve* (1947) and *Bodyguard* (1948). If he'd had a strong prior interest in film-making, California was the place to go to follow up this little pair of breakthroughs – there would have been worse rising stars to hitch his wagon to than Richard Fleischer, who directed *Bodyguard*. Instead he moved to New York, almost the caricatural expression of the desire to be a serious writer rather than a pleaser of crowds.

If that was the plan, it didn't work. In 1949 he moved back to Kansas City, where he took a job making educational and promotional films for the Calvin Company. (It's a style of apprenticeship he shares with his temperamental opposite Peter Greenaway, who made and edited films at the Central Office of Information for fifteen years.) The head of production at Calvin was Frank Barhydt. So it was Frank Sr, ten years older than Altman, with a background in broadcasting and journalism, who supervised his grounding in the technical side of film-making.

Frank Jr had a similar career trajectory to his father's, studying journalism at university before working in print media. I don't imagine he took a job on a Californian health magazine with a view to gathering material for a screenplay – seven years in the job seems more than enough research time. I'm making this up as I go along, of course, but perhaps Altman got Frank Jr to work on the screenplay of *Quintet*, adapting someone else's material, before he worked on his own story. By the time *Kansas City* was taking shape he had all the specialised skills required for the job – taking notes while his father and Altman reminisced about the town's sordid glory days, when Altman was a teenager and Frank Sr was a young reporter. I imagine Frank Jr being kept on short rations in terms of drink, his glass topped up relatively rarely, to make sure that marks of some sort reached paper. That's how I'd write the scene in a screenplay of my own, and Altman's fondness for a joint didn't supersede his taste for booze.

I'm not particularly attracted to the notion of the director as control freak. Part of the stereotype comes from Erich von

Stroheim, who wore riding costume (jodhpurs and boots) on set and shouted through a megaphone, necessary props to substantiate his claim of being a Prussian aristocrat when in fact his Jewish father made hats, but there's also a tyrant of a softer type – examples would be Hitchcock and Kubrick – who plans every moment in advance, framing and cutting in his head. It's true that Kubrick could seize the moment, moving quickly during the shooting of *A Clockwork Orange* to secure the rights to 'Singin' in the Rain' after Malcolm McDowell started quoting from the song during a rehearsal of some 'ultraviolence' – something that made me warm to Kubrick a little, though it couldn't make me like that particular film. The Clouzot who came so disastrously unstuck on *L'Enfer* was a control freak who lost control, and had no other way of working on his pet project than making impossible demands.

Altman is at the other end of the spectrum in this respect, not a coercer but a collaborator, but perhaps there are drawbacks to this approach also. Sometimes he seems to know what he wants but not how to make it happen, like a laboratory researcher whose discovery depends on the right spore landing in the right Petri dish at the right moment. There's being lateral, and there's getting lost. There's cultivating the pleasures of the flâneur, and there's having no sense of direction. Perhaps that's why I feel the need to find a hidden purposefulness in Altman's collaborations with Frank Barhydt, Sr and Jr, to see *Kansas City* as a long-dreamed-of culmination, blessedly free from over-emphasis (the usual fate of the personal project), rather than just another happy accident on the long list of hits and misses, a film that somehow, for no particular reason, failed to be a failure.

A Prairie Home Companion (2006)

I didn't see Altman's last film, *A Prairie Home Companion*, based on Garrison Keillor's long-running radio show, at the time of its release, though I'd had plenty of mild delight from Keillor's spin-off writing about the imaginary Minnesota settlement of Lake Wobegon. I thought it sounded rather safe, when it's actually the safe films that can go most badly wrong. Keillor's screenplay (from a story written with Ken LaZebnik) has a notional plot, about the arrival of the Axeman, played by Tommy Lee Jones, at the theatre from which the show is broadcast, sent by the new owners to look around a property they plan to tear down. There's a private-eye voice-over (Kevin Kline as Guy Noir) and a glamorous woman in a white trench coat, played by Virginia Madsen, who turns out to be the Angel of Death, though a good-hearted one. These various genre elements hardly even try to get any traction, and mostly the film is made up of songs and chat, interrupted by adverts for products (such as Powdermilk Biscuits, so 'tasty and expeditious', and Jens Jensen's, the tinned herring you never tire of) that more than half deserve to exist.

The whole film takes place in two stylised settings. There's a neon-lit diner for the prologue and epilogue that can hardly avoid associations with Edward Hopper melancholy, though it also evokes the seductive Las Vegas of Coppola's *One From The Heart*, but the bulk of the film takes place in the welcoming tatty plush womb of the theatre. Even that title, *A Prairie Home Companion*, describes a sharp arc from the wild outdoors to cosiness and sociability. Altman's camera does what it has done for decades, both responsive and enabling, patrolling round the actors like the perfect waiter, invisibly topping up their invisible glasses. Time seems have to have stopped here, and so long ago that no one can even be sure when it happened – there are echoes of pre-war and even pre-twentieth century styles of entertainment, monologues and parlour songs. The emotions on offer are entirely conventional but treated with respect. Familial sorrow melts into religious acceptance on 'Goodbye to my Mama', sung without condescension by Meryl Streep and Lily Tomlin. The faint fond trace of satire in the anecdotes, mainly about the gloomy temperament of Norwegian Americans, doesn't extend to the songs, though naturally the singing cowboys Dusty and Lefty (Woody Harrelson and John C. Reilly) are a little rough around the edges. In one comedy song they even mention Viagra, whatever that is, the scamps.

The values put under such pressure in *The Long Goodbye* (loyalty, keeping your promises) seem to have survived in this protected environment. It helps that the usual causes of tension are absent. 'GK', the master of ceremonies (Garrison Keillor), was supposedly once involved with Streep's character Yolanda but there's no backstory. The only people currently involved in a relationship are the veteran singing heartthrob Lee Akers (L. Q. Jones) and the Lunch Lady played by Marylouise Burke, elderly singletons having a quiet bit of fun. The cast includes a young woman, Lola Johnson, played by Lindsay Lohan, but no one who could realistically be a love interest for her. There's a whisper of generational conflict between Lola and her mother, Yolanda, though it's mainly about singing, with Lola shrinking from the spotlight while Yolanda urges her to continue the family tradition of musical performance. We're far from monstrous stage-mother territory here. Nor is Lola bratty or even sulky, just occasionally a little exasperated that her mother should insist on writing the script for her life.

The communal values on show define community fairly narrowly – this isn't a racially diverse audience, any more than Minnesota is a racially diverse state. When Jearlyn Steele has a singing spot, it seems like tokenism – not that she isn't a magnificent vocalist, but she's introduced under her real name and has minimal interaction offstage with the rest of the cast. None of the characters in the film are more than sketched, but she isn't even a sketch, no more than a voice and presence. I don't mean to suggest that she's been drafted in to give the film a broad appeal it doesn't deserve – Steele is an Indiana native who moved to Minnesota, where she appeared at venues that sound less plausible than those biscuits and that ever-reliable herring, St Paul's Penumbra Theater, for instance (or the Old Log Theater in Excelsior), and made many appearances in the radio show on which the film is based. On radio, too, race makes its presence felt differently, and what she contributes to the show is the extra intensity of gospel, the fervour that makes white Lutheran and even Catholic lives seem like low-stakes games by comparison. Moderation is a useful brake but it doesn't take you anywhere.

The mild conflict between Lola and Yolanda is really, in its attenuated way, a debate about the nature of art. Lola fills notebooks with narcissistic, nihilistic poems, an allegedly creative and expressive activity that leaves her as it found her, entirely enclosed in self. Yolanda doesn't originate the material she sings on stage with her sister, but she is engaged in multiple acts of dialogue, with musical tradition, with family, with audience.

Will Lola agree to perform, at the last possible moment before the theatre curtain comes down for the last time? Well, yes, of course she will. Forget the Axeman, forget the private eye and the Angel of Death, this is the only bit of dramatic development the film has to offer. The question is, what will she sing? Diluted Kurt Cobain angst or warm Carter Family melancholy? Thirty years before, it was a scene of a woman taking control of a microphone that provided an Altman film with its climactic scene, though climax in Altman tends to be a relative term, sharing a soft border with anticlimax. In *Nashville* Barbara Harris's character Albuquerque was able to calm a turbulent crowd, while giving her career a kick-start, by singing in the aftermath of a public shooting.

Naturally the context is less dramatic in *A Prairie Home Companion*. Lola plans to perform her miserabilist songs but drops most of the lyric sheets in her hurry to reach the stage from the dressing room. Consequently when she's fully committed, actually on stage, she must rely on a standard. The band strikes up 'Frankie and Johnny'. These lyrics, too, she can't remember in full, so all she can do is produce a helpless inadvertent mash-up of the two: 'He was her man, but he was a jerk . . . he was her man, and that's all she wrote.' Never mind. It's enough, she's proved herself. And the tiny element of conflict in the set-up melts sweetly away. It isn't every director who would accept the limitations of such a project and work within them, content to capture the homely flavour of sarsaparilla in an age gone mad for salted caramel.

It's a bit late in the day to be owning up to human weakness, but I admit that before I reviewed films, and even afterwards, I tended to react against the ones that came with an underground following, like *Performance* and later *Eraserhead*. (Seeing films before other people is obviously one of the pleasures of reviewing them.) I saw *Performance* at a college society screening, armoured against its esoteric glamour, but I never got round to seeing *Eraserhead* at the late-night shows that seemed to be that dark creature's natural habitat. The rather different-seeming David Lynch who made *The Elephant Man* (1980) was a wonderful shock, the film being so well controlled. If *The Hunchback of Notre-Dame* is a version of *Beauty and the Beast* in which the

Beast doesn't get the girl, *The Elephant Man* is a version in which there isn't a girl, but the Beast gets the consolation prize of winning the love of the world in general.

I enjoyed *Dune*, though Lynch clearly struggled with the amount of narrative to get through, and reviewed *Blue Velvet* for *The Independent*, but it wasn't one of my sharper pieces. I'd read Pauline Kael's review of the film in the *New Yorker*, which was certainly a mistake and contrary to my usual way of working. In general I try to avoid other people's opinions of what I'm reviewing, though in the case of books it may involve removing any press releases and pleading inserts (the dust jacket must go, of course), even tearing the covers off proofs when endorsements are printed there, to make sure that I'm not subliminally absorbing formulas of praise every time I shut the book or pick it up again. It's not my job to be right, but the least I can do is be sincere about what I read or see. It may be that Kael's rhapsody inhibited my own enthusiasm, as if I was trying to strike a balance, when I need to ignore everything but the film.

I had another chance when *Blue Velvet* was re-released in 2016, and the TLS let me discuss a couple of films with a bearing on it.

Blue Velvet (1986, re-released 2016)

The press copy for the BFI's re-release of *Blue Velvet* describes David Lynch's film as 'a potent dissection of the American psyche, its social mores and its sexual proclivities', which makes it sound like *Peyton Place* rather than American cinema's purest exercise in psychodrama, innocent of social critique. The re-release coincides with two documentaries screened at the 2016 London Film Festival, *Blue Velvet Revisited* and *David Lynch: The Art Life*, both of them reverential and without commentary, but valuably exploring a unique director and his defining film.

Lynch gave Peter Braatz, a young German fan, permission to attend the 1986 filming of his new script. Braatz documented the shoot (in Wilmington, North Carolina) on Super 8, and recorded conversations with members of the cast and crew, though sound and image remain separate in *Blue Velvet Revisited*. From the footage it's clear that Braatz's presence wasn't universally welcomed – a crew member jocularly crosses his index fingers as if to ward off a vampire – and there were times when actors were talking to him when they were needed for filming.

The most revealing comment comes from Dennis Hopper, who plays the feral psychopath Frank Booth (and was himself a film director), when he remarks that Lynch isn't a film buff, so that if his work converges on Buñuel territory it doesn't necessarily mean that he has seen Buñuel's films. The other American directors to emerge in the 1970s, Coppola, Scorsese, De Palma, Spielberg, were saturated in film tradition, and this has become the rule, with Quentin Tarantino, for whom a world outside the cinema hardly exists, representing its extreme development.

Lynch's training was in fine art. Jon Nguyen and Rick Barnes's film *David Lynch: The Art Life* gives him an opportunity to talk about this part of his life, still important since he continues to paint. (The word 'film' itself is only mentioned a long way into *The Art Life*, and refers to Lynch's first filmed ventures, which were animations.) Here again there is no sense that an artistic training involves engagement with tradition. It seems a simple matter of devoting years to the activity of painting, until the images in your head are satisfactorily visible to other people. A severed ear covered in ants is the starting point of the plot of *Blue Velvet*, discovered by Jeffrey Beaumont (Kyle MacLachlan) after visiting his father in hospital, and this would seem to be an image with Dalí's fingerprints all over it, but there is no sense here of the referential or the borrowed.

One of the childhood memories passed on in *The Art Life* recurs very vividly in *Blue Velvet*. Lynch remembers playing outside with his brother one summer evening, aged about five, when an unknown woman appeared on the street, naked and bleeding. He wanted to help her, but this was hardly a possibility, and he had no sense of what world she might be from. In *Blue Velvet* Dorothy Vallens (Isabella Rossellini), naked and bleeding, appears outside Jeffrey's home, traumatised and seeking refuge. Accounts of artists' primal scenes are necessarily suspect, above all when they dovetail seductively with the imagery or tone of the work, whether it's Magritte's mother, drowning herself in a river, supposedly with her nightdress wrapped round her face, or Mahler running into the street as a child to avoid his parents' quarrelling, and hearing 'Ach, du lieber Augustin' played on a barrel organ, so that a permanent link was created between uncontrollable emotion and second-hand sentiment.

A recurring idea in David Lynch's perception of the world is that there are two realities, capable of displacing each other but not of merging. This principle seems also to have governed his early working practice – in *The Art Life* he describes the physical impact of warmth and sunshine when he arrived in Los Angeles to take up a scholarship at the American Film Institute, yet the film he made there, working at night shut away in the institute's disused stables, was *Eraserhead*, about as dark and cold a film as can be imagined.

In *Blue Velvet*, Jeffrey's daylight world, made up of dates with wholesome fair-haired pink-and-white Sandy (Laura Dern) and work in his dad's hardware store, is supplanted by the dark blues and reds of Dorothy's world, with its mystery, pain and knowledge. (The lack of overlap makes it hard to imagine who in wholesome Lumberton would buy drugs except the drug dealers themselves.) The arrival of the terrifying Frank is somehow linked to the collapse and hospitalisation of Jeffrey's gentle father. Frank is pure id, both brutally adult and infantile, insisting on playing the role of Dorothy's baby while he rapes her. Jeffrey watches from a hiding place in her wardrobe, but the hallowed theme of voyeurism is given a perverse twist, since she knows he is there. Her husband and son are being held hostage, so she must submit to Frank's assaults and also keep Jeffrey's existence secret. When this young man becomes her lover, she insists on a continuation of maltreatment. At first he resists, then responds.

Synthesis has no part to play in David Lynch's cosmos, and even this, his most tightly constructed screenplay, offers no resolution. Frank is destroyed and Dorothy, reunited with her son (too bad about her husband), lightens up on the blue eye shadow and red lipstick until she's just another mom watching her little boy playing. Jeffrey returns to Sandy and to his reconstituted and enhanced family – Dad's out of hospital, and Sandy's parents visit – unchanged by his perverse experiences. The mutual attraction of innocence and damage seemed to be written deeply into the plot of the film, but it has evaporated as a theme before the final credits. The ending has an elaborate absurdism, with an unconvincing mechanical robin munching on a beetle in echo of a dream Sandy recounted earlier in the film, in which robins represented a restoration of happiness.

If *Blue Velvet* has aged well, it's partly that it was only masquerading as a 1980s film in the first place. Its musical reference points (the title song, best known in Bobby Vinton's version, and Roy Orbison's 'In Dreams') are from the early '60s, when Lynch would have been of college age, like Jeffrey. Dorothy's apartment is straight out of the 1940s. Only Jeffrey's discreet earring and the women's hairstyles testify to a later period (there's a startling moment when Isabella Rossellini reveals that her dark mane is in fact a wig). The film wasn't lavishly funded – Lynch was contracted to make another film for Dino De Laurentiis after the failure of *Dune*, and chose to work with a small budget on the condition that he retained artistic control. Preparation was meticulous. Dennis Hopper, as recorded in Braatz's film, was both impressed and exasperated by the time and trouble taken in getting the lighting exactly right.

It's strange to hear David Lynch talking (also in Braatz's film) of how much computers could assist the film-making process, since he seems temperamentally unsuited to any device postdating the gramophone or perhaps the slide rule. In fact he expresses an interest only in non-visual shortcuts, not wanting to digitise backgrounds or use post-production special effects but dreaming of weightless lighting rigs, a floating camera. On location for *Blue Velvet* he made lettering out of tape for anonymous signage to be used in the film, scrupulously trimming the edges with a craft knife, though if there was ever a job that a director might profitably delegate it must be this one. Perhaps it was a displacement activity to reduce anxiety, the great disadvantage of a move from fine art to film-making being that it gives you so much less to do with your hands.

At the time of *Blue Velvet*, and already a long-standing practitioner of transcendental meditation, Lynch was cigarette-free, though in *The Art Life* he smokes almost continuously and alternates stillness with fidgeting. It may seem a strange relaxation technique whose successful practice is compatible with acquiring (or relapsing into) a heavy smoking habit, but that may be to misunderstand meditation, to see it as a way of resolving internal stress rather than surviving it.

If he took on lowly lettering duties for *Blue Velvet*, Lynch must also have been involved in the make-up or model-making for the damaged heads and bodies that are the most striking images towards the end of the film. One man is somehow still standing, though catatonic and badly injured, the other is dead. Their wounds are less euphemistically rendered than is customary in cinema, but there is still the sense that they have a valid claim to beauty. This is what makes David Lynch so unusual as a film-maker, and what entitles him to any amount of meditation and smoking to balance his unique internal apparatus, that in his best work (*Blue Velvet*, *Mulholland Dr.*, parts of *Twin Peaks*) he seems to be reproducing charged images with no predetermined weighting of excitement and dread. As if the film itself had been edited, but the impulse behind it had not.

That balance, of David Lynch being in control of his medium without having intellectually filtered the impulses that drive him, is bound to be precarious. Since *Blue Velvet* I've seen Lynch films that have been disappointing (*Wild at Heart*), baffling (*Lost Highway*) and plain unbearable (*Inland Empire*). The most surprising success of his career and that least imaginable of things, a David Lynch film released by Walt Disney, came in 1999.

The Straight Story (1999)

The opening images of David Lynch's last film, the thrilling and baffling *Lost Highway*, were of tarmac filmed at night and at high speed, the broken stripe in the middle of the road pulsing and jittering. When that stripe recurs in Lynch's marvellous *The Straight Story*, its progress is daylit, extremely slow and has a very different visual texture. Even the film's title seems to be announcing a U-turn – hasn't everyone always taxed Lynch with his refusal or inability to tell a story straight? Except that this is the slyest sort of U-turn, one which allows him to change direction dramatically and then go on doing exactly what he's always done. It's the same with Angelo Badalamenti's score. Despite the bluegrass tinge, the sound world is continuous with *Blue Velvet*.

The screenplay, by John Roach and Mary Sweeney, is based on real events: a man of 73 by the name of Alvin Straight, living in Iowa, travelled to visit his sick brother some 300 miles away in Wisconsin. Lacking a driving licence because of poor eyesight, he drove the only vehicle available to him, a lawnmower, with a trailer behind it for him to sleep in and to carry reserves of gasoline and sausage. It took over a month. This must be the strangest road movie ever made, but it is also one of the most lovable.

Richard Farnsworth, who plays Straight, is older than the part. He first appeared in the movies in 1937, when he answered a casting call for stunt riders and appeared as part of the Mongol horde in *The Adventures of Marco Polo*. He spoke his first word on the screen in *The Duchess and the Dirtwater Fox* in 1976. A man who waited almost forty years for his first speaking part won't have minded the extra twenty-odd of waiting for a great one.

Alvin Straight is gentlemanly, shy, reserved, drily funny, undeceived. He can also turn a piece of road kill – not his road kill, the lawnmower can barely squash bugs – into venison steaks and a pair of antlers to decorate his trailer, though our director, not normally squeamish (to put it mildly), doesn't show us the process.

A certain amount of sentiment appears in the film, and something else shows up that has never been a concern of Lynch's: Nature. While Lynch's previous landscapes were essentially expressionistic, versions of the characters' inner worlds, autumnal America in *The Straight Story* is independently there. The film measures out its story in cupfuls, showing us situations and events first, their meanings later. It's only near the end that Alvin's journey is revealed not as an eccentricity but a pilgrimage, even a penance.

Lynch doesn't always submit to the tyranny of the establishing shot. When Alvin has his first beer in decades, having crossed the Mississippi, the significant interaction we see is not with the bartender, visible from the beginning, but with another customer, revealed only late in the sequence. It was with *Twin Peaks*, which won and then lost a mass audience, that Lynch showed most clearly his ambivalence about narrative: the first episodes of that series created a powerful need to know, which later ones only teased and mocked. There is a pair of passages in *The Straight Story* which seem to comment on this ambivalence. In the first, we are looking out of the windows of Alvin's Iowa home at night, from the point of view of his daughter Rose (brilliantly played by Sissy Spacek). A white ball rolls into a pool of light. Eventually a small boy appears to reclaim it.

Later, Alvin explains the history and depth of Rose's feeling (she lost a child), in a sequence that recapitulates some of what we have already seen. And it's as if Lynch was asking his audience to tell him the truth. Hand on heart, didn't you prefer the images soaked with mysterious emotion to the explanation of what, exactly, the emotion was? The world of *The Straight Story* is benign, but it isn't bland. It's not reassuring – it contains rather too much of the arbitrary for that.

If there is another director on whose territory the film might be said to encroach, it would have to be Robert Altman, but David Lynch proceeds by opposite means. He achieves effects of warmth and inclusiveness not by way of intimacy and improvisation but by absolute distance and control. It's somehow all the more satisfying for having taken the long way round.

Altman as a touchstone, again. It's funny how often he crops up, and *The Straight Story* as made by Altman would almost have been the opposite of what Lynch offered audiences. Wouldn't he have made it socially panoramic rather than sweetly existential? Early Jonathan Demme, the Demme who made *Handle With Care* and *Melvin and Howard*, might have been drawn to the story, but he too would have come up with something quirky rather than mysterious. In fact you could use *The Straight Story* as a strong endorsement of the idea that a film wholly belongs to its director, however many other people made a contribution (the 'auteur' theory). The material isn't personal to Lynch (his work doesn't show much interest in family, for instance) but he has found a way to make it resonate as if it was.

I'm surprised that I didn't mention the film's best visual joke, a slyly witty use of film language. As Alvin Straight pootles off on his lawnmower at one point, the camera slowly rises into the sky above him. This is usually a way of creating a soft transition between scenes, by cutting to another view of the sky and moving down into another scene. In *The Straight Story*, the camera simply reverses its movement after briefly contemplating the sky, to show Alvin Straight still pootling off on his lawnmower, having made only a few yards' progress in the intervening seconds.

In another scene I don't mention, Alvin has a conversation with a female hitchhiker in the course of which he compares family to a bundle of twigs, stronger than the elements that make it up. The next day when he comes out of his trial he finds that she has left him just such a bundle of twigs. By a strange piece of synchronicity, a bundle of twigs played a significant role in another film of 1999, rather better known – *The Blair Witch Project* – where it carries an almost opposite meaning. The three students in that film, camping in the woods, find it outside their tent one morning. In this context the artefact (hardly counting as anything so grand) means *We were here while you slept and you didn't wake up. We could have done anything.* It's the smallest possible unit of menace, and very efficient for its size.

One of the things I enjoy about film is that it hasn't lost its cultural centrality. University students doing a degree in English will cheerfully admit they haven't read any book you happen to mention, but are routinely up to date with the latest mainstream releases and often have knowledge in depth of particular genres. When I was teaching creative non-fiction to MA students at Greenwich, and we were looking at the personal essay as a form, I suggested writing something about film. Film is the medium that seems to reach everyone, without the rival sub-cultures that arise in the case of music. And, as it seems good practice for the tutor who sets the task to do it too, I wrote my own, about ageing in films.

'Ode to Richard Farnsworth' (2011)

If there's one subject, or one object, that cinema has made its own, it's the face: the human face filling the screen. There are directors who have made faces, particularly female faces, in close-up carry the whole weight of a film, like Bergman again and again, like Dreyer in *The Passion of Joan of Arc*.

Cinema has always been hard on faces, particularly female faces. The lighting of early silent films was so harsh that it exposed the imperfections of most complexions aged more than 25. That was the world in which Lillian Gish held sway, at a time when the movies were in their own strange a matriarchy. In the silent era the picture palace was a temple of female dreams, and it was the men's genres, like the Western, that were the exceptions.

Female stars had more power than ever before or since. Stars like Gish or Mary Pickford and Gloria Swanson were the producers. They hired directors and knew what they wanted. MGM had Lillian Gish on contract for several films and more or less set out to break her power with a run of lousy scripts. She rewrote the first couple and made successes of them, but the third one defeated her – and then the whole power struggle turned out to be about nothing, when Greta Garbo came over from Sweden and got more money than Lillian Gish would have dreamed of asking for.

In those days it was possible to leave the building of celebrity. Garbo could live in New York, visibly invisible, without being molested unduly. She was able to outlive her beauty without being humiliated, in the way that is now compulsory, to the point where it can seem that the period of idolatry is really only a softening-up process. The real event is the punishment doled out to those who had seemed to claim exemption from the ordinary process of ageing.

One shameful milestone on the way was *What Ever Happened to Baby Jane?* in 1962. You could only call Robert Aldrich's film a 'vehicle' for Bette Davis and Joan Crawford if you were thinking of a hearse being driven off a bridge. The whole point of the film was the gloating examination of stars past their prime, denied the consolations of becoming costumes and tactful make-up. These two actresses had never been soft or endearing, they were tough, and still Davis wept when she saw herself in the daily footage. That was the film's *raison d'être*. It was Hollywood's bush-tucker trial of 1962, and even the toughest trouper can have trouble making those marsupial glands go all the way down.

Some actors have another centre of artistic gravity, the stage, where the face is only one of the instruments contributing to the total effect. It was on stage, after all, that Sarah Bernhardt could play Hamlet into her sixties, with a wooden leg, without raising any sort of laugh. Not everyone has the training or the opportunity to refresh themselves in this alternative universe, but it has certainly helped to sustain Judi Dench. An ageing face innocent of surgery, such as she presents to the viewer in, say, *Mrs Brown*, is so rare an object in the performing arts today as to have a sort of alien integrity and eloquence, testimony from beyond the grave of youth and beauty. The taboo against the ageing face gives some dark sort of power to those not intimidated by it.

Yet every passing crone and granddad in a documentary of a little-filmed country has radiance. Perhaps the much-mocked 'primitive' idea that the camera sucks the soul is true after all, it's just that the spell is slower-acting than anyone suspected.

Lillian Gish made films in eight decades (from 1912 to 1987), but she is given a run for her money by Sylvia Sidney, whose working years were 1929 to 1996. Gish had great grace and an eerie wholesomeness, but Sidney had real range. She gave the single deepest emotional performance in a Hitchcock film, as Mrs Verloc in *Sabotage* (1936), and worked three times for Fritz Lang, but she still had something left to give Tim Burton in *Beetlejuice*, where she's the bureaucrat of limbo (a place staffed exclusively by suicides) whose inhaled cigarette smoke emerges through the slash in her throat, and in *Mars Attacks!*, where she's the ailing granny whose country-and-western music makes the aliens' heads explode.

Yet in spite of Sidney's eminence, and even recognising the way the dice are loaded against women in Hollywood, I have to give the award for the most glorious long film career, the greatest slow-burn, the most ridiculous progress through an addled industry and a self-sabotaging art form, to a man. To Richard Farnsworth, 1920–2000. Farnsworth was born in Los Angeles, and got a job in a local polo stable when still very young, after his father died. He learned to look after horses. He learned to ride them. After a few years he started doing stunts in movies. He would ride in chase sequences. It didn't matter if he fell off and was hurt – filming wouldn't be interrupted, as it would be if someone important came to grief. He was promoted to stand-in work and appearing in fight sequences. Over time he doubled for Kirk Douglas, Henry Fonda, Steve McQueen and even Roy Rogers.

He appeared in *Gone with the Wind* and in *Gunga Din* when he was nineteen, in *Fort Apache* when he was in his late twenties. About the same time, Howard Hawks was making *Red River* with Montgomery Clift. Clift was an extraordinary actor as well as a man whose love-hate for his own beauty charged his performances with a remarkable tension, but he was a stranger to cowboy body language. He lacked hat skills and horse skills. He couldn't roll a cigarette. Wearing a gun belt more or less made him forget how to walk.

Howard Hawks asked Richard Farnsworth to show Clift these aspects of life. Farnsworth was now being paid ten dollars a day to smoke, walk, ride and wear a hat, while being followed and copied by a film star whom he liked but hadn't the faintest desire to replace. How could it get any better than that? It was a lot more than they paid at the polo stable.

But it did get better. He did some ranching, and had the option of hiring his horses out for films, though eventually Westerns went out of fashion. But then he was working as an extra on a film called *The Stalking Moon* when it turned out that they needed someone who could deliver a little dialogue. He caught the eye of Alan J. Pakula, the producer. Maybe he was up to speaking a line or two? He was.

Here was his big break, and he wasn't even looking for a break. It was 1968, and he'd not been in the movies for thirty years yet, and here he was getting to say lines! He had reached the end of his own personal silent-movie era. A short decade later, Pakula was no longer a producer but a director, making a film starring Jane Fonda, filming on location, called *Comes a*

Horseman, and he needed someone to play a supporting role, the old-timer who helps her to run her ranch. Again what was needed was someone who could walk the right way, approach a horse the right way, someone whose hat didn't look either brand new or as if it had been artificially aged by costume consultants. Alan Pakula remembered that there was this guy who could get from the beginning of a line to the other end without falling over, and tried him out.

After only 39 years in front of the camera he was playing a character, someone with a name as well as a hat. He got a nomination for best supporting actor for what he did in *Comes a Horseman*, and even though Christopher Walken won the trophy, for what he did in *The Deer Hunter*, Richard Farnsworth was now officially an actor. He may even have got himself an agent, I don't know.

The work came steadily from that point. There was usually a hat and a horse in the frame somewhere, but it wasn't as if he needed them. He was in the film *Misery* in 1990, and in the 1994 remake of Peckinpah's *The Getaway*, where he was relieved that he wasn't required to join in with the general orgy of profanity. It was one of his proudest boasts that he never uttered a cuss word in a film. People liked to cast an authentic rancher and cowboy in their films (even someone who learned about horses at a polo club, not exactly a blue-collar hangout), but they didn't always know what to make of one when they got him.

In his late seventies he had already had cancer for a couple of years – but then he'd been declared 4-F at the time of the Second World War, disqualified from service in uniform, for having spots on his lungs. Rolling cigarettes is a fine manly habit which everyone should acquire, as long as they remember not to smoke 'em. Then he got a leading role which required him to be on screen for more or less every frame of the film, one of the great studies of stoicism and solitude. His director had one of the most perverse sensibilities ever to be in charge of a film, so it was good news all round that the studio making the film was Disney (I always thought I'd have to be tortured to say that) and that David Lynch the director wasn't writing the script. The film was *The Straight Story* (1999), and it was the true-life story of an old man named Straight, Alvin Straight, in poor health, who decided to pay a visit to his estranged brother. It's one of the oddest vehicles in the movies, and for once I do mean, literally, vehicle. He drives the three hundred miles, along back roads, on a lawnmower.

People often talk about the lack of vanity in a performance, but vanity works differently in male and female lives. Male vanity is a real thing, but it's a sort of fever with known casualties (I suppose I'm thinking of Warren Beatty) rather than a chronic condition no one is allowed to opt out of. Ruggedness, even cragginess, these are habitable territories for male humans, even on film.

A 'fearless' performance from a male actor is code for 'you can see his bits' – as you can see Michael Fassbender's bits in the Steve McQueen's *Shame*. When an actress is 'fearless' it means she has allowed herself be seen as unattractive, or old, or both. I suppose a case in point would be Shirley MacLaine, in her mid-sixties, taking off her wig in *Postcards from the Edge*.

In the case of Richard Farnsworth and *The Straight Story*, vanity doesn't even apply. He knows how to be in front of a camera, in full geological integrity, but the camera has never been allowed to suck his soul. Perhaps it didn't get to him young enough. He was allowed to build up over time the layers of failure we call character. Farnsworth's relationship with himself didn't pass through a lens, which paradoxically enough made him absolutely available, at this late moment, to be filmed.

The movie camera is a dog which fawns on you just so it can get close enough to piss on your leg. It kept well away from

Richard Farnsworth until he was old enough to tell it to scram. He didn't need it – which meant that the camera decided, as dogs do, that this was in fact a man it wanted to fetch sticks for. Nobody has ever had such a lucky career as Richard Farnsworth, who got his greatest role when his body was already dying (he finished the job himself with a shotgun the year after the film was made). No one has ever waited so long for success to come looking for him – if he was even waiting – and no one's hand, no one's face has ever been licked so devotedly, when it trotted up at last, by that dog the camera.

A piece for *The Guardian* gave me a chance to broaden the argument.

'Fighting the Seven Signs of Ageing' (2015)

Male careers in the movies have always been longer than female ones, but until recently there was only one real route to virtual immortality, to the certified gold-standard agelessness of Cary Grant, not just appearing opposite a younger woman in *North by Northwest* (55 to Eva Marie Saint's 35) – a routine benefit in this line of work – but having his screen mother played by someone a year younger than him (Mildred Natwick). Suavity is the key principle, the refusal to break sweat, sophistication with the faintest hint of self-mockery, letting us know he knows how silly this all is. There are still disciples following that path up the mountain to the sunny uplands of longevity – perhaps we should think of the mountain being reconfigured to include a huge stone likeness of Grant himself, like the ones he scrambled over so urbanely in the same film. Over there, do you see? There are George Clooney and Hugh Grant in their hiking shorts, twinkling away for dear life as the career shadows fall, and a little further down is Colin Firth, trying to make sense of the map. Richard Gere is sitting cross-legged on a boulder and seems to be meditating, though he may just be taking a nap.

Suddenly they all freeze (though with Gere it's hard to tell). What's that sound? Gunfire. But it seems to be coming from *further up the mountain*. And this isn't a spooky echo but a real event – there is now apparently no age limit to an action career in Hollywood. The expendables are no longer unemployables, and actors in their sixties and even seventies are still high-kicking in the can-can routines of choreographed violence, fighting the seven signs of ageing in the most literal way. After making a third Indiana Jones sequel in his mid-sixties, Harrison Ford was over seventy when he joined the grizzled crew of *The Expendables 3* (with Sylvester Stallone weighing in at 68 and Arnold Schwarzenegger at 67). *Indiana Jones and the Crystal Skull* was weakened by its routine action sequences, with the camera keeping its distance from Ford's stunt doubles (the charisma of an ageing action star has more to fear from obvious fakery in fights – and the implied loss of limberness – than from facial close-ups, where the genre doesn't necessarily require more than rugged scowls and glares of baleful defiance). Tom Cruise, now 53, and strongly committed to stunt work, has just appeared in a fourth *Mission Impossible* film and signed up for another. By the time of its scheduled release, in 2017, he will be as old as Bruce Willis was in the first RED film, when he was Retired (though admittedly also Extremely Dangerous, to complete the acronym of the film's title). For Tom Cruise it seems that the real mission impossible would be calling it a day, as far as international intrigue and high-speed chases are concerned.

A loophole seems to have opened up, almost a wormhole in the fabric of Hollywood space-time. Through this portal an entire generation of veterans is currently trooping – and it's Liam Neeson who has made the most drastic and yet the smoothest journey across the genre universe, with *Taken* and its sequels. Spielberg's Schindler, agonising over whether he might have managed to save one more life, has been made over into a killing machine. His *Taken* character, admittedly, Bryan Mills, is a civilian (ex-CIA) always acting to rescue and secure his family, which makes a difference. It greatly enlarges a film's potential popularity if it can combine elements of sharp and sweet, to produce a sort of salted-caramel-popcorn crossover appeal. As *Gladiator* showed, audiences attuned to romantic self-sacrifice (traditionally female) will accept a fair amount of violence, and it also works the other way round, with the stereotypically male element willing to identify ungrumblingly with a man who has lost the love of his life and never looks for a replacement.

What's Neeson's secret? His physique? Hardly – he has never been one of Hollywood's Shirtless Ones, hasn't even spent much screen time in a singlet. No doubt he has a fitness regime beyond what most civilians would contemplate, but he seems to have no interest in projecting bolts of testosterone to the back of the auditorium. He moves like a big man who has learned to be light on his feet.

He has had the advantage of a late start, though it can hardly have seemed like an advantage at the time. There were plenty of male stars from Hollywood's classic period who couldn't easily be imagined young, among them the ones who most seem to symbolise integrity, Humphrey Bogart and Spencer Tracy. A young actor can embody idealism easily enough (James Spader, say, in *Sex, Lies, and Videotape*) but integrity is something that needs to have been tested over time, if not actually by time. For actors like Bogart and Tracy (plus James

Cagney and Edward G. Robinson, though less reliably virtuous), their heyday was middle age. Wrinkles formed part of their appeal, rather than undermining it. Maturity was their present tense, and they had no visual history, lacking Facebook pages to archive the mistakes of adolescence.

In early roles, such as Gawain in *Excalibur*, made when he was under thirty, Liam Neeson doesn't look especially young, and youth is something that cinema requires, adores and finally punishes. The fact that more people are living long lives doesn't necessarily make ageing easier, and stardom has become a complicated business, with any amount of toxic undercurrent, ripples of projected narcissism and rancour. Stardom has changed because fandom has changed. Fandom in cinema increasingly follows the model of Kathy Bates's Annie Wilkes in *Misery*, revealing devotion as something essentially raging and vengeful. Obsessive love becomes malign stalking. Fame has always had its drawbacks but now it seems all downside.

For most of its history cinema has been our dominant source of visual imagery. Television seemed to offer a threat, but changed the rules of engagement much less over half a century, as it turned out, than mobile phones have in a couple of decades. Celebrity has become an incurable condition, without remission. I can almost find it in my heart to sympathise with film stars who ban eye contact on set, or from their staff. Fame is a treadmill, and having your own gym doesn't seem to make the legwork any easier.

When Gore Vidal said of Truman Capote that his death was a good career move, it was mere waspish provocation, but the same assertion could be made without irony about Jean Harlow, James Dean and Marilyn. The flesh-and-blood person is surplus to requirements once an icon has been created, and often becomes an active embarrassment, like the flesh left over at the end of the magic trick in *The Prestige*: sordid matter to be disposed of. (This is fair disclosure under the statute of spoiler limitations, since the film came out in 2006, its source novel as long ago as 1995.)

The French are fond of calling cinema the Tenth Muse, but if there's a figure from the Greek pantheon who fits this context it has to be Tithonus, granted immortality thanks to the intervention of his lover Eos (the dawn) but lacking the sense to stipulate eternal youth as well. Yes indeed, terms and conditions apply, and it's natural enough that the goddess of the dawn should be attuned to beginnings rather than endings. When Tithonus became shrivelled and unable to move she intervened again, and he was turned into a cicada.

The prophetic document of the transformation of fame from safe haven into torture chamber was Robert Aldrich's hideous 1962 film *Whatever Happened to Baby Jane?* Davis in particular seemed punished by being put in childish clothing, portrayed as being trapped in the past when her screen persona had always been non-standard and her choices often inventive – fading actress Margo Channing in *All About Eve*, for instance, being by Hollywood standards a stingingly honest portrait of vanity made monstrous by despair.

It's easy to feel that the main event of celebrity culture is now the showing-up of the failing flesh, and all the acclaim of youth and freshness that goes before is only a pretext. When identification fails, when the idol fails to opt out of time, things can turn nasty. Films are so centrally about youth and beauty that ageing on screen is a real taboo. We don't feel sympathetic when our idols reveal themselves as mortal, we feel betrayed. They've let down their side of the bargain, and fans become feral. This used to be primarily the experience of women in films, but now the impossible choices are becoming unisex. These days there's almost as full a range of options and delusions available to male movie stars as to their female counterparts.

We've seen male stars go too far down the path of plastic surgery, and others who have relied too much on what they were born with. There's the temptation to have a lot of work done, as revealed by Mickey Rourke to gasps of audience horror in *The Wrestler*. And there's the temptation to put your faith in Mother Nature and let it all hang out, as exemplified by Gérard Depardieu to gasps of audience horror in *Welcome to New York*.

The current incarnation of youth in films isn't in the equivalent of a John Hughes comedy, but in Richard Linklater's high-concept *Boyhood*, in which Ellar Coltrane is made to age convincingly from child to man by the drastic decision to film him over twelve years – achieving by design the effect that in the case of, say, David Lynch's *Eraserhead*, was the result of waiting around for the money to finish the film to trickle in. *Boyhood* seems to have outwitted the enemy, containing and controlling the poignancy of the passage of time, but that's just how it looks now. There's no inoculation against mortality on film, except, strangely, tragic early death. If Coltrane is spared, then one day soon he'll be snapped unshaven and with bags under his eyes (Paparazzo is everyone's middle name now), and then he'll be all over the media world, the shaming image appearing alongside the dewiest frame of him from the film.

If Liam Neeson's physique isn't the key to his durability, then perhaps it's worth considering his face. A broken nose can have a whole little range of overlapping meanings. It suggests a bad boy rather than someone who abides by the rules, though there are many ways of suffering a facial impact and relatively few of them corroborate such a character sketch. The decision not to have the nose straightened seems to offer more reliable testimony of a character indifferent to vanity. Even if this is a false impression, a broken nose takes away the potential stigma of prettiness from a male face. It's certainly a mark of experience of some sort, and an imperfection that can somehow enhance appeal.

There's no equivalent in female iconography for a facial characteristic that communicates, however misleadingly, fearlessness and lack of vanity. The closest equivalent might be diastema, the gap between the front teeth that can qualify as both an imperfection and an added allurement (Anna Paquin, Vanessa Paradis), but it's not close. Its symbolic meaning isn't just approximate but arbitrary – the folk tradition associating diastema with lustiness that goes back to the Wife of Bath and beyond. Diastema isn't the result of experience, as a broken nose is by definition, so it seems pretty clear that in film terms experience seems to add to a man, subtract from a woman. Men can have been around the block a few times but women are condemned to the repetition of freshness. It's as if a man can live off the interest of the time and effort invested in making movies, with a real prospect of earning the adjective 'distinguished', while a woman is always spending the capital of her looks, jeered at when she runs into debt or has to borrow youth from a surgeon.

Heavyweight dramatic actors often venture into comedy as a way of extending their durability in the marketplace. Meryl Streep has turned herself with some effort and after a fair few duds into a performer who can raise a laugh, while Robert De Niro has by now spent more time spoofing his persona than exploring it. Self-parody has existed in the movies since at least Dietrich's performance in *Destry Rides Again*, but it's a new development for it to be a whole career in itself. Of course it's tempting for writers and directors to inoculate their films against laughter by pre-empting it. A dusting of comedy is the standard industry procedure for increasing the appeal of ramshackle film projects, though it's a perverse approach to making something superficially appetising. Why sprinkle sugar on a hot dog?

Liam Neeson may or may not have a sense of humour – certainly his appearance on Ricky Gervais and Stephen

Merchant's *Life's Too Short* on television was as excruciating as anything since De Niro's turn in Scorsese's *The King of Comedy*, but that was the desired effect. Comic relief is certainly not part of the organising principle of *Taken* and its sequels, though the incongruity of Neeson as a skilled assassin was built into the structure of the first film – there was a certain amount of genre disguise involved, impossible to carry over into subsequent instalments of what has become a successful franchise. At the beginning of the story Neeson's character Bryan Mills was presented as an overprotective father, unable to move on from a broken marriage and spending altogether too much time worrying about his teenage daughter Kim's safety, seeking to control her movements.

This could be a psychological drama of divorce, with some of the synthetic sourness of *Kramer vs. Kramer* – but then it strays into *The Bodyguard* territory, when Bryan agrees to help out some old friends, hired to provide security for a moppet pop star's gala concert, who are a man short. In due course there's a murder attempt, fitting the Kevin Costner/Whitney Houston template, and a moment of intimacy in its aftermath, but this too is a false trail, revealing the hero's combat skills but not yet explaining them (he's an ex-CIA operative). Two genre feints in a running time of only 93 minutes – that's not bad going. Only when Kim (Maggie Grace) goes to Paris and is abducted does *Taken* move up decisively in terms of octane rating. Liam Neeson plays it grim and straight.

The level of brutality is modest by (for instance) Tarantino's standards, and is excused in plot terms by a number of factors – Bryan being far from home, one against many, racing against time and so on. But it isn't every actor who can make an audience accept the hero leaving a villain plugged into the mains after he has no more information to give, or shooting a woman without warning to make sure her husband understands the gravity of his situation. 'It's only a flesh wound,' growls Neeson, as if he'd done no more than spill red wine on his hostess's dress.

Gravitas is an indispensable term in this context, the moral stature that can not only complement physical power but make it irrelevant, and it seems to be defined culturally as a male preserve. It's hard to define, though, even as it applies to men – perhaps it's simplest to describe it in negative terms, as 'what Tom Cruise will never have'. Some have gravitas and some don't. Boyishness and gravitas don't go together, and an eager-beaver quality kills it stone dead. The script of the 1992 film *Far and Away*, for instance, required Cruise, in desperate straits, to assert his authority over a horse with a punch (it's the Oklahoma Land Rush, and he's in a hurry to stake a claim). As a bit of business it simply didn't come off. There were film actors at the time who could have made it work, and it's the same ones who could get away with it today, nearly a quarter-century on: Clint Eastwood, Sean Connery, Harrison Ford. It's not a matter of physical strength, since after all no horse is actually being hit. It's down to gravitas – old-style stardom without the benefit of moisturiser.

Is gravitas even possible for women in the movies? Of the possible claimants, in terms of seniority and eminence, Meryl Streep more or less disqualifies herself by her reliance on acting technique, her disinclination to establish a consistent persona across a range of roles. Helen Mirren relies on a disarming insolence, and her confidence that she will never run short of desirability seems justified so far. Perhaps being ogled by Michael Powell's camera swimming naked in *Age of Consent* while still in her teens has given her some sort of immunity. She can have a love interest her own age, or even fractionally older (like Brian Cox in RED) and she's so offhand about it that nobody even notices how exceptional this is. Of this select group, only Judi Dench is defined not by being looked at but by looking. In her best work she outstares the viewer, astringent, judging, refusing even the admiration she has earned with her refusal of conventional approval.

There seems to be a shortage of intelligent ways of presenting an older woman to a grown-up audience. Anyone who has seen Almodóvar's *Women on the Edge of a Nervous Breakdown* will have seen the director's cheeky casting of Francisca Caballero – his mother – as a television newsreader. Women who work in front of a television camera and are unwise enough to pass their fortieth birthdays are losing their jobs all the time, but one look at Almodóvar's film should convince any sensible person that newsreaders in their forties aren't slightly too old but much too young. What you want, when it's time to hear about the day's events, isn't some glamour puss but someone who's been around for a bit, someone who's seen a few things in her time, a few wars, floods and Oscar nominations. It gives a bit of context, a sense of proportion.

Film-making, of course, is not about proportion. Stardom has strange acoustical properties, variously amplifying, suppressing and distorting frequencies of the personality involved. It's hard to turn such an apparatus into a loudspeaker for consciously conveying messages, though it's sometimes been tried. Subtext needs to stay buried. When Mark Rydell's *On Golden Pond* reunited Jane and Henry Fonda on screen in 1981, the family reunion seemed to stand in for something more ambitious, the rehabilitation of a prodigal daughter. The star who had aligned herself most intensely with the counterculture of the 1960s, 'Hanoi Jane' herself, was sending the message, using her father as a stand-in, that all she had ever wanted was to be loved and accepted by conservative America. No wonder the film felt strained – it had an agenda as fraught as the AGM of a failing company.

Film stars, offering themselves as screens on which audiences can project their fantasies, can't expect to control the process except in the most indirect way. A shrewd film star is both a work of art and its curator. The supreme practitioner in this line must be Dietrich – when you hired her, you got her lighting man too, so that she retained full control over the product. Alongside the erotic mystique she had a strong *hausfrau* side, which didn't show up on film, but she certainly kept her glamour swept and dusted. The professionalism extended to her home, where she received visitors in a chair placed under a spotlight, with a silver stripe painted down her nose to correct the proportions that didn't meet her standards. Without any such crude mechanisms Cary Grant maintained an astonishingly consistent persona over the decades, defending his narrow range (stylised ease, controlling suavity) against any possible challenge.

It can happen that stardom simply evaporates, leaving talent intact, which would be one way of describing Al Pacino's career – he's still a performer with magnetism but has shed what made him so fascinating in the 1970s, the physicality with elements of both innocence and the feral. And sometimes a star persona takes a dogleg, moving into new territory without an actual break. John Wayne's last starring role in *The Shootist* (1976), for instance, was enriched by the cancer diagnosis shared by the actor and the character he played. Sometimes a film star can have two different and contrasting heydays, as happened with James Stewart. In his early career, up to *The Philadelphia Story* in 1940, Stewart embodied an idealism that didn't necessarily exclude slyness (in *The Philadelphia Story* he makes Cary Grant seem smug and obvious). When he started making films again after his distinguished military service, he had changed. He was like a bell with a hairline crack, the fundamental note unchanged, the overtones tending to jangle, and offering rich new resonances of uncertainty (*Vertigo*), strained folksiness (*Anatomy of a Murder*) and despair (*It's A Wonderful Life*) to the directors he worked with.

The first *Taken* film was made before Neeson's wife Natasha Richardson died suddenly in 2009. If it seems crass to connect a film star's changing persona with his life experiences, then it is a crassness that was built into the workings of stardom even before modern communications made sure that there was no such thing as a secret sorrow. Film is porous. An event like Neeson's bereavement echoes backward in time, filling his segment of *Love, Actually* (widowed father tries to teach his son how to approach the girl he's besotted with) with new associations, though it's anything but classic material in itself. His persona has been enriched with pain and the guilt of the survivor, which adds depth to the action hero's trump card, the willingness to take punishment, winning not because he's the better fighter but because he doesn't care about himself. Neeson's presence was always sombre rather than blithe, so that the sorrow and strain we project onto it only accentuates what was there before. With the right director he might yet match what James Stewart achieved in the 1950s Westerns he made with Anthony Mann (the series that started with *Winchester '73* in 1950). To have gravitas means to inhabit your history, and not to be diminished by your losses. And if that isn't quite the same thing as real-world maturity, on the big screen it's the best we're going to get.

Mortality is more often the subtext than the subject in films, something that can't be eliminated rather than something that is consciously addressed – mortality was hardly even the subtext of Christopher Nolan's *The Dark Knight* (2008), for instance, until Heath Ledger died before the film was released. An exception was Michael Haneke's *Amour*, the first film by a feted director that to my mind moved beyond cold manipulation.

Amour (2012)

Casual television watching can offer the same face twice in a weekend, in different versions like phases of a moon, Wendy Hiller's, say, with her crusty cameo in *Murder on the Orient Express* (1974), then as the vibrant heroine of *I Know Where I'm Going* (1945). Between them Jean-Louis Trintignant and Emmanuelle Riva, appearing together in Michael Haneke's film *Amour*, bring more than a century's worth of past selves to lay at the feet of their writer-director.

These two actors seem to have moved crabwise through their careers towards this meeting. It happened that they made reputations in the best-known sexy films of their period, one lowbrow and the other highbrow, *Et Dieu Créa La Femme* (1956) and *Hiroshima Mon Amour* (1959), so that Trintignant got his start as a hunk opposite Bardot, in front of Roger Vadim's possessively salivating camera, while Riva delivered existential-erotic anguish for Alain Resnais. If their subsequent careers have been a slow spiralling towards each other, then their gravitational fields certainly grazed when Riva played Juliette Binoche's mother in Krzysztof Kieślowski's *Three Colours: Blue* (1993) and Trintignant had a larger role in *Three Colours: Red* the next year.

In the past Michael Haneke has shown something of an obsession – in films as different as *Funny Games*, *The Piano Teacher* and *The White Ribbon* – with cruelty and humiliation. Though the same statement could be made about *Amour* it would be entirely misleading, since the film's subject is the struggle for dignity at the end of life. Coupled with Haneke's preference for emotional distance, this sounds like a hellish prospect for the audience, but the film's tone is restrained rather than cold, the texture fluid rather than stiff, and it moves towards intensity.

Anne and Georges are in their eighties but mobile and far from housebound. In the opening scene they attend a piano recital given by (as it turns out) a past pupil of Anne's who has gone on to great things. Their byplay has a dry, low-key intimacy. When the two of them get home after the concert, he helps her off with her coat and asks if she'd like a drink. She says she's tired, but he says he'll have one anyway. 'I'm not stopping you,' she says, though the French dialogue ('Fais comme chez toi') makes the delicacy of her teasing more evident.

From then on the camera stays in the couple's flat, which is spacious and comfortable, though the grand piano is perhaps a stern rather than a luxurious presence – it's an invitation to the discipline of practice rather than the sensuality of listening. At breakfast one morning Anne has a long moment of mental absence. It seems possible at first that she is practising passive resistance, piqued that she is expected to fill the salt cellar when her husband can do it perfectly well himself. Soon it is clear that something is seriously wrong.

Hollywood produces films with similar storylines, and normally they amount to sequenced hammer blows of pathos. *Amour* is very unlike that, though it's also remote from the more *engagé* British tradition, which would tend to see terminal care as (among other things) a social issue. When Anne loses her mobility and independence it isn't clear what help Georges could expect from the state, if any, since he chooses to go it alone. He hires private nurses by the hour when his labour needs to be supplemented.

There are the equivalents of Stations of the Cross in grave illness, rites of passage, inescapable farewells to particular experiences or faculties, but *Amour* comes at them unpredictably, with a syncopated narrative and a number of shifts of emphasis. When the couple's daughter Eva first appears, her scene contains some casual surprises. She's played by Isabelle Huppert, at the warm end of her admittedly cool emotional spectrum as an actress. Eva wants to know what's the matter with her mother, but the health bulletin Georges gives her makes it clear that we too have been kept in the dark. Since the last scene shown, Anne has gone for tests, accepted the need for an operation with a 95 per cent success rate, actually undergone the operation and then learned that she falls in the category of the 5 per cent who don't benefit. 'It's all terribly exciting,' says Georges, with wintry humour.

The effect of these little revelations is to put the audience in the position of Eva, lightly winded, struggling to keep up with developments, when we had seemed to be trusted with at least the outline of events, though not perhaps with the deepest recesses of feeling. Unpredictably the script defends the couple's right to privacy. Eva mentions that as a child she always found it reassuring to hear her parents making love, a statement that would lead any therapist to clear time for extra sessions but also supplies a missing dimension to the audience's understanding of this enduring couple. Their marital tenderness is very inexplicit. At one point Anne tells Georges that he's a monster, but very kind.

The effect of closeness is produced more by naturalism of performance than any enactment of warmth. At one point Georges, wanting to check that Anne hasn't wet herself, lifts up a corner of the blanket and takes a quick sniff in passing to make sure that all is well. Intimacy could hardly go further.

One of Haneke's strongest decisions is to enlist his director of photography, Darius Khondji, in the task of resisting claustrophobia on the audience's behalf, even when illness closes in on Anne and there is no way out. For hints about sick-room atmospherics the film-makers have been looking less to Munch than to Hammershøi, whose domestic interiors hum with a strange peace. Simple scenes, such as Georges giving Anne a shampoo, have the sort of inexplicable beauty that Bresson strove for – how can there be so much visual interest here, in the slightly different pale blue tones of three ordinary objects, two of them towels and one of them the small enamel saucepan he is using to rinse her hair? There's an extraordinary sequence towards the end of the film which is simply a leisurely montage of some of the paintings in the flat, shot so as to occupy the whole screen, without the implication that anyone other than us is being refreshed by these wall-mounted reservoirs of space and otherness.

Little flourishes of film language derail any obviousness of response. In one sequence we see Anne, in health, playing the piano – until the shot changes and we're looking at Georges sitting by the CD player, whose little lights are lit. The first shot seemed to be taking place in Anne's memory, but now we understand it as his. It might be a tiny homage to the Resnais who gave Riva her start, arch-refractor of memory. Earlier on, she was lying in bed when a piano piece started playing. Then it broke off, and she called out to ask why Georges had stopped. It's the only indication that he too is a pianist – but then we are told almost nothing about him, not even what he did with his life before retirement, just a few routinely piercing anecdotes from childhood.

The early parts of *Amour* are modest in the demands they make on Riva's tolerance of exposure. At moments of great potential shame Trintignant's body is between hers and the camera. Later on we move into new territory, with documentary frankness superimposed on a lightly fictionalised narrative. This is the point (as with Wilfrid Brambell in the last part of Terence Davies's trilogy) where viewers are driven to celebrate the greatness of acting by a reflex combining protectiveness and terror, as they imagine what it must be like for an elderly actor to be rehearsing so publicly the preludes to death. Riva treads this path of no return so convincingly that (logically enough) it seems impossible that she should return from it, and scenes of flashback or fantasy involving her previous self seem to be calling on the services of a stand-in bearing only a moderate resemblance.

The film departs from sentimental views of how families come together in crisis. Without actual reproach, Georges sees his daughter as an irrelevance if not an obstruction. Eva's suggestions about her mother's care are batted aside without real interest. She's an outsider, quite apart from the fact that her husband Geoff (which everyone pronounces as the disyllable its spelling suggests) is likely to bring his English humour, tolerable only in small quantities, to bear on Anne's situation. It's true that at her unresponsive mother's bedside Eva talks about her investment worries, but she is at least offering the sound of a familiar voice, and most of us would do, perhaps have done, something similar.

A dispute between Georges and one of the nurses, though hardly a shouting-match, seethes with rancour. He says he hopes that one day she will be on the receiving end of the sort of treatment she doles out. All we have seen is some brusque hair-brushing, and the sort of inane chivvying that assumes a mental age in single figures, while Anne's is variable. The nurse wants Anne to admire her pretty face in the mirror, while Anne looks fiercely away. Again, most people would accept this sort of unthinking cruelty as inevitable when personal care is rendered impersonally, or would find a way of influencing it short of raging dismissal. There is something potentially overwrought about this insistence on the absolute presence and primacy of the dying, whether it should be ascribed to the character or the film itself. Anyone who has seen Haneke's *Caché* will remember the effectiveness of its single isolated moment of extremity. He works the same trick here with a dream sequence, to warn his audiences against too serene a contemplation of last things. Computer Generated Imagery in a Michael Haneke film! It's like stumbling on Thomas Pynchon's Facebook page. Yet he continues to manipulate us with extraordinary skill into imagining we're being left alone with our own thoughts and feelings.

The only non-human visitor to the flat is a pigeon that gains access through an open window in two scenes, and must be coaxed to return outdoors (the second time Georges has to capture it under a blanket). Might this be a symbol of some sort? Hard to set aside the sublimity suggested by even a grubby style of dove. Never mind that the pigeon is the only sub-standard performer in the whole film, all too clearly pecking at the grain (perhaps withheld on this occasion) that has been used to lure it indoors. It's like a second-rate method actor, knowing its motivation and nothing else.

Is it significant that the Bach-Busoni transcription played by Georges, and then abandoned, is the chorale prelude on 'Ich ruf zu dir, Herr' (I call on thee, O Lord)? The choice can hardly be an accident in so scrupulously composed a film, but the simple fact of its breaking off doesn't make it become a prayer abandoned in hopelessness, because this is a general rule rather than an exceptional occurrence. There isn't a great deal of music used in the film, by modern standards, and not a single piece of it – not the various pieces of piano repertoire, not even 'Sur le Pont d'Avignon', which Georges tries to persuade Anne to sing along with as a way of gingering up her speech centre – is allowed to finish.

This is a remarkably brave move at a time when film and music score seem locked in a mutual debauch more or less worldwide, with music called on to supply emotional meaning in a way that ignores its other powers, while making such things as visual storytelling and subtle acting essentially irrelevant.

The recent television version of *Parade's End* (2012) is an obvious example, with the music constantly stressing the crudest associations (world war an ominous prospect, love a troubled sweetness), adding nothing and thereby subtracting everything – and all this to tell the story of a man whose emotions are supposed to be rather less obvious than a bad case of acne. Recommended for medals, everyone else. Sent for court-martial (named and shamed), Dirk Brossé. Only obeying orders? Save it for the tribunal. The sooner television remote controls make it possible to banish an aggressively insipid score – without sacrificing dialogue – the better.

'Mutual debauch' may not go far enough. It's more like the accidental suicide pact at the end of *The Mill on the Floss*, with two people drowning because one of them can't swim and won't stop clutching the other. Haneke's film refuses to follow the formula. Death is not the completion of a pattern. A person's last breath has nothing in common with the last note or chord of a piece of music. If you are trying to make an honest film about death then it follows that you will not allow music to have the last unlanguaged word. Although (or even because) *Amour* concerns itself with endings, it withholds such formal completions on the soundtrack. Music too must be made to break off, denied its claims to offer a consolation that is meaningless when not actively insulting.

The only time Georges leaves the flat, after the evening of the concert, he goes to the funeral of an old friend. This is relatively early in Anne's illness, when she is still able to hold a conversation. She insists on being given an account of the event when he returns. Reluctantly he tells her. It was distressing. The urn of ashes was placed on a trolley intended for a coffin and then trundled ludicrously towards the hole dug for it. Worst of all, someone had brought along a tape-recorder, which played 'Yesterday'. The response of at least some of the mourners, according to Georges, was not sorrow but appalled laughter. *Amour* itself avoids any sort of play-out. The rest, for once, really is silence. Michael Haneke's film, among its other distinctions, is highly unusual in respecting this logic.

My admiration for Michael Haneke didn't survive the release of *Happy End* in 2017, a sort of semi-sequel (with Trintignant in a similar role but not the same one) seeking to trade on the reputation of the earlier film but hardly in a position to draw out a story that had come to the most definitive of conclusions. In *Happy End* connection is equated with delusion and self-knowledge means wanting to die. Nihilism comes in various versions, ferocious and feeble, crisp and soggy, and the one on offer here was hardly cogent or appealing. Haneke had laid aside his dogmatic negativity for the duration, along with his need to preach and scold, but the urge was too strong for him to abstain for long.

Coda: Second Sight

I chose *Second Sight* as the title of this book because I had no physical record of much of the material it contains, the reviews dictated over the phone to copy-takers at *The Independent* from sheets of A4 that are almost certainly preserved in a box *some-where*, or word-processed for *The Times* on a computer that has been pushing up silicon daisies for years. This has been only my second sight of my weekly reviewing self, and though overall I'm not thrilled by the performance on offer I'm not shocked either. It's not a job I'd want now, but then I've been spoiled by – generally – a greater allocation of thinking time. I normally stick with my first impressions, it's the making of the case for them that sometimes seems clumsy or rushed.

Inevitably there are films I have reviewed that I don't even remember seeing, but one additional surprise in looking back over my *Times* columns is that in Top Ten listings published under my name I routinely recommend films that I know I've never seen – *Snatch*, *The Luzhin Defence*, *Chopper*. So maybe I have second sight after all.

It's not an original title, I admit, but there are other virtues. In the Preface to his 1929 novel *Summer Lightning*, P. G. Wodehouse described his discovery that he wasn't the only person to have used the title. There were several rivals on the market. Still, he sticks to his choice and ends by saying, 'I can only express the modest hope that this story will be considered worthy of inclusion in the list of the Hundred Best Books Called *Summer Lightning*.'

My rivals are many. My rivals are legion. I don't even include in the count titles like *Love at Second Sight*, of which there are a fair few, starting with Ada Leverson's novel of 1916. I do include *Second Sights*, an Enriched Life Movement (ELM) anthology edited by Josh Langston and published in 2014, because of its splendid subtitle – *From Wrinkled Writers*. The fourteen contributors to the book have a combined life experience pushing a millennium, ELM being 'a learning organization for seniors' in Marietta, Georgia.

There are books called *Second Sight*, most of them novels, by Alan E. Nourse, by Denise Moncrief, by Kara Sevda, by Maximilian Pereira, by Patricia Fox-Sheinwold (author of *Too Young To Die*), by C. S. Conwell, by J. F. Althouse, by Maria Rachel Hooley, by Elizabeth Cooke, by Elizabeth Martina Bishop, by George Hoepfner, by H. K. Savage, 'an avid writer in the frozen tundra where half of the year is best spent behind a computer'. There's a *Second Sight* by D. L. Taylor, another by Debbie Mumford, one by Mary Tannen, one by Cecilia Bartholomew. Sinclair Smith has written a *Second Sight*, and so has Sally Emerson. Amanda Quick has written one. Basil Wells saw no reason to be left out in the *Second Sight* title stakes, and Sherry D. Ficklin wasn't going to let Griselda Gifford monopolise the market. There's plenty of room on the *Second Sight* shelves for Kat Green, for Janine Burke, for Lindsay Welsh, for Rickey Gard Diamond, Sidney Bigman and Anne Redmon. *Second Sight* is a broad church, and can shelter within its mighty nave the contributions of David Williams, Beth Amos and Gary Blackwood, of Paula Newcombe and Lotus Token.

'Second sight' is primarily a phrase used to denote clairvoyance – 'Deuteroscopia', as W.A.F. Browne, psychological consultant at the Crichton Institution of Dumfries, uses the word in the subtitle of the *Second Sight* he published in 1876. He defines the phenomenon as 'an involuntary affection, a supersensuous impression, involving a portent'. He acknowledges a supposed connection with the Highlands and Islands of Scotland, 'even to Skye and the vexed Hebrides, where the burst-boom of the mighty Atlantic echoes and expends itself amongst the gigantic cliffs which wall in the semi-sterile hills . . .' But no area or individual has an exclusive right to the phenomenon, nor to the title. Judith Orloff, MD, needs no licence to call her book *Second Sight*, certainly a crisper formula than her subtitle: 'An Intuitive Psychiatrist Tells Her Extraordinary Story and Shows You How to Tap Your Own Inner Wisdom.' (In one AbeBooks listing, the author is described as Inuitive rather than Intuitive, making her therapeutic approach even more gloriously bespoke.) Sharon Neill is less keen for others to develop supersensuous gifts of their own, and goes with the subtitle 'spine-tingling tales from Britain's leading blind psychic'.

Of all the *Second Sights*, the one by the mystic Sepharial (also known as Walter Gorn Old) bearing the tantalising subtitle 'a study of natural and induced clairvoyance', seems to have had the longest active life in the market. There can't be many writers of Old's generation (1864–1929) whose work is sufficiently in demand for an e-book to be made available.

The phrase 'second sight' summons up the idea of seeing and then transcends it – it's about seeing beyond what the eye can make out. But there's no arguing with Charlotte Sanford's right to give her 'Miraculous Story of Vision Regained' the title *Second Sight*. And why shouldn't an ophthalmologist like David Paton use it for his memoirs, subtitled 'Views from an Eye Doctor's Odyssey'?

Come one, come all. It's only with Cheryl B. Klein's *Second Sight: An Editor's Talks on Writing, Revising, and Publishing Books for Children and Young Adults* (2006) that I begin to feel that someone is hitching a free ride on the unstoppable *Second Sight* bandwagon. What plausible argument could Klein make, in front of an oversight committee, to stake a claim on the coveted title? She would have to lean hard on that word 'revising', with its etymological hint of looking-at-again, yes, plausibly, seeing-for-a-second-time, and I still think the decision could go either way.

My own *Second Sight* isn't even the first to be a collection of film writings – Richard Schickel got there nearly fifty years ago, with his book subtitled 'Notes on Some Movies, 1965–1970'. Like a virus, or a Rob Bottin special effect, the title sends insidious filaments across the genres. Art historians aren't immune, whether their subject is Australian photographs in the National Gallery of Victoria, printmaking in Chicago from 1935 to 1995 or the paradox of vision in contemporary art. There was even a *Second Sight* series put out by the the National Gallery Publications department in London, examining works by pairs of artists – Claude and Turner, Rubens and Gainsborough, Mantegna and Degas. Poets have more resistance, or are more proudly independent of trends, though Dinah Livingstone succumbed in 1993 (*Second Sight: 33 Poems*) and Dabney Stuart gave up the struggle to resist a few years later (*Second Sight: Poems for Paintings by Carroll Cloar*).

One *Second Sight* is a science-fiction action-adventure stealth video game released in 2004. Another is a farcical comedy in one act, subtitled 'Your Fortune for a Dollar', dating back to 1887. A third is a six-part graphic novel published in 2016. Language is no barrier to the cosmic travel of *Second Sight*: the individual volumes of Kathryn Cline's trilogy, published by Klopp Erika Verlag, may have German subtitles (Tödliche Träume, Gefährliche Stille, Verlorene Seelen) but the name of the series as a whole needs no translation. Perhaps *second sight* is on a linguistic exchange programme with *doppelgänger*.

In a world where every book seems to be called *Second Sight* subtitles take on special importance, so that a particular production can stand out from the ruck. Mr Richard Smith (so styled) seems not to have grasped this principle, to judge by the subtitle of his *Second Sight* – 'The Second Sight Chronicles'. Charles McCarry's *Second Sight* is the seventh of the Paul Christopher novels, which may give some potential readers their bearings. The *Second Sight* by Philip R. Craig and William G. Tapply, similarly, is 'a Brady Coyne and J. W. Jackson Mystery' so fans of those know what to expect.

Indicating genre can be a handy shortcut to a readership, with George D. Shuman's *Second Sight* being labelled in its subtitle as a 'novel of psychic suspense'. A subtitle can even perform the function of the trailer for a film, as it does in Jake Buchan's *Second Sight*, with the subtitle 'Can John Steadman Find the Links between a Trail of Bizarre and Macabre Murders?' Not bad – but it takes something close to genius to come up with a genre description that tantalises without offering any real clue about what to expect. Hats off, ladies and gentlemen, to Carly Fall's *Second Sight* of 2015, which is subtitled 'A Paranormal Military

Romance'. That's right – not 'normal paramilitary romance', paranormal military romance.

I can only express the modest hope that this collection of writing about film will be considered worthy of inclusion in the list of the Two Hundred Best Books called *Second Sight* (I'm allowing for inflation), though obviously in the matter of subtitles I can't hold a candle to Carly Fall.